Best w[...]

Douglas Lamb.

C000181087

A Pub on Every Corner

Douglas Lamb

The Black Swan Hotel, Pond Street

A PUB ON EVERY CORNER

Douglas Lamb

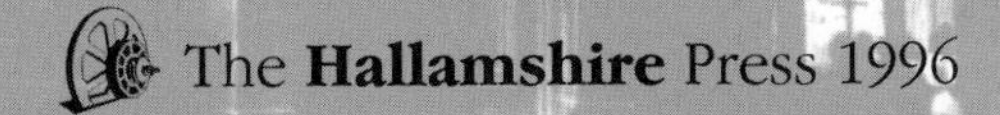
The **Hallamshire** Press 1996

Published by The Hallamshire Press Limited
Broom Hall
Sheffield S10 2DR

Reprinted 1998 and 1999

Typeset by Interleaf Productions Limited
Printed in Great Britain by The Cromwell Press, Wiltshire

All rights reserved. No part of this publication may be reproduced, stored in a retrieval system, or transmitted, in any form or by any means, electronic, mechanical, photocopying, recording or otherwise, without the prior permission in writing of the publishers.

British Library Cataloguing in Publication Data
Lamb, Douglas
A pub on every corner
1.Bars (Drinking establishments) - England - Sheffield - History
I.Title
647.9'5'42821

ISBN 1 874718 55 5

Contents

Preface 7

Introduction 9

Origins of Some Public House Signs and Names 19

The Sporting Angle 44

Sheffield Beer and Breweries 51

Old Sheffield Public Houses and their History 66

Public Houses as Social Centres 110

On the Outskirts, Some Interesting Pubs and Pub Stories 115

Old Buildings, New Pubs 125

Bibliography 127

Photographs 129

Public House Lists and Maps 145

This book is dedicated to Wilf Banks. Without his research the history of many public houses mentioned in this book would have disappeared forever. Wilf died in 1995 aged 86, before the completion of this edition of 'A Pub On Every Corner'. He would have enjoyed reading it.

I should like to give my special thanks to Stephen J. Reaney, who did so much invaluable work on the photographs which are reproduced in the book; and also to Keith Yule, without whose patience and technical assistance, this book may never have got past the planning stage.

Preface

The discovery and listing of the huge number of public houses, beerhouses and inns which have, at one time or another, existed in Sheffield is the product of many hours of painstaking research by Wilf Banks. The main text, together with much additional research and relevant historical material, is by Douglas Lamb and the photographs are by Wilf Banks, Keith Yule, Douglas Lamb, Tony Robinson, Stephen J. Reaney and others and through the courtesy of Sheffield City Library and its archives; the map work is by Keith Yule and Douglas Lamb developed from the original maps by Wilf Banks.

It wouldn't be an overstatement to claim that here is a unique document. There have, over the course of the years, been a number of books produced which have in varying degrees of depth covered the subject of the public houses of Sheffield. However, this book must be unrivalled in the sheer number of old public houses that it mentions; pubs, previously lost, which have been rediscovered, catalogued and located on an accurate map of the area.

In addition to this wealth of information, many of the public houses, both in the city area and in the suburbs, are the subjects of pen portraits designed to bring to the attention of the reader the little nuggets of information which make this book far more than just a list of old pub names.

Also included, apart from the many photographs of public houses both living and dead, is a complete range of maps, several interesting 19th century advertisements, a certain amount of gentle local history, a survey of old Sheffield breweries together with a short history of brewing and many other little 'odds and ends' which might be of interest to the reader.

The area covered is mainly the 'old' town of Sheffield—where it all began. This area includes the city centre, Attercliffe, Crookes, The Moor, Darnall, West Bar, Shalesmoor, Burngreave and parts of Hillsborough, Owlerton, Walkley and Broomhill. The boundaries are rather fluid and certain liberties have been taken to enable the inclusion of additional pubs. There are pubs which have been ignored as being too new and most of these are either in the city centre or the surrounding new estates.

While it would be a fine thing indeed to be able to claim that this book is a full and complete inventory of all the public, beer and alehouses that have ever existed in Sheffield, it would be untrue. The city has, over the last two hundred years, grown and developed; been built up and knocked down; streets have disappeared and new ones been laid. All this makes the tracing of this kind of history difficult. After all, the opening or closing of a humble beerhouse was not exactly an important historical occasion.

There will be pubs that I know about, but can't pinpoint, pubs that I have missed or about which there is no record apart from old peoples' memories. There will be readers who find mistakes or who know about a pub that I haven't included. To them I can only say that I am sorry, but surely 1,500 pubs are enough! Aren't they?

The local historian, R.E. Leader, writing in 1905, said:

> There are three things which must strike forcibly anyone who looks into the history of the old Sheffield taverns. The first is the prominent position that the landlords, in past days, took in the affairs of the town and the manner in which the learned professions were recruited from their sons. The second is the disappearance of many inns once foremost in rank—**a disappearance so complete that not even the sites can now be identified**. The third is the intimate part these houses played in the life of the town, when they were the accepted meeting places of the leading citizens, and the rendezvous where all public and a large measure of private business was transacted.
>
> The endeavour to discover traces of the old inns which have vanished might be expected to be easy. On the contrary it is surprisingly difficult!

Introduction

In The Beginning . . .

As Britain and its industrial base grew and expanded following the Reformation, the village of Sheffield developed into a small town. This increase in industry as a way of life and its attendant prosperity for the upper classes, did little for the quality of life of the workers—the coal miners, steel and cutlery workers who made up the bulk of the population. The conditions were no better in the 18th and 19th centuries. Far worse indeed than those which had been enjoyed, if that is the correct word, by the inhabitants of the rural villages which had until then been the usual pattern of living in Britain.

Homes were built with little skill and poor materials. There was no building control to impose any kind of order over the development of the town. The result was a filthy, cluttered area with ramshackle cottages and workshops centred on a small region around a market place. This area was linked together by a network of about thirty-five narrow, dark, winding streets and alleyways. Some of these—or at least their names—are still in existence: Fargate, High Street, Campo Lane, Balm Green, Waingate, Castle Green, Dixon Lane and others.

As the town grew, the original timber-framed buildings of the previous centuries gradually deteriorated and either fell down or were demolished. Today in the city only one original building, the Old Queen's Head (formerly known as The Hawle in the Pondes), is still standing. Now a public house, it is thought to have previously been a laundry, it dates from around the 15th century and is considered to be the oldest commercial building in the city.

In those days, the population had little or no idea of the importance of hygiene or sanitation and disease was widespread. Sewage disposal consisted of dumping all types of waste into the open drainage ditches which ran down the centre of most streets. These ditches were flushed every month or so when the waters from the ponds at Barker's Pool were released and all the filth was swept into the River Don. At least that was the general idea!

The Directory of Sheffield, 1797 states that: 'About this time was built, in Pepper Lane, the first brick house in Sheffield which was viewed by the inhabitants of the town with wonder and ridicule, they supposing it to be built of such perishable materials that it must soon yield to destruction'. This was in the year 1696!

The Old Queens Head

In 1615, a survey was carried out on behalf of Gilbert, 7th Earl of Shrewsbury, the Keeper of the Castle. This showed that the population of the town was 2,207 and it gives a fair insight into the miserable way of life endured by those people:

> By the survaie of the towne of Sheffield made the second daie of Januarie 1615 by twenty-four of the most sufficient inhabitants there, it apeareth that there are in the towne of Sheffield 2,207 people; of which there are 725 which are not able to live without the charity of their neighbours. These are all begging poore.
>
> 100 households which relieve others. These (though the beste sort) are but poor artificers; among them is not one which can

> keepe a teame on his own land, and not above tenn who have grounds of their own which will keep a cow.
>
> 160 householders, not able to relieve others. These are such (though they beg not) as are not able to abide the storme of one fortnights sickness, but would thereby be driven to beggary.
>
> 1222 children and servants of the said householders; the greatest part of which are such as live by small wages, and are constrained to worke sore, to provide them necessaries.

In 1672, a tax was imposed on hearths and a survey showed that there were 224 cutlers smithies in the town—a ratio of 1 per 2.2 households. These were merely small lean-to extensions to the cottages or small out-houses standing in the backyard. In 1678, the population was about 3,000 and by 1750 it had grown to 15,000 and was rising rapidly. It was probably inevitable that with a fast-growing and largely ill-educated and poorly paid population, Sheffield developed, in the 18th and 19th centuries, into a town which had, almost literally, a 'pub on every corner'. One example is Bailey Street—in 1840 it was fifty yards long and contained 192 houses, 40 workshops and 5 pubs!

Inns, hotels, public houses and alehouses were in an abundance. The vast majority of which bore little or no comparison to the well-lit, clean and comfortable establishments of our century. Some being often little more than the front room of a terraced house with a couple of barrels of home brewed beer in the back yard. In these houses, usually alehouses, it was common for the wife to attend to the customers during the day, while her husband went out to work; he would take over in the evenings. Many of these houses made little profit for the landlord. Others, in better positions such as the town centre or surrounded by workshops, often carried a sign outside which read: 'Drunk for a penny, dead drunk for two pence and clean bedding straw free!'

A list of the prices for beer and ale shows that this sign was probably true. In 1400, best ale sold for a penny halfpenny a gallon; in 1500 the price was threepence and in 1600 the West Riding Quarter Sessions ordered that no ale was to be sold at more than one penny a quart. In those days, of course, there was no Excise Tax on ale but it was to come very soon.

These were the days of rough, cheap, strong ale; poverty, filth, crime and violence. There were no really effective licensing laws until an Act of Parliament was passed in 1822. This piece of legislation was also aimed at stamping out the practice of serving short measure pints of beer, which had been a common offence for years. In 1790, 22 persons, most of them ale or beerhouse keepers, were brought to court and fined for 'keeping short pints'.

An extract from that Act was published in the Leeds Mercury, 1822:

> Caution to publicans. On Friday 11th October, instant, the Act of Parliament which was passed in the last session regulating the granting of licences to alehouse keepers came into full operation. By the provisions of that Act all alehouse keepers are required, under penalty of 40/-, to sell their ale, both in and from their houses, in pewter measures sized to standard, and in no other manner, and it must be so served to the customer; by being brought into his presence in such measure, it may be put into any other vessel to be drunk or carried out of the house. As one moiety of the penalty goes to the informer and the other to the poor of the parish, it behoves alehouse keepers to be on their guard . . .

This act did nothing to control the times that public houses opened and, if the landlord thought that it would pay, as it usually did on pay nights or Saturdays, many would stay open as long as there was money to be spent and the trouble was under control.

With drunkenness an increasing problem, two debtors prisons were opened in 1756, in Scotland Street and Tudor Street (there was already an older prison in Pudding Lane, now King's Street) and these held a large number of men and women jailed for alehouse debts. It was possible to be jailed then for any debt above sixpence! In 1787, there were 161 licensed victuallers in the town (these were public houses with a full licence enabling them to sell beer, wines and spirits) and many more alehouses. The temptation to drown out some of the harsher aspects of life must have been irresistible. The poverty and wretched living conditions being as much to blame as human weakness. Many men were paid their wages in public houses, which was the custom of the day, and then proceeded to drink themselves insensible leaving their wives and children to exist on a few pennies for the rest of the week.

In 1830, the Beerhouse Act permitted any householder to retail beer from his premises on payment of two guineas for the licence. The purpose of this was to reduce the sales of spirits, especially cheap 'gin', by making beer more accessible and cheaper. When this act was rescinded about forty years later, many of the alehouses which had appeared were allowed to remain, as they were by then considered to be well-established businesses.

In 1852, it was found that the incidence of drunkenness in Sheffield was far higher than in towns of a similar size. Sheffield then had a population of 135,000, and there were 392 public houses and a further 335 alehouses. In the best tradition of British local government, a committee was set up to investigate the problem. It suggested, after due deliberation, that the sale of alcoholic drink to those under seventeen years of age should be banned, public houses should be made to close at eleven o'clock at night and the custom of paying workmens' wages in public houses should cease. Like many council committee suggestions then and now, it was filed and forgotten. In 1900, when the building of the huge steelworks in the East End of the, by then, city had pushed the population past 400,000, there were 514 public houses and 651 alehouses. In 1990, in an area roughly the same as the one considered in 1900, there were 188 public houses and no alehouses. The last beer-only house to change to a full licence did so in 1990 and is The Forest Inn, off Rutland Road.

In 1869 and 1872, the Government passed Parliamentary Acts which allowed the local justices to exercise some measure of control over the public house trade and, together with the appearance of several well intentioned temperance societies, some restraint was obtained. With the coming of the First World War, far more restrictive licensing laws, which have only recently been altered, were imposed on the country and for the first time ever, public drinking habits were severely curtailed.

Population figures

This table gives some idea of how rapidly the population of Sheffield increased over the years:

1571–**1,676**	1801–**45,755**	1851–**135,307**	1893–**333,962**
1615–**2,207**	1821–**65,275**	1861–**185,157**	1911–**455,081**
1672–**3,000**	1831–**91,692**	1871–**239,947**	1926–**523,300**
1736–**14,531**	1841–**110,891**	1877–**282,130**	1990–**550,000**

Why the decrease in drinking establishments?

In Sheffield one hundred years ago, there were about 1,800 premises where it was possible to buy alcoholic drink. This, of course, was long before supermarkets appeared and the 'four pack' of lager became available to all. This total was split up three ways—the straightforward public house (inn, tavern or hotel), the beerhouse with a licence for on-the-premises drinking and the beerhouse with only an 'off licence'. These latter premises were usually also normal shops, where, along with provisions, the customer could buy drink. This was often supplied, as in a public house, from a barrel, the customers providing their own containers. There were about six hundred such premises and a similar number of beerhouses with 'on' licences. These were almost the same as public houses, but were not allowed to sell spirits or wines. The public houses were, I suppose, the top of the heap in the pecking order of drinking establishments. In these places it was possible to buy the full range of alcoholic drinks which could be consumed either on or off the premises. There were over five hundred of these houses in Sheffield.

Today, there are no beerhouses in the city and the number of public houses has dwindled to between two hundred and two hundred and fifty, depending on how far the survey area is spread. There are several reasons for this, one is not that Sheffield townspeople have lost their taste for drinking, rather that the country and the way of life has altered. At the turn of the century and before, many of the jobs followed by the workers of the city were either hot or dusty or both. Cutlers in the grinding shops, file makers and tool makers of all kinds worked, more often than not, in a fog of dust, dirt, smoke and heat and anyone who has ever walked through a rolling mill will not need to be told of the sort of conditions that those men had to tolerate.

Now, regrettably, the bulk of these jobs have gone and with them the many corner beer-offs, constantly busy during the day as the workers sent out 'the lad' for beer to replace the fluid lost in sweat. Also gone are many of the corner pubs, which were always popular for an hour's drinking after the shift had ended—and sometimes during it! Also, in the second half of this century, huge slum clearance programmes were launched and not only whole streets, but whole communities were swept away with the rubble. With them went the little corner pubs and beerhouses, never to be seen again.

Another reason for the fall in the number of drinking places must be the view of successive governments that the beer drinker is fair game, always good for a penny on a pint every time a budget comes around. The trouble is, that together with increases from the breweries, the price of the humble pint has become hard to find for ordinary working people with other calls on their purses. The night out at the pub is becoming a once or twice a week affair and six pints have shrunk to four or less. Pubs are struggling, so the price goes up to compensate for lack of sales, so the sales fall—and so the spiral continues.

It is a fact that during the 20th century far more public houses have been pulled down or converted to other uses than have been built. This situation has become even more pronounced recently. In the late 1980s, the government passed legislation aimed at breaking the stranglehold the brewery conglomerates had on the industry. The idea was that the large breweries would be made to reduce the vast number of public houses that they controlled—Whitbread Brewery has since shed roughly 2,000 pubs but still controls 6,000—and that these public houses would be sold off to spread the area of ownership. This would, so the reasoning went, increase competition and reduce price increases. It was a good idea. If the public houses released onto the market by these big companies had been snapped up by eager buyers and run efficiently, the future of the industry would have looked a good deal rosier.

This, however, hasn't happened. Instead, many of the public houses for sale have either failed to attract a buyer and have remained boarded up and pathetically derelict, or they have been bought and opened as free-houses only to fail as a business through lack of financial and brewery backing or expertise. Still more public houses are struggling to exist as the big breweries drive increasingly harder bargains with their tenants in a bid to achieve the same financial return with less outlets. Hence, more overheads—increased prices. Not much, as far as the ordinary drinker is concerned, has changed!

Probably the most important result of the legislation in Sheffield, was the closure in July, 1993 of the 170 year old Exchange Brewery, Bridge Street. Formerly owned by Tennant Bros, this brewery was taken over by Whitbreads in 1962. Not only have scores of people lost their jobs because of this, but a brewing legend has also disappeared.

This, of course, is a fairly simplified outline of the situation as it stands at the moment, but it covers the main principles. Since this book was begun several dozen well known, and well used, public houses have put the towels over for the last time. It is a tragedy! This is the reason that I have decided

Pictured soon after closure 1993

it would be pointless to include, as once intended, a list of the public houses still open in the area researched.

Many of the pubs which have gone over the years were nothing special, to be sure, but each had it's hard core of regulars and were meeting places for all sorts of clubs, societies and games' leagues. They were the heart of many neighbourhoods and will be sadly missed. The future, as I see it, is of a few profitable beer dispensing houses, with a faceless person running things from behind an electronic money collecting machine!

If this book does what it is meant to do, then its readers will remember the old pubs that they once knew and used, the streets that they once graced, the people that used them, and the memories conjured up will bring them, if not pleasure, then at least a pause from the hard-nosed world of today and a quiet thought about how it used to be.

The East End of Sheffield

With the construction of the huge steelworks in the east end of the city at the turn of the century, a large number of new houses and shops also appeared in the adjoining areas. Along Carlisle Street East, the steelworks were on one side of the road and the houses, shops and public houses along the other. With the majority of the workforce being employed on a three shift system, the pubs were ensured an almost continuous supply of customers, either going on shift or coming off, from both the works and the neighbouring dwellings.

On the maps covering Attercliffe, there is a fair representation of how the pubs were sited in relation to the steelworks and the list given below shows how these pubs were interspaced with the shops and houses:

	No.	
Carlisle Street East:	No 5	**Firth—Carlisle Street Hotel**.
	43	Stacey—coffee shop.
	49	Shopkeeper.
	51	**Crookes—Rock Inn**.
	65	Mason—householder.
	73	Lamber—shopkeeper.
	77	Short—tailor.
	83	Thorpe—shopkeeper.
	87	**Fox—Woodman Hotel**.
Harleston Street		**Henry Jackson—Crown Inn**.
	89	Willis—shoemaker.
	101	Morris—hairdresser.
	103	Ricketts—shopkeeper.
	109	Sawyer—tobacconist.
	113	Samuel—shopkeeper.
	115	Rose—householder.
	121	Hall—shoemaker.
	123	Atkinson—shopkeeper.
	125	Curran—tailor.
	127	**Smithies—Palmerstone Hotel**.
	131	**Mellor—Atlas P.H.**
	133	Tin plate worker.
	135	**Little Atlas P.H.**

137 **Rifle Corps Hotel**.
139 Bates—coffee shop.
141 Taylor—shopkeeper.
143 **Wilby—Coach and Horses P.H.**
145 Davidson—tobacconist.
147 **Robinson—Wrekin P.H.**
Courts 21, 23, 25, 27 Hartley—coke merchant
235 **Parker—Corner Pin P.H.**

When the east end of Sheffield was in full industrial production, there were, at one time or another, over fifty public houses and beerhouses between Wicker Arches and what is now the Meadowhall shopping centre. Now, there are only twelve remaining. Recent casualties were The Excelsior and The Lambpool which were demolished in July, 1993.
The remaining pubs are:

The Bulldog, The Sportsman, The Carlton, The Dog & Partridge, The Horse and Jockey, The King's Head, The Station, The Travellers, The Greyhound, The Pheasant, The Carbrook Hall and The Commercial.

The Excelsior

The Lambpool

Origins of Some Public House Signs and Names

Many of the public house names and signs which were and are found in the City are, of course, common throughout the country, but there are some which underline the development of the iron and steel industries and the cutlery trade in Sheffield. There are also some public house names which are strange or unique to Sheffield.

There must be, as with all historical accounts, many 'possibles and probables' in the text and few 'certainties'. It is better to be like that, than to make a positive statement which is incorrect.

Pub dates

Dating the public houses listed in this book was very difficult. In the 18th and 19th centuries, there must have seemed little need to bother with the dates when a pub opened or closed. This has thus posed many problems when trying to accurately date the life span of the huge number of these establishments.

Many dates though have been tracked down, but rarely have both certain opening and closing dates been found. Where a date for a pub being open is given, it means just that; the pub was open on that date, although it may have been open much longer. Finding out the date a pub closed has been much easier and where these are printed, it usually means the actual date on which it closed, although, in a few instances, it may mean that it is the nearest date which could be found and that the pub closed a few years earlier. For example: The Lambpool, Attercliffe Common (1870–1988, building demolished 1993). This means that the pub was open in 1870, but it could have opened a dozen or fifty years earlier. It closed in 1988.

Inn Signs and Their History

In the middle ages, it was rare for a man to be able to read or write and along with most other businesses, pubs found that it was to their advantage to advertise their existence by the display of a recognised sign or token. During the 18th and 19th centuries, which was the time when most of the public house signs in Britain first appeared, as well as using natural, mythical, mystical or religious objects, it was common to use the names and likenesses of the popular figures of the day.

Britain was different then. The creation of the largest empire in the history of the world was underway. The army and navy were almost always involved in action somewhere around the globe, heroes were not hard to find, and with the slower pace of life, they lasted longer.

The aristocracy of the day also played a more important part in common peoples' lives, having a huge say in the running of the government, as well as often being the local major landowner and benefactor. Few of the persons whose names and effigies appeared on the public house signs would have ever have been seen, let alone have visited the neighbourhood. Life then was only as fast as a horse could travel, and travelling itself was a rare event to most people. They remained almost legendary figures, except perhaps to returning sailors or soldiers. These veterans would be able to ensure plenty of free beer in exchange for their tales of derring-do in the company of the Lords' Nelson and Wellington.

The Wellington Inn, Henry Street, now the Cask and Cutler

An 'ale stake' was one of the earliest public house signs. This was simply a pole or log of wood attached to the front of the building or sunk into the ground outside, in clear view, beside the road. Often it had a bundle of barley, hay or ivy attached to it. Later additions such as a painted, carved effigy were the forerunners of the pub signs as we know them today. As well as informing the customers that here ale was for sale, they also informed the ale conner that a new batch of ale had been brewed and was available for testing.

The Ale Conner

This man was usually appointed by the local lord of the manor; the first of these officials was recorded as operating in London in 1377. He was, in effect, a rough and ready quality control inspector, who was expected to taste the ale and evaluate it's condition. He also informed the owner of the alehouse of the current prices to charge. At that time, the price of ale was closely linked to the price of bread as both were considered basic dietary items.

One tale, which cannot be verified, but is worth telling, states that: 'the conner poured a measure of ale onto the seat of a wooden stool and then sat on it in his leather breeches and didn't move for half an hour. If, at the end of this time he found that he was stuck to the stool, then the ale was "a good drop of stuff" '!

This job of ale taster must have been one of the better ones around at the time, but it did have its drawbacks. Henry Andrew, who was ale taster for the area of Ecclesall in 1753, was attacked by one Samuel Hill of Little Common, who was presumably an ale or beerhouse keeper. Mr. Hill was fined 3/4d for 'making an affray and drawing blood upon the person of Hy. Andrew'!

There was a rhyme concerning an ale conner:

> A nose he had that gan show,
> What liquor beloved I trow,
> For he had before seven long years,
> Been of the town the ale conner.

It doesn't scan too well, but I only find them, I don't write them!

Royal Signs

Many of these are common and self explanatory: Victoria, Albert, Prince or Princess of Wales, Princess Royal, King's Head etc. Most royal persons had at least a handful of public houses named after them.

The George or Royal George probably refers to King George IV, 1762–1830. He was the eldest of King George III's seven surviving sons, two more died in infancy, and between them these offspring have huge numbers of pubs named after them. This is rather curious, because most of them, as far as I can make out, weren't particularly popular with the general public. As well as public houses, many street names derive from this royal family. King George IV was more famous as The Prince Regent, The Regent or Prinny.

He became Regent when his father, George III, proved incapable through bouts of madness to be able to continue. He was also, as the king's eldest son, Prince of Wales and pub signs such as The Three Feathers or Feathers are derived from the three feathers which make up the prince's insignia.

The George Hotel, Boston Street/Arley Street

He was not a great success as a king, had a disastrous marriage, but was literally a larger than life character, being hugely fat, who seemed to have been liked or loathed in about equal proportions. When he died, the country was in dire need of reforms. These were partially supplied under the premiership of the Earl Grey, who is mentioned later. George IV's wife was named Caroline, the daughter of the Duke of Brunswick, which gives the reason for the several pubs in Sheffield which had Brunswick in their names—these have all closed.

The second brother, Frederick, Duke of York and Albany, 1763–1827, was commander in chief of the British army for many years and missed out on

The Frog and Parrot, formerly The Prince of Wales

being king by dying too early of dropsy. Four pubs in Sheffield had names associated with him: The Duke of York, Main Street, Darnall and The York Hotel, Fulwood Road; these are still open. The Albany pubs in Gloucester Street and Surrey Street are not.

The next brother, William, Duke of Clarence, 1765–1837, became in his turn, William IV. He is usually commemorated in William or King William named pubs, of which there were several in the town, or Clarence of which there were four.

The two eldest sons of King Edward VII were the Dukes of Clarence and York. It is possible that some pubs were named after them. Several pubs were named after Edward's wife, Alexandra of Denmark.

The seventh brother was Adolphus, Duke of Cambridge, 1774–1850. A military man and reasonably popular, he was probably the most stable and sensible of all the male offspring of King George III. He had no mistresses that anyone knew about and had three children by his wife, Princess Augusta of Hesse-Cassel. He had three pubs named after him and one of Sheffield's most famous streets.

Prince Leopold, a minor German aristocrat, was the name of one pub in Sheffield. He married Charlotte, daughter of King George IV, who died in childbirth aged about twenty-one. He became King of the Belgians. The pub was in St. Phillips Road and is no longer open. It is possible that this pub was named after Leopold, Duke of Albany, a son of Queen Victoria.

The King's Head, Attercliffe Road

The King's Head is popular everywhere. Other variations are The King's Arms and The King and Miller. There were a dozen so named pubs in Sheffield. It is believed that before the Reformation, when King Henry VIII broke away from the Roman Catholic Church, many where called The Pope's Head. These were swiftly and diplomatically changed. It was best not to upset people like King Henry VIII.

Aristocratic Names

Many of the upper layers of the British aristocracy are well represented in pub names, especially around Sheffield and its immediate area which has always had its fair share of dukes.

The family of the Dukes of Norfolk undoubtedly have the commonest 'aristocratic' names to be found in Sheffield with streets, buildings and parks named after them, as well as public houses. In the past there used to be at least eighteen public houses alone called The Norfolk Arms and many more variations of that. It is not surprising, as this family have been major landowners in and around the town for centuries.

This family also accounts for the name of The Earl of Arundel and Surrey, Queen's Road. This is a minor title held by the duke and is usually used by his son and heir as a courtesy title. This corner pub still flourishes.

Pubs with the name of Howard, Gower and Fitzalan are also using Norfolk family names. The two other pubs with Arundel in their names took it from Arundel Castle, the family seat in Sussex—The Arundel Castle, Arundel Lane and The Arundel Cottage, Arundel Lane—both are closed.

Rutland comes from the Dukes of Rutland, who owned a shooting lodge on the outskirts of Sheffield and large amounts of land. Two pubs were named after these dukes—The Rutland, Neepsend Lane, now closed and The Rutland Arms, Brown Street which is still in existence.

The Rutland Arms, Brown Street

Portland is from the Dukes of Portland, who once owned a huge and stately mansion in Clumber Park near Worksop. Earlier this century, the duke at that time became so angry during an argument with the government about taxes that he had it pulled down. There were two Portland Arms in the town, in Portland Street and Rockingham Street. The dukedom, which was created in 1716, has recently become extinct—July 30th 1990, although there is still an Earl of Portland—a title which was created in 1689.

The Dukes of Devonshire and their family have left a lasting mark on both the pubs and street names of Sheffield. Three Devonshire Arms existed in the area covered by this book—in Eldon Street, closed in 1917; South Street, Moor; open in 1825, bombed in 1940; and Ecclesall Road, recently rebuilt and still open. The Granville Inn, Granville Street, now closed, was named after the Ist Earl of Granville, who married Harriet Cavendish, sister of the 6th Duke of Devonshire. The family name of the Earls of Granville is Leverson-Gower and is remembered in various street names and a pub.

Another of the Duke's sisters, Georgiana, married the 6th Earl of Carlisle and two pubs commemorated this—the Carlisle Street Hotel, which is still open, and the Carlisle Tavern, Carlisle Street, which closed in 1910.

The Burlington, Burlington Street, which closed in 1957, was named after the Earl of Burlington, a minor title of the Dukes of Devonshire.

The Carlisle, Carlisle Street East

It is possible that The Egerton Hotel, Fitzwilliam Street, now closed, was named after Admiral Francis Egerton, husband of Louisa Cavendish, sister of the 8th Duke of Devonshire.

Earls have had their share of pub names: The Earl of Newcastle was remembered with The Newcastle Arms in Newcastle Street which closed in

1905 and became a lodging house. This earl took Sheffield Castle in 1643 in the King's name during the Civil War, after first decimating Rotherham.

The Earls of Shrewsbury also figure with three pub names, two of them in South Street, and one in Broad Street. The 4th Earl had custody of Cardinal Wolsey at Sheffield Manor, and the 6th Earl, one of the husbands of Bess of Hardwick, had charge of Mary, Queen of Scots, both at the castle and manor.

There is a legend that when the 1st Earl of Shrewsbury was killed with his son, in 1453, whilst fighting the French, so many Hallamshire men were killed with him that 'there was no family or house in Hallamshire that did not lose a father, or brother, or husband, or son on that fatal day'. It is a story of the times, true or not.

There used to be a Marquis of Waterford public house and six with the name of Talbot. These also derive from the Earls of Shrewsbury and the family name. The first title was bestowed on the family in 1442 and they are the Premier Earls of England and Ireland. The present earl is the 22nd. There is no Marquis of Waterford now and the title has been absorbed to make up the Earls of Shrewsbury and Waterford.

The 4th Earl built the Shrewsbury Chapel in Sheffield Cathedral in the reign of Henry VIII. It was probably a shrewd move in those days, as it helped to keep both your titles and your head if you kept in well with Big Hal!

The chapel, in my opinion, is too overtly ornate to be considered beautiful. It is, however, said to be crammed with 'sepulchral monuments of great beauty'. Not my words, but from an early 19th century book called 'Hallamshire' written by the well known contemporary historian, Joseph Hunter.

There is an interesting and rather gruesome account concerning the Shrewsbury Chapel in the book and I thought that it had merit and 'colour' enough to justify its inclusion in a book about pubs. The vaults under the Shrewsbury Chapel have a considerable interest attached to them. Hunter makes out a list of eighteen persons buried there. He gives the following account of a visit he paid to these vaults in 1809:

> By eight or nine steps from the chancel we descended to an upright door, which we found so decayed that it fell from its bolt and hinges on a very slight force being applied to it. We were then admitted to a room about 10 feet square and six feet in height, its stone roof supported by a rough hewn pillar, rising in the centre. We found only two coffins lying on trestles.

The vaults were again entered on 18th May, 1858, for the purpose of making a search in connection with the celebrated Shrewsbury Peerage case, then pending in the House of Lords. The following particulars were given in a local paper of the time:

A list had been made of seventeen members of the noble family buried in the vaults, beginning with Ann, Countess of Shrewsbury, daughter of Lord Hastings, early in the sixteenth century and ending with Henry Howard Esq., 1787. In the open part of the vault were

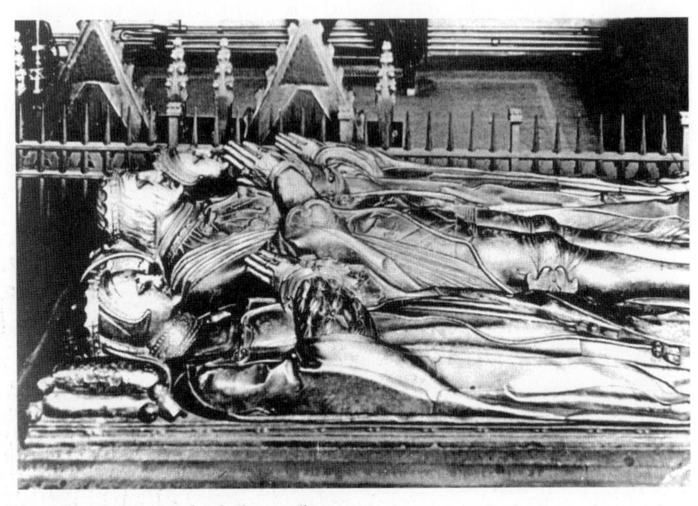

Tomb of the Earl of Shrewsbury

found two coffins, one of them Gilbert, Earl of Shrewsbury, who died in 1616, and the other of Mr. Henry Howard. The wooden coffin of the Earl had been several times renewed, and in 1774 a brass plate put upon it, containing the inscription found on the lead in which the body was enveloped. On opening the coffin, it was found that the lead covering the body was not in the form of a coffin, but wrapped about it after the manner of the envelopes of an Egyptian mummy. The lead bore an inscription containing the full titles of the Earl.

Mr. Hunter had supposed that the other coffins were walled up on the north side of the vault, under the tomb of George, the 4th Earl and the founder of the chapel; and in order to find them an excavation was made in that direction. After this had been prosecuted for about four feet, it was found that it had reached the original foundation of the church. No trace of a vault or of any human remains were found.

A search was then made under the floor of the vault. Here was found a body encased in lead. The lead tore like coarse paper, and being removed from around the face it disclosed the skull, evidently of a male person, on which there still remained some reddish grey hair. There was, however, no inscription. Two coffins were found under this one, one containing the body of John Sherborne, gentleman, and the other his widow, Ruth. There were also the remains of an empty wooden coffin, without date or name. A great number of loose bones were found, with no trace of the coffins.

The conclusion was that at some time the vault had been ransacked, the lead stolen, and the contents buried here. After excavating the floor about six feet, the labourers found themselves stopped by solid rock.

Personally, I'm a great believer in cremation!

The Wentworth House Hotel, Milford Street

The Earls of Oxford, the De Veres, who supported the usurper, Henry Tudor, used the sign of the Blue Boar as their emblem, while the White Boar was used by King Richard III and the House of York. After the Battle of Bosworth, in 1485, many White Boar signs were prudently and quickly repainted blue so as not to appear to oppose the new King Henry. It paid to be fairly fast on your feet in those days. There used to be three Blue Boar public houses in Sheffield, but they are all now gone.

The Earls of Wharncliffe, another local family, have had two pubs named after them: one in King Street and one in West Street.

The Earls Fitzwilliam, also local, have had two pubs with the family name and four named after Wentworth House, their former family seat on the fringes of Sheffield. This huge house, not at the moment inhabited on a regular basis, has the longest frontage of any house in England. It is, however, devoid of any trace of the possessions of the Fitzwilliams, who no longer own it and it must, although kindly, be considered a white elephant of a building—a too large and ungainly relic of a former age. One pub carrying the Wentworth name is still open in Milford Street. The Earldom, created in 1746, became extinct during the 1980s following the death of the 8th Earl.

The Effingham Arms, Sussex Street, was named after the earls of that name who are, I believe, yet another branch of the Duke of Norfolk's family. The 3rd Earl has been the most prominent member of this family. He was a descendant of the Lord Howard who commanded the fleet which defeated the Spanish Armada in 1588. He lived at Thundercliffe Grange, near Rotherham.

The 3rd Earl was opposed to the Government's policy during the American War of Independence and did in fact refuse to join his regiment and serve in America. He made an impassioned speech on the subject in the House of Lords, this was said to have been the best speech he ever made. His stand on the war was soon forgotten and he became Deputy Earl Marshal of England from 1777 until 1782. He was then appointed Treasurer of the Royal Household, a Privy Counsellor and George III made him a colonel in the army.

His rise to prominence didn't stop there—in 1784, he obtained the lucrative post, salary £5,500 per year, of Master of The Royal Mint, a post he held for five years. In 1789, he became Captain-General and Governor of Jamaica, where he died in November 1791 aged only forty-four. He and his wife are buried in Spanish Town, a long way from The Effingham Arms, Sussex Street, Sheffield!

There used to be one public house named The Lord Ratcliffe, Lord Street, this also had a connection with the Norfolk family. Lord Ratcliffe was the 3rd Earl of Sussex and his mother, Elizabeth, was the daughter of Thomas Howard, 2nd Duke of Norfolk.

There were two public houses named after the 2nd Earl Grey (1764–1845), who was a Whig statesman under whose Premiership, 1830–34, were passed

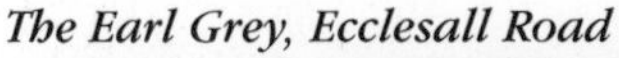
The Earl Grey, Ecclesall Road

the Reform Bill of 1832, a Bill which abolished slavery throughout the British Empire (1833) and the Poor Law Amendment Act (1834). He is also commemorated in a particular type of china tea. He was a good man and deserved to have had far more pubs named after him. These two pubs were in Moorfields and Ecclesall Road.

Other pubs named after British Prime Ministers were The Sir Robert Peel, Carlisle Street which was open in 1862 and closed in 1917. Peel, who died in a riding accident in 1850, was Prime Minister from 1834–35 and 1841–46. He was famous for creating the modern police force. The Aberdeen House, Aberdeen Street was possibly named after George Gordon, 1784–1860, 4th Earl of Aberdeen and Prime Minister from 1852–55, during the Crimean War. The Palmerston Hotel, Carlisle Street was named after Lord Palmerston, who was Prime Minister from 1855–1858 and from 1859 until his death in 1865.

The Burgoyne Arms, Langsett Road

The Burgoyne Arms, Langsett Road is still open and was named after Sir Montague and Lady Burgoyne. She was a member of the Bamforth family who were for many years Lords of the Manor of Owlerton.

It is not known what connection the Earls of Normanton had with Sheffield, they must have had some link as there is still a pub called The Normanton, in Grimesthorpe Road.

The Chandos, Rockingham Street took its name from Richard Grenville, who was created Duke of Buckingham and Chandos in 1822. His wife, Anne, whom he married in 1796, was the daughter and heiress of the 3rd Duke of Chandos. The title is now extinct.

The Lord Nelson, Arundel Street

Patriotic and Military Signs

These have always abounded in England, and Sheffield was no exception. Army and navy heroes were especially popular—Lord Nelson, The Duke of Wellington, Lord Raglan, Lord Rodney, General Gordon, Lord Cardigan, Cromwell. Even two foreigners get into the game—Blucher, who possibly saved the day at Waterloo by arriving with help on the left flank in the nick of time; he was a Prussian general, Napoleon wasn't and was on the other side.

Many Sheffield pubs were named after regiments or had other military connections: The Old Hussar, The Hussar, The Great Gun, The Big Gun, The Evening Gun, The Cannon, The Guard's Rest, The Rifleman's Canteen, The Rifle Corps, The Rifle Tavern, The Old Light Horseman, The Royal Lancers, The New Barracks, The Barrack Tavern, The Yeomanry, The Garrison Arms, The Soldier's Return, The Queen's Bays, The Life Guardsman, The Artillery Man etc..

The Old Light Horseman, Penistone Road, now demolished

The Hero and His Horse, Langsett Road, was named after the Duke of Wellington and the name was eventually changed to that.

The English have always liked to show how patriotic they are and have long named streets and pubs after battles—The Alma and The Inkerman were from the Crimean War, both streets and pubs; Waterloo pubs came from the Napoleonic Wars and The Standard after the defeat of the Scots in 1138. Don't ask me where.

One name, The Crooked Billet, is often associated with the steel industry, but it is also used in connection with the Battle of Towton, near York, 1461. This was one of the bloodiest battles fought during the Wars of the Roses.

The Blue Ball (Old Blue Ball)

This is said to represent a fortune tellers crystal ball, but modern usage associates it with more sporting activities. There were five pubs of this name in Sheffield: on Pond Street, Broad Street, Castle Foulds, Pye Bank and Bradfield Road—the latter is still open.

Bear Signs

Associated usually with the cruel, but popular sport of baiting a tethered bear with dogs. The sign is usually a Brown or a White Bear. There used to be a White Bear in High Street and there is still a Brown Bear in Norfolk Street.

Several public houses in the Ecclesall area of the city, then a separate village, are recorded as being centres for bear baiting in the 19th century. The Hammer and Pincers was one. This 'sport' was only staged here about once a year and ceased altogether after the landlord was 'worried' by a bear. The Rising Sun, near High Storrs, often provided both bull and bear baiting 'entertainments'.

Stables in Attercliffe once used to house the bears, used in bear baiting

The Monument

From the beginning of July until the end of October, 1832, a cholera epidemic ravaged Sheffield. 1,347 people caught this terrible disease and 402 people died from it, including the Master Cutler at the time, John Blake. The Cholera

Monument was erected in 1834–35 and the cornerstone was laid by James Montgomery, the local poet and newspaper editor. There used to be three Monument pubs in the town, but they too have died. Two of them were situated in South Street, Park, and one in Button Lane. There followed another outbreak of the disease in 1849, which accounted for 205 more lives.

The Ram

This was a common public house sign in cloth making areas. It was the emblem of the Clothmakers Company. There were four in Sheffield, rather strangely as this area is not renowned for cloth making. They were in Pea Croft, Kenninghall Street, Rockingham Street and Ecclesall Road.

The Greyhound

This was said to have been the badge first used by the King's Messengers until the late 18th century. It could also originate from the sport of hare coursing—take your pick. There were six Greyhound pubs in Sheffield, one still exists in Attercliffe. It was open in 1830.

The Green Man

This sign represents the spirit of fertility, the rejuvenating power of nature. It was a popular medieval image and appeared in many church carvings and in May Day dances. Sheffield had two, both now closed, in New Church Street and Broad Street.

The Union

This sign almost always referred to one of the Acts of Union—England and Scotland (1707) and England and Ireland (1801). Obviously popular, there were twelve pubs so named.

The Chequers

At one time there were five pubs in the town with this name. It probably is derived from the ancient checkered board, which was used in the early and middle ages as a method of calculation, much as an abacus is used in the Middle Eastern countries. Another idea is that it is possibly taken from the chequered pattern of the armorial bearings of ancestors of the Norfolk family, the Warrens. This family can be traced back to William de Warrenne, Earl of Warrenne in Normandy, a kinsman of William the Conqueror. Whatever the true answer, all five pubs with this name are gone.

The Plough

This almost always refers to the agricultural implement which was, in the middle ages, almost sacred. It was blessed and decorated on the Sunday or Monday following the twelve days of Christmas and then taken in procession around the village to raise money for the 'plough ale'.

The Eagle and Child

Sheffield had one pub with this name. It is taken from part of the family crest of the Earls of Derby. Seven pubs were just called The Eagle, but all have gone. There are also many pubs with Derby in the name. Sheffield had one in Smithfield, which closed in 1917.

The White Horse

Originally a pagan emblem, the standard of the Saxons and the badge of the county of Kent, referring to the white horses cut into the chalk hills. The galloping white horse was the heraldic device of the House of Hanover. There were seven White Horses in Sheffield at one time, but they have all trotted off into the sunset!

The White Hart

This was the shield badge of the ill-fated King Richard II (read your history!). This sign was well represented in the town with five pubs, two of which are still open—St. Phillips Road and Russell Street.

Pub emblem on The White Hart, Worksop Road, 1825–1992

The Oak Tree

This most English of symbols is usually seen as The Royal Oak or The Old Oak. It is said to commemorate the future King Charles II's escape from his enemies by hiding in an oak tree following his defeat in battle in 1651. These signs didn't, of course, appear until after the Restoration of the Monarchy. There were nineteen pubs in Sheffield with 'Oak' in their names and only four have survived: The Royal Oak in Hollis Croft, open in 1825; The British Oak, in Oak Street; The Bull and Oak, Wicker and The Royal Oak, Cemetery Road, which has recently changed it's name to The Brewing Engine and is now a freehouse. The site where the Bull and Oak stands was previously the assembly hall when Wicker was known as Assembly or 'Sembly Green, (this is covered elsewhere).

The Rising Sun or The Sun
This sign is thought to refer to King Edward III, the Son (Sun) of York. The Sun was his heraldic badge. It could, of course, just mean the sun! There used to be, but are no more, twelve pubs connected with this name.

Signs Associated With Brewing
Sheffield had plenty of this type of sign, which is not really surprising, as in 1891 there were many breweries listed in the town. The Brewery House, The Brewery Tap, The Brewer's Inn, The Brewer's Arms, The Three Tuns,

The Three Tuns, Leopold Street, closed 1987

The Barley Corn, The Barley Mow and, most popular of all, The Barrel, with eleven pubs. There were also The Tankard, The Old Tankard, The New Tankard, The Little Tankard and The Punch Bowl.

The Barley Corn, Cambridge Street, now demolished

The Beehive, there were six of those, was a reminder of the days when honey was used to sweeten beer and mead—before sugar became the usual thing. There is a surviving Beehive in West Street which was open in 1825, and two Barrels: Broad Lane, which was open in 1825 and London Road, which was open at the same time.

The Fleur de Lys (Lis)

Pubs with this emblem as a sign take it, so general opinion goes, from the arms of King Edward III (1327–1377) who was king of both England and France. The Fleur de Lys being the heraldic emblem of France. There were three pubs with this sign in Sheffield, but all have now gone. There is one in Totley which is still open and mentioned elsewhere, as is the one formerly in Attercliffe.

Burns Hotel or Head

Either John Burns, a late 19th century militant Socialist or Robert Burns, the Scottish poet, gave rise to the naming of The Burn's Head, Townhead Street, open 1833 until 1900 and The Burn's Hotel, Sheffield Road, now closed.

Admiral Rodney

This admiral led the British fleet to victory over the Spanish at Cape St Vincent in 1780, and the French off Dominica in 1782. The Rodney Arms, Fargate closed in 1898 and there was another, in Leadmill Road, which is also now gone. Out of town, there is an Admiral Rodney on the way to Bradfield.

Trade and Craft Signs

It will come as no surprise to find that the majority of these are associated with the iron and steel and cutlery trades. It is surprising, though, to find that there were so few public houses named after the coal mining industry, as at one time there were dozens of coal mines in the area. The Duke of Norfolk had his own Coal Company and was powerful enough, when the Sheffield and South Yorkshire Navigation Canal was being planned, to insist on a branch of it to serve his mines.

Signs associated with the town's main industries were:
The Three Whitesmiths, The Three Merry Smiths, The Moulders, The Sawmaker's Arms, The Scissormaker's Arms, The Anvil, The Plumper's Arms, The Blademaker's Arms, The Grinder's Rest, The Foundry, The Steelmelters, The Forge, The Turner's Arms, The Cutlers, The Filesmiths, The Vulcan, The Mason's (or Freemason's) Arms and The Grindstone.

The Three Horse Shoes and The Farriers are of course well known all over the country. Less well known were two pubs called the Bay Childers, one in High Street and the other in Bridge Street. This name comes, I believe, from Flemish weavers. Bay was a sort of cloth and the word 'childer' is an old English dialect word meaning 'to bring forth'.

There used to be a Collier's Arms in Duke Street and four pubs called The Miners in various parts of the town. All seven Filesmiths and all Cutlers pubs have gone, except the one in Worksop Road. In case you didn't know it, plumpers were men who stirred up the molten metal in a wrought iron works. The modern name for a whitesmith is tinsmith.

The Durham Ox

This is a popular name for pubs in the north of England and is reputed to be in memory of a huge ox which was bred by a Mr Charles Collins, who came from Ketton, County Durham. It died early in the 19th century. A Durham Ox pub still exists in Cricket Inn Road, although boarded up.

Yorkshire Stingo

This name is at least two hundred years old and is derived from a very strong, barley wine type Yorkshire ale. There was one such pub in Sheffield, which was open in 1833, but it is now closed.

Wheatsheaf or Baker's Arms
It is possible that a pub bearing the Baker's Arms sign was both a bakery and a pub. The sign is often 'borrowed' from the arms of the Baker's Company. There was a Baker's Arms in Clarence Street, and seven Wheatsheaf pubs, all of which have closed.

Woolpack or Woolsack
As wool was the chief source of national wealth in the middle ages, the industry left it's mark on public house signs. They are often found on communication lines and in the vicinity of the great sheep walks. As well as Woolpack or Woolsack, other common names were The Fleece, or as an indication of the wealth that it brought, The Golden Fleece, Wharf Street, also The Pack Horse, West Bar, and The Shepherd, Duke Street. The five public houses which bore this type of name are all gone. There was a Woolpack in Percy Street and a Woolsack in Upper Allen Street.

The Pack Horse Inn, West Bar, 1825–1902, went to allow for road widening

White Swan

This sign is taken from the badge of Edward of Lancaster, who was killed at the Battle of Shrewsbury. There were two in Sheffield, one at West Bar and one on Charlotte Street—both are gone.

The Elephant

The Elephant or The Elephant and Castle is the crest of the Cutler's Company. There are many of these in England. A notable one in London now refers to a whole district of the city. Sheffield, perhaps surprisingly as a centre of the cutlery trade, only had three, The Elephant in Norfolk Street; The Elephant and Castle in Arundel Street and The Elephant and Castle beside Lady's Bridge. There are also possible religious connections with this sign as it occurs in church decorations, especially in choir stalls. There is also a theory that the name is a corruption of Eleanor of Castille, who was the first wife of King Edward I (1239–1307).

The Elephant Inn, Fitzalan Square, 1825–1968

Falconry

Many inn signs are descended from this popular medieval pastime of the rich; very common are The Bird in Hand—Sheffield had four: Church Lane; Bridge Street; Broughton Lane and Brightside Lane and The Falcon—Sheffield had three: Flat Street; Leicester Street and Pea Croft.

All the following signs have religious associations:

The Angel, The Star, The Old Star, (not the Star and Garter, that is an order of chivalry), The Lamb, The Mitre, The Lion & The Lamb and The Noah's Ark. Also possibly The Fleece.

One of the Lion and Lamb public houses in Sheffield, which was in Pea Croft and closed in 1900 to become a lodging house, had the following rhyme on its sign:

> If the lion should kill the lamb,
> We'll kill the lion if we can,
> But if the lamb should kill the lion,
> We'll kill the lamb to make a pie on.

The Noah's Ark, Crookes

Also popular were Lions of various colours, a total of 34 in Sheffield at one time or another, but the Red Lion is sometimes thought to refer to John O'Gaunt (1340–1399), again taken from his shield emblem.

The Salutation is a popular pub name with religious overtones. It is the old English word for Annunciation and should represent the Archangel Gabriel saluting the Blessed Virgin with the words 'Ava Maria'. The three Salutation Inns in Sheffield: St. Phillip's Road; West Street and Attercliffe Common are all closed. The Cock and The Cross Keys are both symbols of St. Peter. The Anchor originally symbolised the theological virtue of Hope.

The Seven Stars sign is to be seen in many areas of the country and it comes from the seven stars in the celestial crown worn by the Virgin Mary. Another explanation is that they represent the Pleiades, a cluster of stars in the constellation of Taurus. In Greek mythology, the Pleiades were the seven daughters of Atlas and Pleione. There was one Seven Stars pub in Sheffield in Trippet Lane (Pinfold Street), it was open in 1787, but this has long since closed.

Sheffield Public House Nicknames

Public House	Nickname
The Norfolk Vaults, 1–9 Dixon Lane	The Cow Sheds.
The Wicker Brewery Hotel, Savile Street	The Hole in the Wall.
The Old No. 12, 27 Haymarket	The Double Six.
The Bricklayer's Arms, Hereford Street	The Mad House.
The Industry Inn, Corporation Street	The Swarf Oil.
The Black Swan, Snig Hill	The Mucky Duck (later adopted as official name).
The Old Blue Ball, Bradfield Road	The Blue Dumpling.
The Prospect View, Gleadless Road	The Cuckoo.
The Sportsman, Well Road	The Boiler's Rest.
The West Street Hotel, West Street	The Bull & Bush.
The Bull's Head, Dun Street	The Devil's Kitchen.
The Lord Nelson, Arundel Street	Fanny's.
The Marshall Tavern, Pye Bank	The Bacon Box.
The Traveller's Rest, South Street, Moor	Billy Lee's.
The Wellington, Brightside Lane	The Rubber Boot.
The Union, Bridgehouses	The Hand in Hand or Old Hand Shakes.
The Three Tuns, Silver Street Head	The Low Drop.
The Crown (or Old Crown), Attercliffe Common	The Long Drop.
The Dog and Partridge, Attercliffe Road	The Dog and Duck.
The St. Phillip's Tavern, St. Phillip's Road	The Monday Morning Knocking Shop.

The Guard's Rest, Sorby Street	The Widows' Hut.
21, Meadow Street	also, The Widows' Hut.
The Washington, Washington Road	The Cripples.
The Owl, Norfolk Street	Shout 'em Downs.

The Bull's Head, Dun Street, Shalesmoor. Once known as the Devil's Kitchen, now offices

The Sporting Angle

Public houses and sports of all types have always gone happily onwards hand in hand. Many pubs have never graduated much further than a dart board in the corner of the public bar and a pack of greasy cards or a box of dominos behind the bar. Others have been the centre of flourishing fishing clubs or have provided feared teams to compete in the inter-pub games leagues—darts, crib and dominos (5's and 3's).

Since the sad disappearance of the many public house bowling greens beneath the tarmac of carparks, very few pubs offer much in the way of outdoor entertainment.

One well known Sheffield pub which is in Upwell Lane, Grimesthorpe, the aptly named Bowling Green Hotel, still displays the remains of its green behind the main buildings. This is in a pathetic state of neglect and will, I suppose, soon disappear altogether beneath some 'new development'. It might as well, for its past use and beauty has been swallowed up by weeds and indifference.

Other bowling pubs were: The Wadsley Jack, Rural Lane, Wadsley, which still has a small green; The Old Blue Ball, Bradfield Road; The Gate, Penistone Road; and in Crookes, The Punch Bowl; The Ball; and The White Lion, London Road.

In the past, several pubs in the area covered by this book provided more outdoor activities than a quiet game of bowls.

The Queen's Ground, formerly The Queen's Hotel, Langsett Road was there in 1825 and is still open today. This public house had a running track situated at the rear and this was much used by professional runners and, presumably, by the bored soldiers from the barracks almost opposite.

On Attercliffe Road,The Pheasant had a sports arena. This pub was demolished in 1927 and a new one built.

The Sheaf House Hotel, Bramall Lane, which has been open since 1816, was another well known sporting pub.

Professional runners were common then, especially in the north of England and handicap running matches were very popular. A successful runner could expect to make a fair living out of it, if he kept himself free

The Pheasant Inn, Attercliffe Common, demolished 1927. A new pub now stands on this site

from injury and placed his bets shrewdly. He could also expect some of the sort of popularity reserved for the pop stars of today.

One man who was world famous for his running and walking exploits was George Littlewood, born in 1859, died in 1912, who was at one time reputed to be the World Champion endurance and distance racer. He used to train locally at Tinsley Park Wood, which has since gone, and his trainer was named Tommy Chick. In 1880, on September 7th, a six days long, distance endurance race began at the Agricultural Hall, London. George covered 406 miles and won the £50 first prize and a gold medal. One race that he lost, but which is one that he is best remembered for, was from Doncaster to Sheffield, a distance of almost 20 miles. His opponent was a horse and trap!

George Littlewood

When he was about a quarter of a mile from the finishing line and it was obvious that he wasn't going to win, he climbed into the trap beside the driver and finished the course in style! He ran all over the world and many times took part in races in Madison Square Gardens in New York, USA. When he retired he was, for a time, the landlord of The King's Head, Attercliffe Common. This is also the building in which Samuel Jackson of Spear & Jackson, the Sheffield toolmakers, was born. A later landlord was Billy Calvert, a lightweight boxer who was born in the area and who fought during the 1960s.

Another man well known in the running fraternity was Harry Hutchens. He was reputed have run 300 yards in an even 30 seconds. Whether this was in Sheffield or not is unknown.

Betting would have played a huge part in these sports meetings, with large sums of money being wagered on the outcome of the races. It must have all been rather 'under the table' stuff, as in those days off-course betting was strictly against the law—betting shops were still a hundred years away!

Boxing, be it with gloves or bare knuckles, has always been a favourite of the drinking classes and Sheffield has had its share of fights and fighters.

Both The Pheasant, Attercliffe Road, and The Sportsman's Group, Penistone Road, which closed in 1989, were popular locations for boxing matches and these attracted both big money and big names. One can imagine that it was also a meeting place for every villain, pickpocket and cardsharp in the area.

First amongst the men who fought in Sheffield must be ranked a man who is still mentioned in all good boxing history books—William Thompson of Nottingham, known to one and all as 'Bendigo'. He has an interesting story and must have led a full life. Said to have been one of triplets, he was born in 1811 and in 1832, at the age of only twenty-one, he became bare-knuckle heavyweight boxing champion of England by fighting and beating William Faulkner. During a long career in the ring, he had a series of three fights with a man named Benjamin Caunt or Gaunt. They fought a total of 192 rounds during these fights and Bendigo won the rubber 2 to 1.

As bare-knuckle pugilism was against the law, most of the fights and their venues were strictly guarded secrets. Bendigo fell foul of the law on many occasions and spent several periods of his life in jail. He turned to religion during one sentence and settled in Sheffield where he was, for a while, the landlord of The Manchester, 42 West Street, originally known as The William McReady and later renamed The Wharncliffe Arms.

Augustus (Gus) Platts was a Sheffielder born in 1891. He was a well known heavyweight boxer and often fought in the city—at The Attercliffe Boxing Hall and The New City Club, Carver Street. He came from a pub background, as his father was the landlord of The Red Lion, Holly Street. This little pub was there in 1825 and has survived much re-development of the area. A few years ago it was refurbished by Stones Brewery and is now known as The Old Red Lion—a small, snug, city pub. Gus Platts himself kept The Blue Boar, West Bar; The Ball, Green Lane and The Barleycorn, Cambridge Street. All these early 19th century pubs have now gone.

The Old Red Lion, Holly Street, previously The Red Lion

Another boxer who kept The Red Lion, Holly Street for a time, came from Staffordshire originally. His name was Harvey Flood and he boxed at lightweight. His mother was the landlady of The Albany Hotel in the city centre and Harvey himself, apart from The Red Lion, held a licence for The Raven, off West Street and The Harp Tavern, St. Phillip's Road. The Raven has been remodelled and was called The Hornblower, until changing recently to O'Hagan's. Harvey built and ran a small gymnasium behind it during his time as landlord and many a young boxer learned the ropes there.

Footballers have always been attracted to the pub trade when their playing days have finished and Sheffield, with two professional teams, has had it's quota over the years, both from Wednesday and United.

Sheffield Wednesday have been represented by: Tommy Cranshaw, who kept The Yorkshireman's Arms, Burgess Street. There has been a pub on this site as far back as 1796. Jimmy Spoors was landlord of The Old Blue Ball, Bradfield Road, a short walk from his old stamping ground. Freddie Kean, well known to pre-war Hillsborough fans, kept The Angel, Button Lane, in the 1930s. Bill Millership was licensee of The Sportsman, Railway Street, which closed in 1960, and also of The Fitzalan, Fitzalan Street, which closed in 1966; Billy Marsden kept The White Lion, London Road for a period. Ted Catling ran a number of pubs for John Smith's Tadcaster Brewery. He was licensee, at one time or another, of The Magnet, Southey Green; The Rose and Crown, Wadsley; The Kelvin Grove, off Infirmary Road and The Anvil, Stannington Road.

One old Wednesday player ran a pub called The Nelson, off The Moor and his wife looked after The Red Lion on Cambridge Street. This house became well known as Nell's bar. It was almost unique in Sheffield at the time for holding a 'supper licence'. This allowed the premises to stay open for an hour longer than the surrounding public houses and for a while, until perhaps other similar establishments appeared, it was a very popular place with young couples and theatre goers. The Red Lion was one of the first public houses to appear on Cambridge Street, then known as Coal Pit Lane, and it was there in 1796. Alas, it is no more.

Ernest Blenkinsop went out of town for his pub and kept The Sportsman, Manchester Road and he is mentioned later.

Sheffield United, which once had a very strict view about players' involvement with the licensed trade, had a couple of well known players who took pubs: The Broomhall Tavern, Broomhall Street, which was open in 1833 and closed in 1964 and The Burgoyne Arms, Langsett Road, which is still open.

Cricket, as it should, has connections with several Sheffield public houses.

The Cricket Inn, on Cricket Inn Road, recently closed, stands near a piece of ground which was used sometimes by the military and sometimes for cricket. This was in the early years of the 19th century. It is still a public open space providing a recreation area for the residents of the flats complex at Hyde Park. It spent many years doing service as a 'flapping' greyhound track, i.e. a track not affiliated to the Greyhound Racing Federation.

One pub, now gone, was involved in the development of cricket in Sheffield in a very important role, the Adelphi Hotel, Sycamore Street/ Tudor Way. This was demolished in 1969, when that whole small area of the city was redeveloped. The site is now dominated by the remarkable 'modern' building which houses the Crucible Theatre. At one time there were over a dozen pubs in this corner of Sheffield, but now the sole survivor is The Brown Bear, Norfolk Street.

On January 30th 1854, when a well known local single wicket cricketer, Harry Sampson, was the landlord, The Adelphi was the venue for a public meeting. This meeting resulted in the founding of a cricket and bowling ground on a nine-acre site leased from the Duke of Norfolk. This is now Bramall Lane, the home of Sheffield United Football Club. This grand old hotel was again used on January 8th 1863, when Yorkshire County Cricket Club formally became a reality.

Before Bramall Lane finally became a 100% football stadium, it was one of the finest cricket grounds in England and hosted both County and Test matches. Some of the feats achieved on the ground have a tenuous connection with public houses. A local historian recalled a scene he witnessed in July 1897. On that day, two Yorkshire batsmen, JT Brown and John Tunnicliffe set the then record first wicket partnership for the county when they put on a total of 378 playing against Sussex. After the batsmen had scored 100, two of his neighbours celebrated by drinking a pint of beer each in the bar. They then agreed to sup another pint for every further 50 runs scored. When the score reached 350, both men were feeling the ale and one of them, staring down at his fast shrinking pocket money said, 'If this goes on much longer, I'll be ruined'!

John Tunnicliffe, in May 1891, playing for Sheffield and Leicester against a Nottingham team, hit the ball out of the ground and into the yard of the brewery in Cherry Street.

In the early days of cricket, there were no scoreboards and various crude ways were employed to keep the score—notching sticks, chalking on stones or counting peas. When cricket was played on Hyde Park, off Cricket Inn Road, the townsfolk were kept abreast of cricket events by a runner who left the ground about every hour and ran down into the town. One famous messenger was known as Pincher. He was easily recognisable by the red suit he always wore as he hurried through the streets to place his news in the window of The Old No. 12, Haymarket. When he died, he was buried, at his request, at the corner of St. John's Churchyard nearest to Hyde Park cricket ground.

One of the most famous cricketers of the 19th century was Tom Marsden. His finest match was in July 1826, when a combined Sheffield and Leicester side took on Nottingham at Darnall. Tom scored 227, only the second ever double century scored in first class cricket, and he also claimed six Nottingham wickets. He became so popular with Sheffield cricket supporters that in 1831, a public subscription fund raised £50 to pay for an inscribed silver cup which celebrated his cricketing exploits. Sadly, after he became landlord of The Cricketers, Darnall, he took to heavy drinking and was dead at the age of thirty-eight. The cup is now in the City Council's silver collection.

Billiards, and to a lesser extent, snooker, were popular games in pubs and many of the stars of the 19th and early 20th centuries played at various pub venues in the city. Local players like Billy Mitchell, the Almond brothers, Laurie Steeples, Jack Seffers, Ken Phelan, Jack Lambert, 'Staffy' Brittle, John

Barrie, Charlie Simpson and others, mixed with legends like Joe and Fred Davies, Walter Donaldson, also a Yorkshireman, and Walter Lindrum, an Australian.

Some of the many pubs which staged billiards and snooker matches were The Maunche, Corn Exchange; The New Inn, Penistone Road; The Grey Horse, High Street and The Shades Vaults, Hartshead. There were a huge number of pubs with a snooker table, either full or three-quarter size. Today there is, but a handful.

Sheffield Beer and Breweries

Brewing as a business didn't really start to be considered a good commercial prospect until the middle years of the 18th century. Up until then, most of the public houses and ale or beerhouses brewed their own or were part of small brewing groups. However, since the setting up of the first 'public' brewery company in the 1750s, there is evidence that from then until the end of the 19th century, there were well over fifty breweries, at one date or another, spread over the face of Sheffield.

Some of these establishments seem to have been little more than glorified 'back yard' set ups, but at the other end of the scale were operations the size of Duncan Gilmours, S.H. Wards, William Stones and Tennant Bros.. These breweries all have a long history in brewing and several of the names still exist today, even in the dog eat dog brewery business. When Duncan Gilmour & Co. Ltd was swallowed up by the Leeds brewers, Joshua Tetley and Son Ltd, the company was able to contribute Lady's Bridge Brewery and some 350 public houses of various size. The brewery site is now beneath the magistrates court complex.

There is some doubt as to which person was the first to have opened a public brewery in Sheffield. According to an account written by Joseph Woolhouse in 1832, 'the first public brewery was (first) established at the top of Townhead Street,(the site of The Warm Hearthstone public house) the proprietor was Mr. John Taylor, 1754'. However, recent researches have discovered an advertisement in The Leeds Mercury for May 17th, 1744 which states that Thomas Elliott had a business established in Scargill Croft known as The Sheffield Brew-house. Thomas Rawson, a local miller and tanner, is usually the man credited in history books with opening a brewery first. This was in 1758 on a site at 28 Pond Street. The brewery continued in business for the next 182 years until it was destroyed by German bombs on the night of December 12th, 1940. The remains of the business, including its chain of public houses, was taken over in 1946 by Duncan Gilmour's Brewery.

In this book there are obviously many references to ale and beer and these days the use of these words has become interchangeable. In fact, ale and beer were at one time different drinks with different methods of brewing. In the old days people understood this, today we don't.

In simple terms, ale is made with water and grain, usually barley or sometimes wheat. The grain is malted, then scalded with boiling water and allowed to ferment. No other flavourings are usually added. Beer, on the other hand, is made by taking the 'wort' produced in the ale making cycle and adding hops to it. This mixture is then boiled and allowed to ferment. The rest of the civilized world seems to have known about this a lot earlier than this country. It was a method used in pre-Christian times. Germany, one of the great beer producing countries of the world and Holland, another beer-loving nation, exported hops and brewing knowledge to England during the 15th and 16th centuries. In the middle ages, most large quantities of beer and ale were produced by the monasteries and the establishments of the local lords of the manor. If the common people did brew, it was probably based on a communal system whereby each member of the group contributed what grain they could afford and received a like amount of the finished product. If honey was available, this was added to produce a type of mead. The production of alcoholic drink was not merely for enjoyment, but being high in carbohydrates, formed an important part of an otherwise monotonous diet.

Beer in the 19th century and probably before was a much stronger brew than that which is drunk today. In 1850, the strongest beer brewed by the Leeds brewers, Joshua Tetley & Sons Ltd, was called XX (Imperial) and it had the extremely high specific gravity of 1094. Their best selling pale ale had a S.G. of 1060 and of the twelve different types of beers they produced, the lowest S.G. was 1059—an average gravity for the complete range of 1074. This can be compared to the gravity of beer sold in 1982, when the average was 1037.

This decrease in the strength of today's beer has two main causes. During the First World War, in order to conserve grain supplies and thus the amount of bread and flour, the amount of grain allowed to be used by the brewers was restricted. This led to a shortage of beer, and unrest amongst the drinking population. The government realised this and in June 1917, it allowed the brewers to increase by one third the amount of beer produced. This concession was on condition that both the price and the strength of the beer was reduced. They went further than that in 1918 and ordered that no beer sold should have a specific gravity of over 1030. The days of rough, strong ales were over!

Another reason for the relative weakness of today's beer is that the method by which duty is levied on beer means that as the gravity of the beer increases, so does the duty payable. Taxes on beer are not new, probably the first time that the brewing trade was taxed was when brewing malt was taxed at 4d per quarter weight in 1614 during the reign of King James I. A few years later, in 1625, while Charles I was king, each barrel of beer was taxed at 6d. In 1689, the tax on beer was raised by 50% and a year later it was doubled. At the time, England was in desperate need of tax revenue to finance endless wars against various European countries, notably France, Holland and Spain.

During the 1690s, the importation of foreign distilled spirits, especially French brandy, was outlawed, while at the same time the restrictions on distilling spirits in England were drastically reduced.

All these measures had the effect of encouraging the manufacture and consumption of cheap 'gin'. This concoction was crudely made and probably lethal, bearing little similarity to the gin drunk today.

In 1729, a Gin Act was passed in parliament which slapped a £20 licence fee on the retailers of gin in the hope of reducing the 'gin flood'. It didn't work!

In 1736, a petition was composed by the magistrates of the county of Middlesex and sent to the government. This stated that: 'the drinking of geneva (gin), and other distilled spirits had for some years greatly increased; that the constant and excessive use thereof had destroyed thousands of His Majesty's subjects; that great numbers of others were by its use rendered unfit for useful labour, debauched in morals, and drawn into all manner of vice and wickedness.'

By 1736, the amount of gin distilled and sold was in excess of 6,000,000 gallons a year, so perhaps they had a point! Employers were paying their workers partly in gin and it was nothing unusual to see men with wheelbarrows selling gin in the streets.

The following was written at the time: 'Gin-shops, or what the English call spirit vaults, are numerous in the vicinity of these poor streets, and are set off with the magnificence of gilded doorposts, tarnished by contact with the unclean customers who haunt there. Ragged children come thither with old shaving-mugs, or broken nosed tea-pots, or any such makeshift receptacle, to get a little poison or madness for their parents, who deserve no better requital at their hands for having engendered them'.

Later in 1736, a new Act was passed which imposed a duty of £1 per gallon on gin and raised the fee for a retailing licence to £50. This did nothing to help the problem either, as smuggling and bootlegging became rife. In the seven years that the act was in force, only two distillers obtained licences, but over 20,000 people were brought before the courts for either making or selling gin or related spirits.

In London in 1739, it was estimated that one house in every six had liquor for sale—one for every forty-seven people!

The problem was finally brought under control by measures which seem to have been the ones which should have been laid down in the first place—licence fees were reduced and put under the control of local magistrates and revenue duties payable on gin were reduced to a realistic level, thereby encouraging distillers to set up proper, legal distilleries and produce a far better quality drink.

By the start of the 19th century, gin had raised its image above the level of the gutter and was beginning to be accepted as a 'civilised' drink along with whisky, rum and brandy.

In the 18th century, there were three popular types of beer or ale—cheap and medium priced brown ales and a higher priced light ale. As the years passed, the custom of mixing all three beers together to form one drink became common practice. It was known as 'three threads', and must have made many a landlord's life that little bit harder.

In 1722, a new beer called 'entire' began to appear on the market. This beer was aimed at providing both the same taste and effect as the three beer mixture. It was probably rather bitter, with a high alcohol content and a heavily hopped flavour. This 'entire' beer became so popular, especially with London market porters, that it became known as porter. It was found to improve as a drink after it had matured for a while and thus the breweries built huge vats for this purpose. The size of these maturing vats increasing with the popularity of the beer. One vat at the Meux Brewery in London was 22 ft high and held 22,000 gallons of beer. On October 17th 1814, it burst it's hoops and the flood of porter released drowned eight people!

Porter was exported to Ireland, became popular and, in 1759, Arthur Guinness began the world famous brewery which still bears his family name to this day.

An advertisement for 'entire' beer brewed by the Wilson Bros Brewery, Sussex Street can be seen in the photograph of The Prince of Wales beer-house, Sussex Street.

Two Small Independents

The Fat Cat, Alma Street and The Frog and Parrot, Division Street.

The days of public houses producing their own beers and ales from small breweries on the actual premises have all but disappeared with the development of the huge brewing conglomerates. Two public houses in Sheffield have recently revived the tradition.

The Fat Cat, formerly The Alma, is looked upon as a shrine to 'real ale' by the growing band of serious beer connoisseurs, and the house regularly wins plaudits from the Campaign for Real Ale (Camra) and has been mentioned in 'The Good Pub Guide'. It is a privately owned freehouse and brews several distinctive beers in the small, but modern brewery at the rear of the premises. One popular beer is 'Kelham Island Bitter'. Formerly, the pub was a small, poky steel-workers pub with not much, at least in the 20th century, to recommend it.

The Frog and Parrot, previously known as The Prince of Wales, is a different type of operation altogether. It is a managed house, owned by Whitbread's Brewery and it concentrates on producing unbelievably strong, barley wine type beers. One popular brew is known as 'Roger and Out';

The Fat Cat, Alma Street, formerly The Alma

others are 'Old Croak', a standard bitter and 'Reckless', a stronger bitter. It is, I believe, popular with the students and young night-clubbers of Sheffield.

Breweries in Sheffield—Past and Present

Thomas Rawson & Co. Ltd. Rawson was a local miller and tanner. He founded what is regarded by some historians (not this one!) as Sheffield's first public brewery on a site at 28 Pond Street in 1758. It was rebuilt in 1780 by a consortium of businessmen made up of Thomas Rawson, Mr Wheat, Mr Eyre and Dr Brown and traded there until it was heavily damaged by enemy bombs in December 1940. The remains of the brewery and its chain of public houses was then taken over in 1946 by Duncan Gilmour's Brewery. There is a mention in historical writings of Mr Rawson's Brewery in the vicinity of Millsands and Bridge Street around the beginning of the 19th century. Rawson's Brewery was the first to brew porter outside London and also had the distinction of employing Samuel Plimsoll (1824–1898) as a £1 a week clerk. Mr Plimsoll went on to better things!

Chambers & Co., Crofts Brewery, 108 Bridge Street was open between 1845 and 1860. A new brewery was then built in Ellin Street and named The

Brunswick Brewery. This was in operation until 1911 when it was sold for £28,000 and the business closed. This small brewery once owned fourteen public houses which were sold to William Stones. Both brewery buildings have been long demolished.

Strout's Brewery Co. Ltd, Burton Road. Established under this name in 1889, it was earlier known as Strout's & Harryman, then in 1872, Strout's & Waterman. It was taken over by Tennant Bros Brewery in 1918 when the company had about fifty pubs. There is a large amount of the old brewery still standing although it is now part of an industrial company.

William Stones, Cannon Brewery, Rutland Road. William Stones began brewing at a site on the corner of Acorn Street and Rutland Road. He then took over the Rutland Road brewery of Messrs Shepherd, Green & Hatfield in about 1860, in partnership with Mr Watts, becoming Watts & Stones. In 1890, the company was registered under the sole name of William Stones and so it continued until the 1950s, the business having transferred to the Cannon Brewery, Rutland Road in 1860. Stones took over Mappin's Masborough Old Brewery, Rotherham and about 100 public houses in 1954 and also Ward's of Swinton, a beer bottling company. Also in 1954, in partnership with Tennant Brothers, they took over Sheffield Free Brewery. In 1968, Stones themselves were absorbed into the giant Bass Charrington empire along with about 250 public houses and 60-odd off-licences. Beer is still brewed at the modern Cannon Brewery.

Joseph Smith, Eldon Brewery, 15 Eldon Street. It was founded in about 1854 as Carter & Smith; in 1871 it was known as Smith & Lofthouse, later Lofthouse & Bell. It ceased trading before 1900.

John Richdale & Co., Britannia Brewery, Bramall Lane. Established in 1860, it traded as Richdale & Tomlinson until 1894. (It is probable that the Tomlinson part was connected to the adjacent Anchor Brewery, Cherry Street). It was registered as Richdale's Britannia Brewery Co. Ltd in 1898, was taken over in 1956 by Hammond's of Bradford and Rotherham and ceased trading shortly afterwards. At this time, the brewery owned twenty-five tied houses and had a large free trade business. The remains of the brewery buildings used to be a garage, but have since been demolished.

S.H. Wards Ltd, Sheaf Brewery, 129 Ecclesall Road. Established in 1840 as Kirby & Wright at Sheaf Island Brewery, Effingham Road, which was renamed Effingham Road Brewery. Septimus Henry Ward joined the company, infused capital and the company took over Latham and Quihampton's Albion Brewery and Bradley's Soho Brewery in the 1870s—both on Ecclesall Road. The company moved to Soho Brewery which was renamed Sheaf Brewery and became S.H. Ward & Co. in 1896, they merged with Vaux Brewery in 1972. After recent extensive refurbishments, little is left of the old brewery except the original gates.

T.J. Parker & Co., Wicker Brewery, Savile Street. Originally C I Stuart & Co., then Wilmott & Co., it became established as Parker's in 1856. Taken over by W H Birk's Brewery in 1880, it ended it's days in the final dreadful indignity of being converted to a vinegar brewery, which, thankfully, has now been obliterated by new buildings. The Brewery Tap, changed to The Hole in the Wall, is all that remains of this brewery and this is now standing derelict.

Sale Advertisement for The Wicker Brewery, 10th April, 1855.

LOT I.
ALL THAT SUBSTANTIAL AND NEWLY-ERECTED
STONE BUILT BREWERY, CALLED THE 'WICKER BREWERY'
eligibly situated in Saville Street, in the Town of Sheffield aforesaid,
as the same is bounded by the River Don on the East,
and the Midland Railway Station on the West,
with good and comfortable
MESSUAGE OR DWELLING-HOUSE
Adjoining thereto, and numerous convenient and well-arranged Out-offices occupied therewith, comprising Stone Square Room, Large Cellar, Wash-house, Barrel Room, Engine Room, Public and Private Offices, Dram-shop, Cooper's Shop, Stabling for Six horses, and Loose Box.
The Premises contain in the whole an Area of 1,503 Square Yards, or thereabouts. The Buildings are all new and in first-rate condition. There is an excellent Spring of Water on the property, which is well adapted for Brewing purposes.
The Brewery is doing a most extensive and lucrative Business, and may be justly classed amongst the first Breweries in the North of England.

The Plant comprises Iron Water Pan, to hold 46 Barrels; Cast Iron Rollers, for Grinding Malt, with Hopper; Mash Tub, capable of Mashing 16 Quarters, and Apparatus, all complete; Liquor Pan, for 33 Barrels; Cast Iron Under-back; Three-Horse Power Steam Engine, with Boiler equal to Eleven-Horse Power; Six Stone-Squares, prepared for 21 Barrels each, with all proper Fittings; Water Pump, complete, &c. The Fixtures, like the Brewery, are new, and of the best and most modern improved description.

Hunt & Co., Old Albion Brewery, 69 Ecclesall Road. Established about 1840 as Hunt's Albion Brewery. In 1859, became Hunt, Fernell and Warhurst Ltd, then Hunt & Co. in 1871. In the late 1870s it was Peter Lowe & Co., but by 1883 it was known as DH Coupe & Co. Then the brewery was briefly owned by Latham & Quihampton, who were taken over by S.H. Ward's Sheaf

Brewery. Between then and 1889, the brewery was known as The Albion Brewery and finally as The Old Albion Brewery Co. Ltd. It was taken over by The Worksop & Retford Brewery Company in 1939 when the company strength was 52 public houses.

Whitmarsh & Watson Ltd, Free Trade Brewery, South Street, Moor. This brewery began trading as William Whitmarsh & Co., 3 Earl Street, which, in 1854 took over William Jepson's Brewery. In 1898 it became Whitmarsh, Watson & Co. by merging with John Watson's Spring Lane Brewery, Broomspring Lane. In 1900 the company took over Wilson Bros, Parkside Brewery, Sussex Street. Then in 1906 was taken over by Duncan Gilmour's Brewery, when the brewery owned 140 pubs. Gilmour's closed down South Street Brewery soon after.

John Roper, Parkside Brewery, Sussex Street. John Roper's brewery began trading around 1849 and was later taken over by Wilson Bros Brewery.

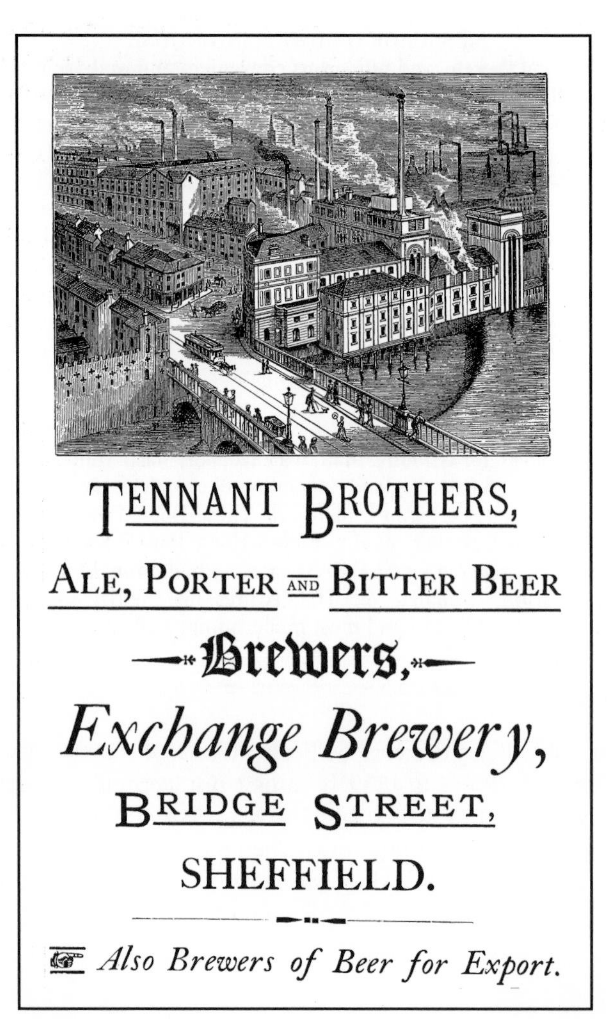

Tennant Bros Ltd, Exchange Brewery, Bridge Street. The original brewery was Proctor's & Co., Market Place in 1820. Business was transferred to the Bridge Street site in 1852. In 1840, Robert and Edward Tennant took over the running of the brewery and in 1847 they were joined by Thomas Moore, a well known Sheffield business man. In 1852, the Duke of Norfolk decided to build a new market on the brewery site and the business moved to Bridge Street. In 1882, the Exchange Brewery became a public company. Tennant's indulged in the usual round of take overs and in 1916 acquired A.H. Smith's Don Brewery; in 1918, Strout's Burton Brewery; in 1924, Berry's Moorhead Brewery and in 1944, the Nottingham Brewery Co. Since then they were involved in a number of mergers until they were themselves taken over by Whitbread's Brewery in 1962. The brewery closed in July, 1993.

Proctor & Co., Haymarket (later the site of the Norfolk Market Hall). Taken over by Tennant Bros Brewery Ltd.

John & William Shaw, Owlerton Brewery, Capel Street, Owlerton. In operation between about 1845 and 1854. Later it became J.L. Cockayne & Son's Owlerton Brewery, 1854–1899. This company was taken over by Allsopp's Brewery in 1899, then by John Smith's Tadcaster Brewery when the company owned fifty public houses. This was closed and demolished in 1913. The site is adjacent to The Mason's Arms, Capel Street.

Turton, Warburton & Co., Don Brewery, Penistone Road. Built in 1832, this brewery became Howe & Smith's, then in 1854, Smith, Redfern & Hanger. Later called A.H. Smith, Redfern, and finally A.H. Smith & Co. In about 1900, this brewery owned eighty-three tied houses which had a value of around £250,000. This means that A.H. Smith's Brewery was one of the senior breweries in Sheffield at the time. It was taken over by Tennant Bros. Brewery in 1916 and closed as a brewery. Some buildings and a trade name, prominent on a side wall, were still in existence until demolition for roadworks in 1994, alas!

H.W. Dearden, High House Brewery, Bamforth Street, off Penistone Road, Owlerton. Established around 1833, then taken over by Duncan Gilmour's Brewery in 1901 and the brewery used as a bottling plant. Dearden's owned few, if any, public houses and relied mainly on free trade sales. Remains of the brewery buildings are still visible between Burton Street and Bamforth Street.

The remains of H.W. Dearden's High House Brewery, Penistone Road

THOMAS MARRIAN & Co., Burton Weir Brewery, SHEFFIELD.

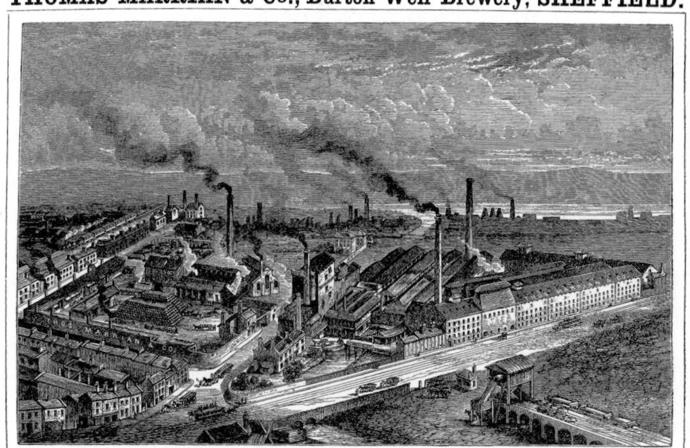

Thomas Marrian & Co., Burton Weir Brewery (formerly Royds Brewery), Royds Mill, off Attercliffe Road. Established in the 1830s, this brewery was taken over by Whitworth's of Wath upon Dearne in 1903 and closed. This company once owned the largest malting complex in Sheffield and these buildings, all that is left of the brewery, are now used by Carter Bond, Manufacturing Chemists and are still visible from Attercliffe Road.

Thomas Berry & Co., originally Parker, Gouldthorpe & Berry, Ecclesall Brewery, Moorhead. Established in 1829, the brewery was rebuilt in 1865 and in 1874 following additional extensions to the premises, it was renamed Moorhead Brewery. Later taken over by Tennant Bros Brewery in the 1940s and demolished. The brewery's peak was probably around 1885, when the company had an output of about 50,000 barrels of beer, employed 100 people and owned over 100 tied houses.

Nanson's Brewery, Bridge Street. Built about 1791. Taken over later by W.H. Birks & Co.

William Greaves & Co., Norfolk Brewery, Broad Street, Park. Established about 1854 as Haselhurst & Greaves. The name was changed in 1880, and in 1910 taken over by Duncan Gilmour's Brewery. The brewery buildings were demolished in the 1960s to make way for re-development works.

Hooson Bros, Park Brewery, Cricket Inn Road. Established in 1865, Hooson Bros was taken over in 1914 by Ind Coope's Brewery, Burton on Trent. It was demolished in 1960. The company also ran the Whitehouse Brewery, Whitehouse Lane, off Infirmary Road, which had been operated by Micah, Gould & Co. The company owned about thirty tied houses and the Union Malt Kilns, Worksop.

Robert Budd, Strong Arm Brewery, 236 Infirmary Road. Established in 1860. Taken over by John Smith's Tadcaster Brewery, it closed in 1914. Some of the brewery's remains can still be seen on the Infirmary Road site.

Samuel Berry, Crown Brewery, Whitehouse Lane, off Infirmary Road. Built around 1840, it was taken over by W.H. Birk's Brewery in 1865. In 1897 it was sold to James Haynes (Crown Brewery Co.) Ltd, then closed in 1910. The site is now a scrap merchants, but the brewery buildings are almost intact and worth a visit.

Carter, Milner & Bird, Hope Brewery, Mowbray Street. Established in 1892 by Christopher Carter, Eleazar Milner and George Bird, the first company operated from a set of semi-derelict houses in Mowbray Street. The company did well and became a public company in 1899. Around 1915, the company was closed down partly due to the deaths of both Milner and Bird. George Bird's son, William, managed to restart the brewery in 1921 and in 1938 the old Hope Brewery was closed and the brewery removed to a new site in Claywheels Lane, Wadsley Bridge. (See following entry).

Henry Tomlinson's Brewery, Anchor Brewery, Cherry Street, off Queen's Road. Set up in 1891, it was badly damaged by enemy bombing in December, 1940. It then joined with The Hope Brewery, Claywheels Lane in 1942 to form The Hope & Anchor Brewery. Taken over by Truswell's Brewery in 1954 and then by Bass Charrington's Brewery in 1963, when the brewery owned 240 public houses. Part of the original brewery offices are now used by Arnold Laver Ltd, Timber Merchants and the brewery's 'Anchor' motif can still be seen on the wall of one of the buildings.

Warwick & Richardson's Brewery, Corn Exchange. Taken over by Newark Brewery.

Wheatley & Bates, Dantzig Brewery, Henry Street, Broomhall. Founded in the early 19th century by John Wheatley.

Rhoden, Freeman & Co., Queen's Brewery, 389 Queen's Road. Established in 1900, it became Queen's Road Brewery in 1905 following the winding up of the previous company. In 1911, this company went into receivership and another new company was formed known as The Sheffield Free Brewery. This company traded until 1937, when a final limited company was formed. This was subject to a joint takeover by Tennant Brothers and William Stones in 1954, when it was agreed that sole control of the brewery should be by Tennant Brothers a year later.

Brook Hill Brewery, 49 Upper St Phillip's Road, Brook Hill. Previously William Harper & Co.(1860), but became, either by name change or take over, Brook Hill Brewery in 1881, it closed in 1892. The brewery buildings have recently disappeared due to a housing development.

W.H. (William Henry) Birks Brewery & Co., Lady's Bridge Brewery, Bridge Street. Established in 1791 as Nanson's & Co. Taken over by Duncan Gilmour's Brewery in 1900—who then began to use the Bridge Street Brewery for all their brewing operations—then by Joshua Tetley until it was finally demolished in 1956.

William Gilbert, Milton Brewery, Button Lane. There in 1854.

Henry Cooks Arculus, Trafalgar Street Brewery, 42 Trafalgar Street.

W.H. Robinson's Scotland Street Brewery, 49 Scotland Street. Opened in 1870 and known as Mower & Pearson. About 1880, it became W.H. Robinson & Co. and a year later it merged with Howe & Alexander, Cromwell Brewery, Newark on Trent, to become Newark & Sheffield Breweries Company Ltd. The Newark part of the operation was bought by Warwicks & Richardson's of Newark and the remains of the company finished trading in 1895.

Shepherd, Green & Hatfield, Neepsend Brewery, Neepsend Lane. Taken over by Watts & Stones Brewery in 1860. Now the site of the William Stone's Cannon Brewery.

John Watson, Spring Lane Brewery, 59 Broomspring Lane. There in 1854. Joined up with Whitmarsh & Co. in 1898 to become Whitmarsh and Watson. John Watson was a founder member of Mansfield Brewery.

Duncan Gilmour's & Co. Brewery, Lady's Bridge Brewery, Bridge Street. This company was founded about 1830 as a wines and spirits merchant, but began brewing in 1860 at Furnival Brewery, Furnival Gate. When this site proved to be inadequate for the needs of the rapidly expanding company, W.H. Birk's Lady's Bridge Brewery, Bridge Street was purchased in 1900. This brewery had previously been owned by Nansons, who had used the site since at least 1791. Gilmours were a go-ahead company and took over Dearden's High House Brewery; Whitmarsh & Watson's Brewery; Greaves Norfolk Brewery and the remains (following war damage) of Thomas Rawson's Pond Street Brewery before themselves being taken over by Joshua Tetley & Sons Ltd, Leeds, when the brewery became a distribution depot. A new depot was opened off Herries Road in 1960. The brewery was demolished in the 1950s to make way for a new development.

Truswell's Brewery Co., 30 Eyre Street, off Norfolk Lane. Built in 1830, in 1860 it became Truswell & Walker. In 1955 it was taken over by The Hope & Anchor Brewery, when the brewery owned sixty tied houses. The buildings were demolished in 1960.

Chamber's Brunswick Brewery, Ellin Street. Originally they occupied The Croft Brewery, 108 Bridge Street, between 1845 and 1860. The brewery closed in 1913.

Robert Bentley, 29 Castle Foulds, later Exchange Street. (Also in Rotherham) Taken over by William Stone's Brewery Ltd.

Bradley & Co., Soho Brewery, Ecclesall Road. Taken over by Kirby & Wright in the 1870s, it was later renamed Sheaf Brewery.

Latham & Quihampton, Albion Brewery, Ecclesall Road. Taken over by Kirby & Wright in the 1870s.

Wilson Bros, Park Side Brewery, Sussex Street. Established before 1849 by John Roper who had previously brewed at 62 Effingham Street. The company became Roper & Co. about 1854, then Matthew Smith, trading at 60 Sussex Street. Wilson Bros were the owners in 1884 and in 1900 it was taken over by Whitmarsh, Watson & Co.

Carter's Brewery, Bank Street.

Thomas Salt, Bank Street.

Samuel Allsopp, Savile Street.

Sowter's, The Warm Hearthstone P.H., 1 Townhead Street. This is the site of Mr John Taylor's Brewery which is believed to have started in 1754.

Samuel Turner, The Shades P.H., 3 Watson's Walk. There in 1825.

John Cadman, 23 South Street. There in 1854.

Joseph Ellis, Twelve O'Clock Hotel, Savile Street/Attercliffe Road. There in 1851.

Francis Parker, Canning Street.

Mrs. Mary Skelton, Broad Street, Park. There in 1854.

Henry Watson, 29 King Street and 15 Watson's Walk. There in 1854

There were two breweries in the Hartshead/ Watson's Walk area, owned by Mr. Ashley and Mr. Whitmarsh. Whether this is the Whitmarsh who joined with Watson to form the Free Trade Brewery is not known.

While this does not pretend to be the total list of all the brewery operations that there have ever been in Sheffield, it is probably the most comprehensive collection that has ever been published together in one book.

Old Sheffield Public Houses and their History

The Crown, Church Street.

The first proper town hall was built in about 1700 beside the church gates in Church Street. At the side of the town hall, at the top of where York Street is now, was The Crown. An early landlord was John Morton, who was Master Cutler 1709–10. It was a meeting place for such public bodies as The River Don Navigation Proprietors and the Town Trustees. John Morton is an example of a victualler who utilized his public position as Master Cutler for the good of his 'house'. During his time in office, the Archbishop of York was entertained at The Crown and The Duke of Norfolk, the largest local landowner, gave a series of dinners for leading townsfolk using 'considerable quantities of plate, pewter, crockery and table linen borrowed of Morton.'

In 1744, Morton's widow announced her retirement from the business and advertised in the Leeds *Mercury* her desire to: 'let that very good accustomed Inn, known by the sign of The Crown, near the church gates and with stabling for 24 horses'. She also wished to sell her household goods and brewing utensils. In 1770, Thomas Vennor acquired the property for his mercers business and in 1772 York Street was established.

The Cock, High Street.

The Cock is the earliest public house which can be traced in Sheffield town. It was owned by Mr. Skinner in 1593. It was then sold by Richard Skinner of Hathersage to William Shemeld.

In 1603, it was the property of Francis Barlow, a chapman (cutlery salesman), and was kept by the Barlow family until about 1686. The Ellison's were mentioned in 1697 and between 1706 and 1737 it was kept by Mr. Woods and his widow. In 1743, its last landlord, Jeremiah Hancock was in possession. In around 1750, it closed down as a public house and became a private dwelling, then a bank and later a draper's shop. Its site was once lost in oblivion, but now it is known to have stood on the north side of High Street, opposite Mulberry Street.

White Bear, High Street.

In 1787, the landlord was David Jones and in 1791 it was the meeting place of the Norfolk Society which was a 'Sick & Dividing Club' mentioned later in the book.

Horse and Cat, High Street.

This pub stood back slightly between George Street and Mulberry Street. It is most remarkable for the number of names that it had. When first opened it was known as the Bay Childers and sometimes the Bay Horse. In 1774 it was called the Horse and Cat. It was rebuilt in 1794 when John Henson was landlord. He was followed by his son, Joe Henson. It was for a number of years known as the Queen Victoria and finally the Westminster. It was bombed in 1940, which probably saved them the trouble of thinking up any more names!

The Blackamore Head, High Street.

In 1675, the Girdler family owned The Blackamore Head, in High Street, on the lower side of Aldine Court. Its name was changed to The Grey Horse in 1787. There used to be a tradition (now thought to have been unlikely) that in 1215, King John stayed at this public house whilst on his way to York. Another story, and this is probably true, is that in 1708, the then landlord, John Trippett, supplied ale for the celebrations in the town when George I was crowned. It finally closed in 1917.

The Rose and Crown, Market Place.

The Rose and Crown, which stood on the south side of the market place adjoining the bottom of High Street, was occupied by Nevil Simmon in 1692. From 1720 until 1742 it was run by John Horsfield and then by his widow. At that time it was regarded as one of the premier inns of the town. From 1742 until about 1748 it was kept by Mr Anderton. Thomas Watson took over in 1750 and was landlord until 1759. Joseph Owen was in charge 1765–71. The last landlord was Samuel Leech from 1773–76, who then left to take up the living of The Angel. The Rose and Crown then closed and was converted into Bardell's Auction Room and shops.

The Rose and Crown, High Street.

The landlord of this pub in 1675 was James Goodie, then in 1681 Thomas Pegg. He was followed by Christopher Pegg, who was possibly his son, in 1700. When he died, his widow Jane Pegg ran the premises until 1723. William Watson, of the well known Watson family, was landlord from then until 1728. Mr Watson had an extraordinary history. In about 1720 he is known to have had a public house 'known by the sign of The Bush', but the location of this pub is unknown. He is thought to have built The George, mentioned below. He was known throughout Sheffield as 'Fecky' Watson due to his interest in the confectionery business. He was a Town Trustee from 1741 until 1784, had 23 children and died, aged 97, at Hag House, Cannon Hall, Firvale in 1791. John Greaves was landlord from 1786 until 1804, then James Heiffer from 1804 until 1807. Thomas Watson followed him and ran the pub until 1812 After this date the pub ceased trading and was converted into shops.

The George, High Street.
After leaving the Rose and Crown, Thomas Watson, who was also a member of the Watson family, moved to The George, which was built on property bought by his father at the bottom of Hartshead Passage. This gennel became known as Watson's Walk. The George stood on the site until about 1782.

The Bodega, Market Place.
It was first opened in 1682 and was sold at about that time to George Hutchinson for £500. Samuel Peech, mentioned later, bought it in 1782 for £1,500. Little is known about this public house, but for it to change hands for what was in those days an enormous sum of money seems to indicate that it was a very successful business. It was originally called the George and Dragon, was often referred to as merely The George and became that before changing, once again, to The Bodega in about 1900. It was destroyed by enemy bombing in 1940.

The Norfolk Arms, High Street.
The Norfolk Arms, which was on the south side of High Street, was kept by Ben Steer in 1742. Later, the name of the public house was changed to The Blue Bell. Later, it was rebuilt and renamed again and was then known as The Clarence House. It stood until it was part of the area swept away to enable Walsh's department store to be built. It closed in 1900.

The King's Head, Change Alley.
The King's Head, which was to become one of the best hotels and coaching inns in the town, was first mentioned in 1572 in the Church Burgess Accounts. The entry read, 'William Dickenson of the King's Head owed 4d for rent.' Mr. Dickenson was at the time the Earl of Shrewsbury's Bailiff. In 1663, Robert Broughton was landlord and he was said to have issued tokens with the King's Head sign on them. In 1700, John Cooke was landlord, then up until about 1732 there were several changes of ownership—Richard Yeomans, Samuel Thompson and George Thompson all had a period in charge. In 1732, it was run by John Woolfe. From 1745, Leonard Webster, the then owner, was a leading citizen of Sheffield and a Town Trustee and the hotel was the centre for meetings of the Cutler's Company. Mr. Webster

himself was Master Cutler 1748–49 and remained as landlord of The King's Head until 1769. James Kay took over from Mr Webster and was landlord until 1801. Situated beside the hotel was a large bowling green and an area of fine gardens, but Mr Webster dug these up and extended Change Alley through to Alsop Field. Houses were erected on the site, because in 1770, John Hawsley, who was a surgeon and who married Mr Webster's daughter, carried out his practice there. Norfolk Street appeared on the street plans for 1771 where Alsop Field used to be. In 1821, the then landlord, William Wright, is said to have driven the first stagecoach over the newly opened turnpike road between Sheffield and Glossop. Mr Wright was landlord from 1808 until 1824. He owned forty-two acres of land beside the canal in Attercliffe and this was mainly used for breeding and training racehorses and also circus ponies. In 1851, William Woodhead was landlord. The building was destroyed by enemy action in December, 1940.

The Cutler's Hall (Bird in Hand), Church Lane. (Street)

The Cutler's Hall has had, over several hundred years, various locations and was, for a period from 1761, based in a tavern, William Truelove was the first tenant. The Cutler's Company, finding it inconvenient to continue to use the building as a public house, gave the then tenant, John Thompson, notice to quit possession. The nearby inn, The Bird in Hand, was considered to be convenient for either supplying liquor for meetings, or for adjourning to the pub's snug parlour afterwards.

The Mulberry Tavern, Mulberry Street.

The present pub of this name is on the same site as the original, which was demolished in the 1970s to allow for development of the whole area. The reason for the name Mulberry evolves from a decree from King James I issued to all Lieutenants of the counties of England that, in order to increase the supply of silk, where possible, mulberry trees, silkworms' staple food, should be planted. As this area of the town had a very high concentration of gardens, many mulberry trees were planted in the vicinity. There is a story attached to this tavern. Many years ago, a commercial traveller booked into the tavern one night and in the morning was found to have fallen to his death through a door in the wall of his room which led to a long drop down to the inn yard. When the body was searched, no identification of any kind was found, but he was in possession of a large sum of money! Enquiries as to his identity were made, but to no avail and his body was eventually buried in an unmarked grave in the Parish Churchyard. I wonder what became of the money?

The Sun, Haymarket.

Murdo Young was the proprietor of the local news-sheet, the *Sun*, and one of his habits, during his period as landlord of this pub, was to put a copy of

The Mulberry Tavern, Mulberry Street, open 1825, rebuilt in the 1980s

his latest edition in the windows of The Sun Tavern. Thomas Wiley, the landlord of The Theatre Tavern on Arundel Street, later took over The Sun and he continued the tradition. In 1832, at the time of the Reform Bill riots, Mr. Wiley travelled from London back to Sheffield in the fast time of twelve hours to put the latest news from the capital in the pub's windows. He steadily built up the house wines and spirits trade and later changed the name to The Old No. 12. There is a later public house which used to be called The Old No. 12, in Exchange Street and this has recently been changed to The Market Tavern.

Sam Hill's Parlour, (Crown & Cushion; The Bull & Oak), Wicker.
The Wicker used to be known as Assembly or 'Sembly Green after the Court of Sembly Quest, which was a people's court. This first started to meet on the site in the 1500s. At this court, the people who considered that they had a grievance or complaint against their fellow citizens could have it discussed and judgement given by their peers. In about 1568, due to international unrest, archery became compulsory for all able-bodied men in England and two practice butts were set up in the area. An assembly house was built there in 1715. It became a general meeting place and later was known as Sam Hill's Parlour. During this period it was a debating chamber for the poet and hymn writer, James Montgomery and his circle of thinkers (although some historians believe they met in the nearby White Lion).

Montgomery was a Scot, born in 1771. He worked for the *Sheffield Register* and when the owner of the newspaper, Mr. Gales, was forced to flee to America to avoid prosecution, because of his unpopular views on the then current French Revolution, Montgomery took control and changed the newspaper's name to the *Iris*. He is best known for the hymns he composed; his poetry, also in a religious vein, is little read. There is a statue of him near the Cathedral and other memorials include the Montgomery Hall, a drinking fountain in Broad Lane, three public houses and Montgomery Road in Nether Edge. He died in 1854, aged 83. Who Sam Hill was is anyone's guess!

In later years, the assembly hall was called The Crown & Cushion and then, in 1780, it was given its present day name of The Bull & Oak. It is the oldest public house site, in the area covered by this book, to be still in business.

Green Seedlings, Bailey Street.
This pub was open in 1825 and closed in 1902. It gained its unusual name from its close proximity to some garden nurseries owned by the Duke of Norfolk.

Hay's Spirit Vaults, Norfolk Street.
The building which used to house the Hay's Spirit Vaults has been renovated by the City Council recently and it now is a small, but interesting art gallery,

The Bull & Oak and The Brown Cow, the Wicker

which offers a range of different and frequently changed exhibitions covering a wide spectrum of the arts. The original public house opened in 1797.

The Old Five Alls, Infirmary Road.
Little is known about this pub, but it is worth mentioning because it used to carry an unusual, but not unique name. The original medieval form of this name seemed to represent: a monk (I pray for all), a knight (I fight for all) and a peasant (I work for all). Sometimes, as in this case, a king was added (I rule over all) and a fifth 'all' representing the devil (I take all).

We Three Loggerheads, Hawley Croft.
Another interesting pub sign would have been found on this pub, which was open in 1830 and closed in 1889. The sign showed two stupid looking faces labelled 'We Three Loggerheads'. The joke was of course that the person looking at the sign made up the third fool.

The Great Britain, John Street.
This public house could have been named after the huge ship, The Great Britain, which was built by Isambard Kingdom Brunel, 1806–59, and which is even now being restored in Bristol having being discovered abandoned and derelict in the Falkland Islands and towed back to Britain.

The Grand Theatre, Spring Street/Coulson Street.
Although to all intents and purposes this was merely a large public house, it also boasted a large stage, gallery and auditorium and was one of the very popular number of pub cum theatres which were centred on the West Bar area of Sheffield during the 19th century (others are mentioned later). It had various names during it's existence. In about 1880, it was called Squints; by 1890 it had changed to Bijou, and in 1893, following refurbishment works, it was known as The Star Music Hall. Business suffered following the opening, in Charles Street, of The Empire Theatre, but it recovered, changed its name to The Grand and prospered until it was demolished in 1920 when moving pictures had decimated music halls.

The Montgomery Public Houses.

There have been three pubs in Sheffield with the name 'Montgomery'. They were named after the Scottish poet James Montgomery, who is covered in more detail elsewhere in this book. The pubs were in St Mary's Road, Montgomery Terrace and Hartshead. This later one was open in 1852, closed in 1893 and was part of the same building that housed the offices of the *Iris* and was possibly the living accommodation, at least for a time, of James Montgomery.

The Beeswing, Hartshead.

This pub was open in 1797 and closed in 1905. There are others of the same name in England and they are possibly named after a famous racehorse of the 19th century. Beeswing won the Doncaster Gold Cup on four occasions—in 1837, and then a hat trick of wins in 1840, 41 and 42. It also won the Ascot Gold Cup in 1842. It is a rather strange name to give either a racehorse or a pub, because as all wine buffs will know 'beeswing' is the name given to the sediment in wine.

Other public houses were named after racehorses: The Why Not Inn, Clun Street, which is mentioned elsewhere, was named after a Grand National winner of 1894; The Cremorne, London Road, which was open in 1833 and is still open, is named after the 1872 Derby winner; The Cossack, Howard Street, which is still open, was named after the 1847 Derby winner. The Black Darling, Talbot Street, open in 1833, sounds as if it might have been named after a racehorse, as does The Well Run Dimple, Fargate, open 1793, closed 1896, and this is mentioned later.

The Tontine Hotel, Haymarket.

The Tontine Hotel was built in 1785, as the result of a meeting between a group of town businessmen. Hence the name 'Tontine', which means 'a financial arrangement by which the benefits of the remaining participants are increased on the death or default of any one of them'. Fifty men each put up £100 towards the cost of building the hotel on the basis of each receiving an equal share of the profits and, likewise, the costs. It was built on the site of the former castle barns and became the largest coaching inn in the area.

It had a large, impressive frontage, a 12,000 sq. ft banqueting hall on the second floor and seven or eight different rooms where various activities such as meetings and dances were held. At the rear, there were extensive ancillary buildings, including stabling for about 60 horses, a brewery and cottages for the hotel staff.

The first landlord was James Watson, of the well known Sheffield public house family, and he developed the business into the most important hotel in the town. Some persons of national importance were entertained at the hotel. These included the anti-slavery pioneer, William Wilberforce MP and Lord Palmerston, who was Prime Minister twice, 1855–58 and 1859–65, when he died. The Duke of Wellington, another Prime Minister and a national hero, also stayed at the hotel. While he was there, he presented the Waterloo Medal to a cutlery worker, Billy Proctor, a former Napoleonic War veteran. Billy lived in Trinity Street, West Bar.

When Samuel Peech of the Angel Inn died in 1809, the then landlord of the Tontine, Mr J. Batty, took over the running of the lucrative Sheffield to London coach business.

In 1825, when Mr Lambert was landlord, the coach was doing the journey in only twenty-two hours. It was the heyday of coach travel and, in 1832, when Mr Brickley was running the hotel, thirteen coaches a day left either the Tontine or the King's Head for various destinations.

In the late 18th century, the Government passed Acts of Parliament which resulted in vast areas of former common land being enclosed and people were denied the use of land which they had enjoyed for centuries. When Crookes Moor and Little Sheffield Moor, a racecourse, were enclosed, a large number of angry townspeople took to the street to give vent to their feelings on 29th July 1791. A large, unruly mob of them assembled outside the Tontine Hotel in Haymarket. From there, they marched to King Street, formerly Pudding Lane, where the Debtors Gaol was attacked and many of the inmates released. There then followed a march to, and a concerted attack on, the home at Broom Hall of the Reverend Wilkinson, the Vicar of Sheffield. Wilkinson was known to have received a large number of acres of land due to the Enclosures Acts. Broom Hall was damaged and several straw stacks fired. A rhyme composed soon after this event went:

They burnt his books
and scared his rooks
and set his stacks on fire!

Although The Rev. Wilkinson seems at this time to have been one of the town's least liked people—he was a town magistrate and was feared for his severe sentences—in later life he became well-liked and there was much sorrow when he died in 1805.

The peace was only restored in the town following the arrival and intervention of a company of Light Dragoons who had been summoned from Nottingham. Following the riot, five men were tried at York Assizes. Four were released, but one man, John Bennett, was found guilty and hanged in September of the same year. Historians have since given the opinion that the root cause of the trouble stemmed as much from the populations' disgust at the standard of justice and punishment as from the new laws.

The next year, on 4th May 1792, another mob gathered outside the Tontine. This time the reasons were the low wages and living conditions and also, again, the Enclosures Acts. The military were set upon the crowd, who fought back. Many windows were broken in the hotel and several of the crowd were injured before peace was restored.

Sheffield must have been a town on the very brink of rebellion at this time, and the Tontine Hotel, possibly because of its size, popularity and central position, seemed to be the focal point where the mobs gathered.

It was once again in the news, on 14th December 1832, following the passing of the Government's Reform Act of that year, which allowed about 3,500 citizens of the town to vote in the elections. This was out of a population total of about 90,000! When the name of the first successful candidate was announced, Mr John Parker of Woodthorpe, it was extremely unpopular with the large crowd which had gathered outside the Corn Exchange, Haymarket, to hear the results. Part of the crowd broke away and gathered outside the Tontine Hotel, where Mr Parker had held his political meetings. They began to attack the hotel's windows with stones and other missiles.

Whilst a rider was despatched to Rotherham to summon help from a regiment of infantry who were stationed there, the mob went on a general rampage through the town, damaging property and attacking the constables who tried to maintain order. Four hours later, at about 10pm, a detachment of the 18th Irish Foot arrived and positioned themselves in front of the Tontine. They were under the orders of Thomas Bosville, a local magistrate. When the crowd refused to disperse and began to stone the soldiers, Bosville was hit on the head and badly injured. The soldiers were then ordered to fire over the heads of the crowd. In the panic and general confusion which followed, five people were shot dead and a sixth later died in the Infirmary. Later, the Coroner recorded verdicts of 'justifiable homicide' in all six cases.

In 1850, with the arrival of the railway in Sheffield, the coaching business began to decline and the Tontine Hotel was bought by The Duke of Norfolk for £7,720, plus £284 for 'other charges'. It was pulled down to build the new Norfolk Markets on the site. These were in turn demolished in 1960.

This site is now occupied by a department store, which at the time of writing has recently been refurbished again, following a lengthy period standing empty. How nice it would be to still have a building like the Tontine standing in The Haymarket.

The Spread Eagle, High Street.

Among the buildings at the top of Chapel Walk in 1794, was the Spread Eagle, whose landlord was James Richardson. He also owned The Grey Horse, which was lower down High Street. The pub was closed in 1890.

The Fleur de Lis, Attercliffe Road.

On Attercliffe Road, near Washford Bridge, at the back of Don Terrace, was a small house called Sugar House. It was built by a widow named Elizabeth Roades in 1671, for when she retired after working for 35 years. On the doorhead was inscribed: 'E.R. 1671'. Norfolk Estate rental records for the years 1671–72 state: 'For stone got out of Dick Bank for Widow Roades at Attercliffe 3/-'.

In 1791, it or part of it, became an inn and in 1882 a drawing made by local artist, William Topham, showed it as an inn called the Fleur de Lis (or Lys). During the time that it was an inn, Jonathan Oakes and his son were scissor makers there. It was later used as a sugar refinery and for the manufacture of ropes. By 1889, it had reverted to a private residence.

The Dog and Partridge, Attercliffe Road.

In about 1860, John Backhouse became landlord of this pub. He was a partner in Parker & Backhouse of Woods (or Bridge) Foundry. They were 'patentees and manufacturers of metallic spring piston plungers', according to an advertisement from 1860. It is still open as a freehouse.

The Old Queen's Head, Pond Hill.

This is a very interesting building, formerly known as 'The Hawle in the Poandes'. It is first mentioned in 1582 in an inventory made for George, the Sixth Earl of Shrewsbury. It is possible that its earliest use was as a wash-house or laundry for Sheffield Castle and Manor Lodge, for it is referred to in an account book in the Duke of Norfolk's estate office. The entry, dated July 17th 1770, says: 'the old house in the ponds, formerly wash-house to Sheffield Manor'. The ponds mentioned were the fishing ponds which were, in medieval times, to be found in the Pond Hill area of the town, adjacent to the pub's site, and which were used as carp breeding waters by the monks from the ancient Beauchief Abbey.

The Dog & Partridge, Attercliffe Road

It was a badly run down building when James Pilley, a nail and rivet maker, made it into a beerhouse by paying two guineas licence money in 1841. At the same time, Joshua Ogden, a butter dealer and mason, occupied part of the building.

The cutlery firm of Rodgers was situated at the side and, with trade improving, Mr Pilley took out a victuallers licence and called the building the Old Queen's Head. Thomas Rawson's, the brewers on Pond Street, owned a lot of land on Pond Hill in the late 19th century, including the lease of the Old Queen's Head, but this lease was taken over by the Truswell Brewery in 1892, when it came under the licencing magistrates. At this time, the pub contained one bar, one bar parlour, one taproom, a kitchen and three bedrooms.

Thomas Berry, the brewer, was the owner in 1884, and the brewers Tennant Brothers, now part of the Whitbread Group, were the owners in 1924. In 1935, the public house was taken over by Sheffield Corporation who leased it to John Smith's Brewery of Tadcaster.

In 1949, extensive restoration work was done on the building, exposing the original outside wooden beams and carvings and removing years of accumulated whitewash and plaster. During these renovations, an old stone fireplace and two mullioned windows were uncovered inside the building and, during excavation work to make a new cellar, a circular well shaft was found.

The pub has recently re-opened following a lengthy and expensive renovation and is now connected to the main buildings of the passenger transport interchange. During these building works, a time capsule, sheathed in stainless steel, was buried in the foundations of the building.

Moseley's Arms, Paradise Street, West Bar.

At the time of publication, there is only one public house standing on West Bar, the Moseley's Arms. This contrasts with the period of time when there were twenty or so inns and taverns in the area. Paradise Street, at the bottom of which the Moseley's Arms stands, used to be known as Workhouse Croft. This is because the West Bar Workhouse, which was built in 1722 and closed in 1829, was near the site. This place was feared by anyone who expected to end their days inside it or a similar institution. It is recorded in 1746 that two women inmates were caught stealing workhouse property and taking it over the wall to sell to a 'fence' in the nearby White Horse public house in Gregory Row (now disappeared). For this offence they were sentenced to spend time in an underground cell, known as the 'black hole', as it was without any natural light. They were then whipped 'until their backs bled'!

In 1828, Thomas Moseley was the landlord of the London Apprentice at 81 West Bar and No. 8 West Bar Green. From 1837 until 1845, George Allender kept the Rose Inn at 41 Workhouse Croft and 73 West Bar. The Poll Book for the 1852 Sheffield Election gives Thomas Moseley as landlord of The Moseley's Arms. Thomas

Moseley had moved to The Rose Inn and re-named it The Moseley's Arms. The landlord at The London Apprentice was Thomas Schwarar. In 1857, the publican at The Moseley's Arms was L. Ibbertson.

The Public Gardens, Saracen's Head, Gardener's Arms and Tea Gardens Hotel, Grimesthorpe Road.

Samuel Staniforth had a linen drapers shop in Castle Street, near the top of Water Lane. He was a tall, sedate old gentleman, who wore a ruffled shirt and top hat. He was a celebrated horticulturist, spending much time in the cultivation of flowers and fruit in his extensive garden. This was a large piece of land enclosed by high brick walls, on Occupation Lane near to Burngreave House. Spending so much time there, he had a garden house built so that he could enjoy it fully. By the side of the garden were a number of cottages where people would come and have tea. In the 1840s, Mr Staniforth left Sheffield and his property was put up for sale. Charles Palfreyman, a mason, rented the garden house and, in 1848, opened it as a beerhouse called The Public Gardens. Later, in 1850, it became a licenced victualler's house called The Gardener's Arms. For a short while it was called The Saracen's Head, then some time later, taking its name from the nearby cottages, it became known as The Tea Gardens Hotel, the name it carries today. Most of the trade would have come from the nearby collieries, the Occupation Road Colliery and the Pitsmoor Colliery, both of which are long gone.

The following list is of all the landlords of this public house up until 1983:

C. Palfreyman	1848.	Johnson	1890.	Lingard	1939.
C. Palfreyman	1852.	W. Sutcliffe	1893.	Raybould	1942.
S. Stones	1863.	B. Wilson	1900.	F. Bedford	1948.
Baker	1868.	F. Exton	1911.	G. Bostock	1954.
W. Earnshaw	1876.	J. Weldon	1915.	J. Broadley	19??.
Usherwood	1879.	Levick	1924.	Rollingson	1973.
Atkinson	1884.	Stocks	1932.	R. Turton	1975.
R. Morrel	1887.	Eames	1938.	K. Pawson	1983.

The Marples Hotel.

In 1876, there was a Wine and Spirit Commercial Hotel, also known at some period of its history as the Old London Mart. This occupied the site of No. 64 High Street, on the corner of High Street and Market Street. It was owned then by a Mr Atley. Mr Marples purchased the hotel for £6,000 and changed the name to his own.

There has been a public house on the corner site ever since, although the seven storey building which was standing on the site on December 12th 1940, was completely destroyed, with the loss of between 60 and 70 lives, following a direct hit by an enemy high explosive bomb at about 11.40 that night.

This night will always be remembered as the worst night of bombing that the city received during the Second World War. Including the raid on 15th

December, the total number of people killed in the city was almost 700, with 1,800 injured and 92 missing. As well as the dreadful loss of life, huge numbers of commercial and private buildings were either destroyed or damaged and, apart from the Marples Hotel, eight other public houses were obliterated: The King's Head, Change Alley; The Angel, Angel Street; The Westminster, High Street; The Royal Oak, King Street; The Bodega, High Street; The Devonshire Arms, South Street, Moor; The Shades Vaults, Watson's Walk and The Three Horse Shoes, Norfolk Street.

The Marples Hotel has long since been rebuilt and is now run by a private company as a free-house.

The Mowbray Inn, Mowbray Street.

Joe Dixon, the landlord of the Mowbray Inn, was also a racecourse bookmaker. In 1898, a championship boxing contest was to be held at the Edmund Road Drill Hall. The boxers taking part included Jack Hare, Tom Chuser, Matt Precious and George Corfield. All these boxers were frequent visitors to the Mowbray Inn. At one o'clock on the day of the competition, all participants congregated outside the issue office to collect their wages. At 2.30pm, the manager came out and said: 'I'm sorry, boys, to have to read such a telegram to you and before I read it, I must tell you that it hurts me very much to have to do so.' He then informed the boxers that the telegram had been handed in at Prince's landing stage, Liverpool, at 12 noon. It read:

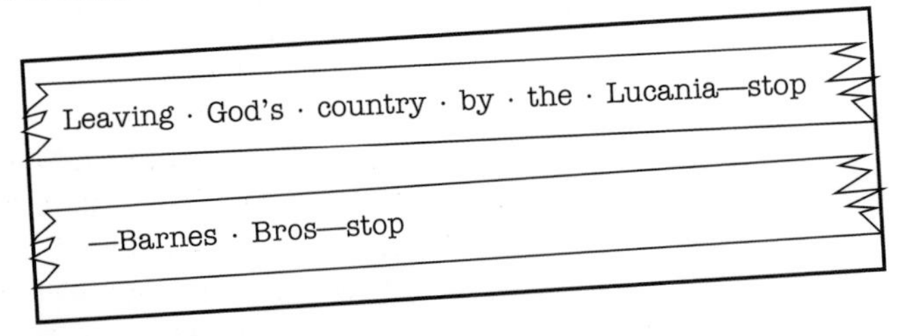

The organisers of the boxing competition had cleaned up all the money and 'beat it'. They left unpaid their hotel bill, the cost of training and the hire of the hall, as well as their staff and boxers.

Jack Hare remained a barman at the Mowbray Inn and a month after the boxing contest fiasco, he knocked out Matt Palmer in five rounds at the Excelsior School of Arms, Furnace Hill, Sheffield.

The Vine Tavern, Hartshead.

In 1807, Samuel Hall had a pawnbrokers shop in the Hartshead. The shop was made into a brewhouse and the dwelling part of the building was turned into a public house called the Barrel Inn. Under landlord George Moss, it became the Jolly Tar. Francis Lilley changed its name again, in 1816, to the Chequers and in 1827 it was kept by Richard Alexander and called the Vine Tavern. Four different names in twenty years! In the 1890s it was converted into a police institute.

The Hartshead area.
To the rear of the north side of High Street is an area of numerous offices, these were served by a number of public houses: The Vine Tavern (1807–1893) at No. 4; The Freemason's Arms (1796–1893) at No. 8; The Montgomery Tavern (1852–1893) at No. 12; The Beeswing (1797–1905) at No. 46; The Dove and Rainbow at No. 25 and The Red Lion (1755–1903) at No. 39. Of these six pubs only the Dove and Rainbow still exists. It was a favourite watering hole for the army recruiting parties that used to visit the town at regular intervals to lure fit young men into the service. Just before Christmas in 1783, a fire broke out in the inn and it proved fatal to the landlord's wife, Mrs Oates, and to a young apprentice who was living there. It was later rebuilt and today there is still a Dove and Rainbow in business but in a slightly different place. There was a pub called the French Horn in Hartshead. It was open in 1780 and closed by 1901. Its actual location is unknown.

There is a passage called Watson's Walk, built sometime after the fire at the Dove and Rainbow. This then ran from Angel Street to Hartshead. It was named after a well known local family which had kept a number of public houses in the town. This short right of way had three pubs: The Shades (open in 1797), was kept in 1805 by Sam Turner, known as 'Gin Sam', this pub was commonly named T'oil in T'wall; The Waterloo Tavern (1833–1905) and The Turf Tavern (1774–1906).

The Shades has an unusual story attached to it—early in the 19th century, a man named Thomas Dunn, described as 'an honest workman', brought his son, William, from his house in Malin Bridge to be confirmed at the Parish Church. They arrived too late. The church was shut and the Archbishop of York, who had officiated at the service, was taking his dinner in the nearby Shades Inn. Mr Dunn approached the Archbishop who interrupted his meal to confirm the young man inside the pub. He then resumed his meal.

The White Bear, High Street.
At the top of High Street, on the south side near Chapel Walk, there were a great many ramshackle buildings. Up a passage in White Bear Yard was the White Bear public house. In 1787 John Burgon was the landlord, followed by David Jones. While Mr Jones was the landlord, new building went on and in 1811, Foster's the Clothiers took over the frontage of the pub to build their new shop. The pub was open in 1780 and closed in 1900.

Cross Daggers, Commercial Street/Change Alley.
Although the actual site of this pub has long been built over, there is some information left about it. In 1791 Robert Sandys succeeded Ann Asline as

landlord. In 1828, it was kept by Richard Greenwood and in 1847 it was a beerhouse let to a Mr Bradley of Soho Brewery and part of the building was used as a warehouse. The pub stood slightly back from the road and when the King's Head, Change Alley, was extended in about 1901, the site of the Cross Daggers was covered. The passage from Fruit Market to Norfolk Street is called Cross Daggers Yard on an O.S. map of 1853.

The Hen and Chickens, Castle Green.

Counterfeiting and forging were considered to be such serious offences in the 18th and 19th centuries that they were classed as treason. In 1838, a man named Henry White was arrested in the bar of the Hen and Chickens, whilst in possession of a large number of counterfeit shillings. In spite of claiming that he was a spy for the Royal Mint, he was convicted and sentenced to be transported for fifteen years. He was fortunate not to have been hanged. This pub is still open.

The Swan with Two Necks, Furnival Street.

In 1837, Joseph Romasarte, an itinerant barrel organ player, stabbed a man in the stomach during an argument in this pub. He was acquitted because of the Italian's 'excitable temperament and the victim's quarrelsome nature'!

The name, The Swan with Two Necks, is really a corruption of The Swan with Two Nicks. Swans were, and possibly still are, marked by having nicks cut into their beaks. A bird with one nick belonged to the Dyers Company, a swan with two nicks belonged to the Vintners Company, while a swan with no nicks belonged to the reigning monarch. The pub was open in 1825.

The Ball Inn, Osbourne Street.

Following a political meeting in Paradise Square in 1874, a crowd rampaged through the town, breaking property, raiding public houses and stealing drink. The riot lasted from the afternoon until the early hours of the morning. At about 1am, The Ball Inn and its surroundings were occupied by a huge and unruly crowd of several hundred people who helped themselves to the beer. Several men were arrested and served short terms of hard labour.

The Clown and Monkey, Paradise Square.

This is an extract from the Sheffield Independent, 1852:

> Saturday—Before J Haywood Esq. and J Bower Esq.
>
> A disorderly beerhouse—Wm Cliffe, of the Clown and Monkey Beerhouse, Paradise Square, was summoned on the complaint of Mr Booth, Surgeon, for not maintaining proper order in his house. From the evidence of Mr Booth and Mr White, one of the detective officers, it appears that the defendant's house is the resort of thieves, dog fighters and the lowest possible company. In the back

> part of the premises there was a rat-pit and dogs and rats were kept for the convenience of those of the 'fancy' who chose to pay for the amusement. Last Tuesday morning, a large concourse of men assembled at the house, and there was continued disturbance and quarrels all the afternoon. After one of these quarrels, the parties turned out into the square, where they had a regular pitched battle, each combatant having seconders etc., after the most approved style of 'the ring'. There were not less than 150 men looking on at the fight, and the disorder may be imagined when it is known that this took place in the middle of the market day, when the square is occupied with earthenware and other stalls. Mr Booth produced a memorial signed by every householder in the square complaining of the defendant's house as a nuisance. He stated further, that the defendant was in the habit of turning rats loose to breed on his premises, in order to supply his pit. The consequence was that his (Mr Booth's) cellars were over run with them . . . The defendant: Was it likely that he should turn them loose when he gave 1/- a dozen for them? . . . Mr Haywood convicted in the penalty of 50/- and 8/- costs.

Enough said. Perhaps his beer was alright! The exact location of this public house in Paradise Square is not known.

Several pubs in Sheffield are known to have had rat-pits on the premises, as this was a popular sport in beerhouses. One landlord, nicknamed 'Fagey Joe', who ran the Blue Bell, in Silver Street Head, which closed in 1903, maintained a very large pit. He is said to have owned a terrier named Bullet. This dog is reputed to have once despatched 200 rats in 13 minutes! Gold medal stuff! Fagey Joe sometimes took the place of his dog with great success!

George Hotel, Boston Street.

On August 25th, 1907, a charabanc left this hotel to take a party of about twenty customers on a day trip out to Derbyshire. On the return journey, the weather turned nasty and, in heavy rain, whilst attempting to overtake a horse-drawn carriage, the vehicle hit a telegraph pole, then a wall and finally turned over. Three of the passengers were killed outright and another died a few weeks later in hospital. Twelve others were seriously injured. The charabanc, number W671, was known as Roscoe, it had been available for hire for about a year—the first vehicle in Sheffield to do so. This was Sheffield's first major traffic accident and it resulted in widespread shock amongst the population.

The Barrel Inn, Pinstone Street.

One evening in 1789, John Stevens and Thomas Lastley, both button makers working for John Hoole of Lady's Walk, Sheffield Moor, were out in the town drinking with three friends named Bingham, Booth and Wharton. Wharton had earlier bought a package of groceries which the others, for a joke, seized and took to the Barrel Inn. Once there, they took out a leg of mutton from the package and cooked it, expecting Wharton to join them in eating it as he knew where they'd gone. Wharton, however, told the local constable, George 'Buggy' Eyre, who traced the four men and arrested them for highway robbery. Despite their explanations and offers to pay for the joint of mutton—a few pence—they were imprisoned and tried at York Assizes in 1790. Bingham was acquitted and the other three men were condemned to death.

Booth's sentence was soon commuted to transportation for life. Support for the remaining two condemned men was widespread with even the Master Cutler signing a petition. This resulted in a reprieve being sent from London to York. It arrived two days too late—Stevens and Lastley had been hanged, still protesting their innocence! There was a system in practice at the time which involved the payment of so-called 'blood money' to witnesses to ensure convictions and many people in Sheffield were aware that, in this case, something like £100 had been paid, presumably to Wharton and Constable Eyre.

Following this event, Booth received an unconditional pardon and Wharton, following such violent attacks on his house and a corner shop which he used to keep, as to 'render it almost scarcely habitable', disguised himself in womens clothing and escaped to Manchester never again to be seen in Sheffield.

It was a drunken prank which started in good humour, but which cost two men their lives and one man his home and friends.

The Rose and Crown, Waingate.

Built in the early 19th century, not closed down until 1926, and positioned in Waingate, this pub must have been somewhat famous for the quality of its ale. At least it was good enough for someone to write a poem about it:

The Rose and Crown,
In Sheffield Town,
The landlord's name George Hartley,
He brews good ale,
It is not stale,
Where 'tis I'll tell you shortly,
It's in Waingate,
Which is not straight,
And leads into the Wicker.
Call as you pass,
And take a glass,
Twill make you travel quicker.

Carbrook Hall, Attercliffe Common.

Standing just back from the main Attercliffe road, Carbrook Hall is a building steeped in history. It was a private residence as long ago as 1176, when the Attercliffe area was countryside. It was at one time the home of the Bright family and one member of this family, John Bright, a Colonel in the Parliamentary Army during the Civil War of 1642–49, was appointed Governor of the then still standing Sheffield Castle when it was wrested from Royalist control in 1644. He was also Governor of York 1649–60 and High Sheriff of the County of Yorkshire 1654–55.

The house passed through a number of owners until, in the middle of the 19th century it became a 'common beerhouse'. Today, it is a well restored and popular public house, with some of the ancient internal furnishings and architectural features intact. The oldest part of the building which is still standing was probably built in about 1620.

East House, Spital Hill, Burngreave.
Formerly an alehouse it was open in 1866. This small corner pub used to be part of the Tetley Brewery empire, but recently it has become a free house known as Morrissey's East House. It is a small pub with a violent episode in its past. In 1960, for the only time in it's long history, it was front page news and for a terrible reason.

On January 1st of that year, just before 11pm, Mohammed Ismail, a thirty-two year old Somali who had lived in Sheffield for about six years, was in the packed bar of the pub where the New Year spirit was still flowing strongly. He was in a state of severe mental depression and, in the grip of this illness, he wished to commit suicide. Ismail, however, was forbidden by his strict Muslim religion to do this and so, he claimed later in court, he heard voices in his head which urged him to commit some bloody murder which would force someone to kill him and thus end his miserable life.

Ismail drew out a loaded revolver in the bar and fired all five shots in the weapon at a group of seven young men who were singing around the piano. Michael McFarlane, a twenty-one year old steelworker, died at once. Two friends, Thomas Owen and Frederick Morris, died soon afterwards and McFarlane's brother, Don, was seriously injured with head wounds which left him, after months in hospital, still alive, but badly disabled. Ismail made no attempt to escape and was arrested, in the pub toilet, only minutes later. He was tried on 25th February 1960, at Sheffield Assizes and the jury took only fifteen minutes to find him guilty, but insane. He was sentenced to be detained at Her Majesty's Pleasure.

A disturbing follow-up to this story appeared later in an article in the *Star*, which revealed that Ismail was released from prison after only twenty-two months. He had been deported back to Somalia. The families of the victims of the crime were, understandably, outraged by this news. Following the publication of the newspaper article, a former friend of Ismail's informed the *Star* that after returning to Somalia, Ismail had once again gone berserk and had shot several of his fellow villagers. This time, however, there was no British justice to protect him and he got his final wish.

The Travellers Inn, Penistone Road.
Although recent road widening works has cost this pub the extensive courtyard which used to front the whole of the building and thereby the previously 'olde worlde' appearance of the establishment, the inside still carries reminders of the building's age. In the part of the pub which used to serve as the kitchen and is now part of a bar, there is a large granite fire-place carved with the initials G.C. and the date 1697.

The Burgoyne Arms, Langsett Road.
In the 18th century, a giant of a man named Hales was recorded as living in a public house called the Burgoyne Arms, Owlerton. This is possibly the same pub which is still standing in Langsett Road. It was said that he weighed over twenty-nine stones and his height was 7' 8". That is seriously big! This pub is still open.

The Albany Hotel, Surrey Street.
This hotel stood on the corner and although the hotel has long since gone, the architecturally impressive three storey building is still there and is now the home of a branch of the Yorkshire Bank.

The Twelve O'Clock, Attercliffe Road.
The sign of this public house was a large clock-face with the hands indicating midday (or midnight). The landlord in 1851 was Joseph Ellis, a well known local man. It is commemorated today by a pedestal clock which stands on the site of the pub which has long gone. In front of the pub, just before the road split into two directions, was the Twelve O'Clock toll-bar. These toll-bars were used to extract money from travellers. This money was supposed to be used for the upkeep of the roads and by 1871 about five thousand persons were employed to collect the tolls. The tolls became increasingly unpopular due to widespread misuse of the toll money and because of the short intervals between each toll-gate (or bar). There used to be, according to historical writings, nineteen tolls on the thirty-three mile stretch of road between Halifax and Sheffield. In 1821, the Broomhill toll-bar was wrecked by angry demonstrators. Tolls began to decline during the second half of the 19th century and the Twelve O'Clock toll-bar was abolished in 1866. Even after toll-bars began to go, there were, in 1867, still sixteen toll-bars covering about twenty-five miles of roads in Sheffield. In 1849, John Sephton, landlord of the Sportsman Inn, Attercliffe Road, was described in a town directory as 'a collector'. This was probably a toll-bar collector.

The Angel, Button Lane.
This pub had a large rear courtyard and stables and when the circus came to town to perform at either the Empire or Hippodrome Theatres, anything up to five elephants were quartered behind the pub. The pub opened

in 1825 and closed in 1956. Up until 1902, it was known as the Crown & Anchor.

Why Not Inn, Clun Street.
John Turley was the keeper of a beerhouse in Clun Street, Burngreave, when a horse called 'Why Not' won the Grand National Steeplechase in 1894. Mr Turley, who had backed the horse, changed the name of his house to the 'Why Not'! Why not? The pub was open in 1864.

The Yellow Lion, Haymarket.
In 1787, Robinson's coach went from this hotel to Tideswell once a week. It was an old fashioned public house relying much on the trade of local farmers. The hotel was demolished in 1927 to allow for the building of the present shopping area.

The Cricket Ball Inn, Sutherland Road.
The landlord of this pub in the 1850s was Matthew Needham and the pub was probably named thus because of the close proximity of the cricket field

known as The Gentlemens Cricket Ground—a forerunner of Bramall Lane—which was on part of a common known as Local Fields.

The Hope and Anchor, Attercliffe Road.

This pub was kept from about 1822 until 1849 by Benjamin Blythe, then by his widow. She was followed by Henry Elam and later by his widow. There was a butchers shop next door which combined its business with the running of the pub. The name was then changed to The Sportsman Inn, the landlord being William Wright, then Abraham Booth, who still carried on the butchery business as well. John Simpson was landlord in 1870, Stephen Simpson in 1896 and Joe Simpson in 1911. The pub is still in business.

The Alhambra Music Hall, Union Street.

This establishment was destroyed by fire in 1882 and it was replaced by the aptly named Phoenix. In 1895, the Empire Music Hall was built on the opposite side of the street.

The Pheasant, Attercliffe Road.

Previous to becoming a public house, the building which is now the Pheasant Inn was a thatched dwelling. It was replaced by John and Joseph Fowler with a more modern, for those days, building and in 1830, John Fowler became the first landlord. A descendant of the Fowlers, Mrs Kimber, is recorded as having stated that, 'my grandparents (presumably the Fowlers) were in the house when Spence Broughton was gibbeted and I have the table on which the body was placed before hanging it on the gibbet post'!

The Royal Albion, Finley Street/Hammond Street.

The beerhouse on the corner of Finley Street and Hammond Street had no name for many years until it became known as the Royal Albion.

The Broughton, Broughton Lane.

The Broughton, now demolished, stood on the corner of Broughton Lane and both were named after a well known, but ill-fated highway robber, Spence Broughton.

Broughton had been born into a well-off Lincolnshire farming family, but drink and heavy gambling led him to crime. On February 9th, 1791, Broughton and an accomplice named John Oxley, robbed the Sheffield and Rotherham mail carrier and made off with the mailbags. These contained letters and a bill of exchange worth £123. Both men were caught later the same year in London; Broughton only finally being arrested after a fierce chase by John Townsend, a well known Bow Street Runner of the period. They were locked up in separate jails—Broughton in Newgate and Oxley in Clerkenwell, from which he escaped under suspicious circumstances and disappeared.

Broughton was transferred to York Castle where he was tried at the Spring Assizes. (Some accounts state that they were both tried at the old Sheffield Town Hall by the church gates and then Oxley escaped) He was sentenced to hang and his body to be gibbeted near the scene of his crime as a dreadful warning to others. He was executed at York Tyburn on Saturday 14th April, 1792 and his body returned to Sheffield where a gibbet had been erected on Attercliffe Common. Broughton's wife is reputed to have viewed the body from an upstairs room at The Harrow (or Arrow) public house, which once stood near the spot, although it has proved impossible to pinpoint the actual site. It could have been the public house which stood in nearby Clifton Street and which was later known as The Yellow Lion.

On the first day of his gruesome appearance, the body encased in an iron cage and coated with pitch, an estimated forty thousand people journeyed to Attercliffe to see his wretched body hanging in its chains. It remained there, 'as late as 1817, the whitened bones of the malefactor could be seen, with the remnants of his clothes fluttering in the breeze'! Finally, the new owner of the land, Mr Henry Sorby of Woodburn, had the post sawn down and removed to his coach house. Spence Broughton had finally left the public eye. His partner, Oxley, was found dead a year after Broughton's execution, in February 1793, on Loxley Moor, again in suspicious circumstances.

In an account of May 3rd, 1867 in the *Sheffield Local Register*, a man named Holroyd was digging new cellars on the site opposite The Yellow Lion, Clifton Street, when he found an upright shaft of seasoned black oak, which had been passed through and bolted to a large wooden frame, all of which had been solidly buried in the ground. These were the remains of the Broughton gibbet, which had been made seventy-five years previously by a man named Gregory. Again, large crowds gathered to witness the find.

A final twist to the Spence Broughton saga is the tale which relates how finger bones from the skeleton were ground and mixed with clay at The Don Pottery, Swinton, to make a mug and a seal embossed with a gibbet!

Fagan's Broad Lane, formerly The Barrel

Fagans, Broad Lane.
This small pub was formerly known as the Barrel and owes its present name to a former landlord, Joe Fagan, who took over the pub in 1951. Mr Fagan's father, Michael, was also a well known landlord. He started off in 1908 at 28 Hollis Croft with a beerhouse known as The Orange Branch, moved to The Royal Oak, 11 Hollis Croft in 1926, then took over The Bridge Inn, Bridge Street until his retirement in 1951.

The Albion, Attercliffe Road.
Before it was renamed The Albion, this pub had other names—from before 1819 until after 1828 the landlord was a stone mason by trade, John Eyre, and he named the pub, The Mason's Arms. In 1841, he was still landlord, but the pub was known as The Odd Fellows Arms. He was followed as landlord by Joseph Charlesworth from 1849 until about 1862; in the 1870s the landlord was Charles H. Johnson. When the pub first began to be known as The Albion is not clear, but it was before 1915.

The Bull and Mouth (The Tap and Spile), Waingate.
This name was a corruption of The Boulogne Mouth, off France, where King Henry VII won a notable sea battle in 1544. The pub was open in 1790, rebuilt and moved in 1928 and is still open. It was known for a long time as The Bull and Mouth, but has recently changed its name to The Tap and Spile and is a free-house.

The Angel, Angel Street.
Built in 1680 out of local granite, The Angel, together with The Tontine, were the two great coaching inns of Sheffield. The first recorded landlord of The Angel is Francis Barlow who owned the pub between 1681 and 1700. He was followed by Mr Pegg who lived there until 1720. The next landlords were John Horsfield, 1720–40 and Mr Anderton, 1740–53.

In the year of 1728, Sheffield had its first theatre building. This was an 'inn yard theatre' and it was built in the yard of The Angel Inn. It was probably similar to those found in London during the 16th century, as the Elizabethan actors had found the inn yards perfectly suited for their purposes. The main archway provided an entrance for the audience, while the galleries offered a modicum of comfort for the elderly or those who wished to be separated from the crowd in the inn yard. The stage was an easily erected platform with direct access to the inn. This type of theatre was readily available, simple in structure, open to the light with little or no scenery and admirably suited to popular drama.

Stephen Green became manager and he led a company of strolling players well known throughout the West Riding of Yorkshire. This theatre appears to have flourished, because in 1730 it is reported to have, 'put

THE  HOTEL,

ANGEL STREET,

SHEFFIELD.

FREDERIC WILKINSON, Proprietor.

Commercial, Family & Posting House.

HOT AND COLD BATHS.

This Hotel is in the most central part of the Town.

ANGEL INN LIVERY & BAIT STABLES,

ANGEL STREET, SHEFFIELD.

GEORGE MITCHELL,

LICENSED TO LET

POST HORSES, WEDDING AND PARTY CARRIAGES,

HANSOM'S PATENT & OTHER CABS,

OMNIBUSES FOR PLEASURE EXCURSIONS,

HEARSES,

MOURNING COACHES, AND FAMILY FUNERAL OMNIBUSES.

forth considerable intellectual and moral pretensions', so much so that prominent citizens' subscriptions supplied it with a good stock of costumes and props. Another record noted how 'on Whit Monday 11th May 1761, the Angel Inn Yard Theatre held a benefit concert and a ball for a Mr Hartly of Old Church Yard, in which seats sold for two shillings in the pit and one shilling in the gallery. First violin player was a Mr Shaw from York and the performance began a half hour after six.'

The last record of a theatre in the Angel Inn is of it being used for displaying commercial travellers' samples and as a hall for public dinners. This may have been in the same large room, which was still visible in 19th century photographs, to the left of the yard and above the iron gateway.

Samuel Glanville was one of the most well known of the pub's landlords. He was born in 1720 near Exeter, served in the Army with a regiment of foot, then came to Sheffield in 1741 where he married a Mrs Smith, she kept a public house in Church Street. He took over the Angel Inn in 1753 and made some big changes. An astute businessman, by 1760 he was running the first ever coach service to London. It took three days and six hours to do the journey, in spite of the use of teams of six horses. Samuel himself drove the coach on its first run.

The first coffee rooms were opened at the Angel Inn in 1763 by Mr Holland and the inn became one of the most popular places in the town.

Samuel Glanville retired in 1779 and went to live at the Duke of Norfolk's Alms Houses. He died in the old Shrewsbury Hospital, built on the site of the modern day Sheaf Market, in 1803.

Samuel Peech left the previously mentioned Rose & Crown and took over The Angel Inn in 1779. He carried on the coaching business, sometimes, if the competition was becoming serious, taking passengers for nothing and also giving them a bottle of wine each. Certainly a genial mine host! He is mentioned by Joseph Woolhouse in his book 'Sheffield—200 Years Ago', which was written in 1832, as 'A very wicked, but honest man!' A strange combination indeed. He also had a farm in the then suburb of Carbrook and occasionally brought his workers by coaches for a feast at The Angel. He died in 1809 and was buried at the Hill Top Cemetery. The Angel was sold by his son to Thomas Walker, an industrialist and pioneer in the introduction of gas. He did major rebuilding works to the hotel, moving its frontage forward about fifty yards.

In 1803, there was one of the famous 'beefsteak dinners' for which the Angel was well known. It must have been a good evening, for the following poem was written to commemorate the event:

> On the thirteenth of April, that mem'rable time,
> Some ladies intended at Peech's to dine,
> For Lent being over, the feast was no crime,
> Oh! the beefsteaks of the Angel, the Angelic beefsteaks.

An extract from the diary of a local business man, Mr Acton, written in 1836 reads, 'A grand dinner was given to Dr Younge at the Cutlers Hall last Thursday. I believe about 170 gentlemen sat down to an excellent dinner provided by Mr Hancock of the Angel Hotel.'

A later landlord was Frederic Wilkinson, who was there in 1862. The livery and bait stables were run by George Mitchell.

In common with The Tontine Hotel, The Angel had its share of politically inspired trouble. On Election Day, in 1857, police had to face a crowd of about three hundred people in Angel Street. The Inn was where the unpopular Conservative candidate had made his headquarters and fifty police stood guard at the entrances. Late in the afternoon, no doubt after the crowd had stoked themselves up well from the alehouses, the police and the crowd began to fight. The police charged and the mob replied with missiles and stones, hitting several of the officers. One man, Edward Prior, was so badly injured that he died a few days later.

The Angel Inn was destroyed by enemy bombing in December, 1940.

North Pole, Sussex Street.

This pub started its life as a private house known as Riverside Cottage. It was a canal-side pub with a rear garden which ran down to a broad mill pond beside the River Don. The attractive 19th century buildings are now offices.

The Labour in Vain, Princess Street.

This pub was first called The Brewery Tap and closed in 1920. This is not a rare name and the sign usually depicts a woman scrubbing a black child in the hope of turning it white. Not the sort of thing that would be 'politically correct' today! It closed in 1920.

The River Sheaf.

Public houses with Sheaf in their names are not uncommon in England, but those in Sheffield were not named after sheaves of corn, but the River Sheaf. This small river starts in the Totley area of the town, where the Totley and Oldhay Brooks merge. It meanders through the suburbs and joins the River Don in the town centre. It is an insignificant watercourse and it is surprising that this is the river from which the city of Sheffield (Sheaffield) gets its name.

It had a moment of glory though, on December 21st 1991, when it burst its banks and flooded the Midland railway station. Such was the force of the water that a log 5ft long, with a diameter of over 1ft, was deposited on the platform. It is still there, adorned with a plaque!

Four pubs have held the name 'Sheaf'—in Sheaf Street, open in 1825, closed in 1900; in Bramall Lane, this one is still open; in Effingham Street; and in Gleadless Road , this last pub is also still open.

The Chantrey Arms, Bramall Lane.

The Chantrey Arms was open in 1830. It was named after the celebrated sculptor, Sir Francis Chantrey RA (1781–1841). Chantrey has been called by people who should know as, 'the greatest sculptor that England has ever produced'. He was born in Norton, then a village outside Sheffield, and began his artistic career as a portrait painter working from a small, rented room at 24 Paradise Square. Many of his fine pieces of work adorn the cathedral. When he died, after a career spent mostly in London, he was buried, as he had requested, in the local churchyard at Norton. There is another Chantrey Arms in Chesterfield Road.

Paradise Square.

This little square is now an attractive, high value property area, much favoured by lawyers and estate agents. A hundred years ago, it was a different story. The square was ringed with beerhouses and a market was held there every week. The Q in the Corner, later The Shrewsbury, and The Clown and Monkey are both mentioned elsewhere in this book. It was a popular place for speakers due to the slight slope of the square, which gave them a natural vantage point above the crowd. John Wesley said, after speaking there once, that he had never had a larger audience for a working day—it was probably a Monday!

It was also the position of the town stocks, which on a Sunday morning sometimes had as many as nine men locked in them, usually for the heinous crime of drinking instead of attending church. The market was popular for the selling and buying of earthenware pottery and cooking vessels and this gave the square it's local nickname of 'Pot Square'.

There was also an annual fair which was known as the Sheffield Statute Hirings Fair. It was held on October 28th, the feast of St. Simon and St. Jude. This was an event when countrymen journeyed to the town to offer their labour, for the span of one year, to the highest bidder. It was a rough occasion, when town and country met and often ended in brawls. It gradually faded out at the end of the 19th century.

The market was also the scene of occasional wife selling. In 1796, John Lees took his wife Margaret to the market, haltered round the neck, and sold her to a man called Samuel Hall, a fell monger, for the sum of sixpence. It is reported that he was charged tax on the deal! The last occasion of wife selling that has been recorded was in 1822, when a man got five shillings and a gold watch for his wife. It was said at the time that the woman concerned was 'not loathe to the transfer!'

Although wife selling was probably a fairly rare event in Sheffield, a street ballad of the period has survived:

In Sheffield market, I declare,
'Tis true upon my life,
A cotton spinner t'other day,
By auction sold his wife.

The Bird in Hand, Church Street.

Previously mentioned, The Bird in Hand in Church Street was at the side of the Cutlers Hall and was the meeting place for cutlers and chapmen (salesmen). The cutlers would bring their wares to the inn and strike bargains with the chapmen for them to take the goods and sell them all over England. These chapmen would load their stocks of cutlery onto mules and set off over the poor roads and bridleways which led out of Sheffield.

Not Famous Enough?

Several pubs in Sheffield are named after men who are, nowadays at least, obscure enough for no information to be found as to who they were and what they did which made them worth naming pubs after: The Paul Pry, open in 1833; The Sir Admiral Lyons, 1833 – 1908; The Sir Francis Burnett, open in 1825, closed in 1910 and The William McReady, open 1787.

It is surprising that so few pubs in Sheffield are named after the men who during their lives left a real mark, both in the city and worldwide: John Brown, Mark Firth, Dr Graves, John Fowler (he built the Forth Bridge and large pieces of the London underground, amongst other things), Benjamin Huntsman and of course, Henry Bessamer, to name but a few out of many. Strange, considering how many men and women owed their working lives to these men!

Strange Names.

Several Sheffield pubs had names which must surely have been unique in Britain: The Ancient Pineapple; The Steam Clock; The African Prince, open in 1795, closed 1833; The American Stores, closed in 1893 and The Australian Arms, open in 1825, closed in 1893. These are the names and why anyone should name a pub thus is beyond me. There must have been some reason though. Any ideas?

The Coach and Horses, Attercliffe Road.

This was one of the oldest public houses in the Attercliffe area, being there in 1819 or earlier. At that time it was owned by Peter Dyson, with Thomas Corker as landlord. He and his brother were well known as cabinet makers and joiners in the area. The name of the pub is not known at this time, but in 1833 it was named The Barrel and owned by Hugh Bradford. By 1838, it had become known as The Coach and Horses. This was a fitting name, as there was a four times a week coach service which ran past the pub to and from Retford and Worksop. After Mr Bradford, the pub was run by Alfred

Johnson and then by his widow, Charlotte. A Mrs Bingley was there in 1876 and she was followed by Albert Fellows.

The Matilda Tavern, Matilda Street.
This pub was built in the early 1840s as a coaching stop—the stable yard is still in existence—and was named after Queen Matilda, wife of William the Conqueror, and daughter of Baldwin, Count of Flanders.

The Earl of Arundel and Surrey, Queen's Road.
This large pub has an unusual claim to fame. It is believed to be the only remaining official Pound House in Sheffield. This means that the pub is obliged to house any stray animals which are captured and taken there, be they cows, donkeys, horses or chickens. It has extensive stabling at the rear of the main buildings and this is where the Vaux Brewery Percheron shire-horses are stabled when they are brought to the town for display purposes. The pub buildings were erected in about 1880.

The Red Lion, Charles Street.
One hundred years ago, this Wards' pub had a popular Victorian 'Palace of Varieties' music hall, with a large audience gathering in the pub's large concert room.

The pub has a small mystery—a century ago, during work on the cellar, a small stone was discovered beneath the flooring flagstones. This bore, in

Arabic, a quotation from the Koran, the sacred book of Islam. How it got there has never been discovered to this day. Open in 1825, it is still in business.

The Travellers Rest, South Street, Moor.
This pub was better known as 'Billy Lee's'. It was a popular public house for entertainment during the years of the second world war and its large concert room was regularly full of locals and servicemen.

Victoria Railway Hotel, off Furnival Road.
Since the destruction of the old Tontine Hotel, a place of accommodation upon a similar large scale was needed in Sheffield. This was supplied by a number of shareholders, rather in the same manner as the Tontine had first been built, at a cost of about £15,000. Called The Royal Victoria Hotel, this spacious building was erected adjoining the station of the Manchester, Sheffield and Lincolnshire Railway. It was opened in 1862 and is still in business today. The five storey building contains large public rooms and fifty bedrooms. The first occupier was Mr George Meyer, from Manchester, who spent £10,000 on fitting and furnishing the hotel.

Napier Hotels, Lord Street and Napier Street.
Two public houses were named after Sir Charles Napier, who was the British Army Commander for the north of England around the middle of the 19th century. He is credited with averting serious Chartist riots in 1839, by his watchfulnesss and firm control of the situation. The Napier Street pub was open in 1833 and is still open.

The Golden Ball, Attercliffe Road.
This pub was firstly called The New Inn. It was owned and run by John Davis in 1828, who was also a shovel and spade maker. He was followed by George Watson and then by George Dawson who kept the house for about thirty years. Mr Dawson was also a farmer and the registrar of births and deaths for the district. His successor was John King.

The Q in the Corner, later The Shrewsbury, Paradise Square.
This was one of several public houses which ringed the square and was a favourite resort of the blind fiddlers well known in the town. In the early 19th century, the most famous fiddlers were: James Knight, Samuel Hawke, Joseph Ward, Alexander Clayton, William Brumby and Thomas Booth. At Christmas time they would go 'Christmas Boxing'—touring the local pubs and collecting a fair amount of ale money in tips. Two of their most popular tunes were: 'Bill Block' and 'The Death of the Tan Topsail'. In 1810 a concert took place at the Assembly Rooms. Admission was 2/6d and there was a ball afterwards. It was called 'a concert for the benefit of the six principal blind fiddlers of Sheffield'.

In the 18th century, one landlord, Samuel Goodlad, had an excellent memory for music and he used to be a popular performer on the fiddle at many public occasions. He commonly used to brag to his patrons that he was the first fiddler in the town to hear the popular London tunes and therefore could play them before anyone else. One evening he played one of these tunes in the pub unaware that a blind fiddler named Stephen had been smuggled into the bar, concealed in a sack, by his friends. Later when Samuel was receiving the plaudits of his friends, Stephen returned to the bar and, primed beforehand, his friends asked him if he could play the tune that Samuel claimed that he alone knew. Stephen, who had an even better memory for a tune than Samuel, said that of course he could, and better than anyone else. Samuel fell for the bait and bet Stephen 'a leg of mutton and trimmings' that he couldn't play it. Stephen, of course, won the bet.

Another story concerns Blind Stephen and The Q in the Corner. Late one evening, Stephen asked the landlord's new wife, who didn't know that he was blind, if he could borrow a lantern as it was such a dark night. The kind-hearted women lent him one and Stephen went on his way. After he had left, the remaining customers asked the landlady why she had lent a lantern to a blind man? Not wishing to appear a fool, she sent a servant girl after Stephen to retrieve the lantern, but he refused to give it up. When the girl argued with him, he told her, 'Does tha think I borrowed it for mi sen? Tell thi mistress that there are so many drunken folks in't street, that if one of them knocked me darn and smashed mi fiddle I'd be ruined. I can't see wi't lantern, but other folks can see me!' Which seems fair enough.

The Wheatsheaf, Bridge Street.

This pub which was almost on the corner with Water Lane has now gone, along with several others, to make way for the magistrates court complex. In the public bar, cemented into the wall, there was, until the pub was demolished, a tombstone. It was dedicated to a well known local character called Tommy Lightfoot. He was a bookie's runner in the days before off course betting became legal. Where it went after the pub was knocked down is anyone's bet!

The Army Stores, Wood Street, off Penistone Road.

Why this public house was called The Army Stores is not known. It later became known as The Clifton and was demolished in the late 1960s. This corner was the terminus for the horse-drawn trams which plied between the foot of Snig Hill and Hillfoot Bridge.

One landlord, in the later half of the 19th century, used to erect a greasy pole outside the front of the pub during holiday periods and the prize for anyone lucky, or persistent enough, to reach the top was a leg of mutton (there seemed to be an awful lot of mutton eaten in those days!). It not

The Clifton which looked more like a warehouse than a pub

only drew crowds outside the pub, but no doubt helped the landlord to fill both his bars and his pocket.

The Royal George, Carver Street.

This pub was there in 1833 and demolished in 1970. At one time it was kept by William Broadhead, a radical agitator and one time Secretary of the Sawgrinder's Union. He was heavily involved with the industrial unrest which became rife in the city during the 1840s and which became known as the Rattening Outrages.

The Royal Hotel, Waingate.

This public house was formerly known as The Reindeer. It was built in 1797 by Mr Godfrey Fox and demolished in 1928. Mr Fox was made 'Gaoler and Liberty Bailiff' by the Duke of Norfolk, at the King Street Gaol. He then became landlord of The Royal Oak, Pudding Lane (now King Street). This pub also had a long history, being built in 1774 and closed in 1941.

The Club Mill Inn, Smithfield.

This pub was also known as The Corn Mill Inn. In 1795, a corn mill was built, on a site beside the River Don at Neepsend, by a group of business men. It became known as the club mill and was, by all accounts, not a success. It is possible that the pub of the same name was a meeting place for the corn millers. The mill is gone, Club Mill Lane remains, but the pub went in 1930.

The Barrack Tavern, Penistone Road.
This pub was demolished in 1926, but in its time it was a popular meeting place for members of the Cutlers' Company, especially for their Forfeits Feast. At this event, first held in Sheffield in 1816, the names of each of the members of the Cutlers' Company were read out several times. Anyone who didn't respond to his name was fined a shilling (5p). A New Barrack Tavern was built further up the road. This closed recently and re-opened as the Hillsborough Barracks Inn in 1995.

The Blew (Blue) Bell, High Street.
In 1710, Robert Blastock, a linen draper, bought land and property for £630 in the High Street, He sold the room above his shop and part of the back, for £230 in silver and one 'broad' piece of gold, to Thomas Bingham, a baker, who put up the sign of The Blew (Blue) Bell. There is still an Old Blue Bell pub in the High Street, it is a modern place, much frequented by younger people and very popular at weekends, but it is now known as Cavells.

The Cutler's Inn, Coal Pit Lane (Cambridge Street).
The Cutler's Hall was housed in several buildings before settling in its present day position. It was once based in the Cutler's Inn.

The Pack Horse Inn, Snig Hill.
William Topliss was the first landlord of this public house, which was built in 1860 when the coaching trade was slowly beginning to decline. The imposing building stood at the bottom of Snig Hill, opposite The Grand Theatre, which was one of the foremost entertainment centres of the West Bar area until it was demolished in 1920. The balcony at the front of the building was used to hold large open air political meetings, at the rear there were extensive stables and a large room where Frank Howson held boxing matches on Saturdays. Berry & Co. (Brewers) bought the hotel in 1890 for £9,000 and sold it in 1900 to the Sheffield Corporation for £25,000. The Corporation wanted the site, to allow road alterations from Bridge Street to West Bar, and so the building was demolished. The site became a bus station and has now been developed into a new magistrates courts complex.

The Mason's Arms, off Attercliffe Road.
This pub stood back slightly from the main road and used to be the oldest pub on the road. In 1862 the building was demolished and a Wesleyan Chapel built on the site.

The Prince of Wales, Sussex Street.

This beerhouse closed in 1902. Advertised in the window was Wilson Brothers' 'Entire Beer'. This was the porter or stout which was so popular at the time. The brewery of Wilson Brothers was only a few yards away in the same street, it closed in 1900.

The Forest Inn, off Rutland Road.

This nice little inn was the last of the hundreds of beer and alehouses which have existed in Sheffield over the years. Following extensive renovations and an extension, it applied for and received a full public house licence during the last years of the 1980s—and now there are none.

The Beehive, West Street.

When, in 1818, the Sheffield Town Trustees, the forerunners of the City Council, wanted to build a road to be known as West Street, they bought a garden area from Thomas Rose. Mr Rose was a beekeeper and, in payment for the land, the Beehive Inn was built for him. For some reason the name of this pub was altered to the B-Hive, but has recently been altered again to the Foundry and Firkin.

The Bee Hive Hotel, West Street

The Old Anvil Inn, Waingate.
This inn was open in 1828 and was demolished in 1926 to make way for Foster's Clothing Store.

The Snow Lane Tap, The Crofts.
The area known as The Crofts was well known for all manner of crime and skulduggery and the many alehouses contributed mightily to this. The Snow Lane Tap, which was once kept by John Poole, was the centre of a court appearance by its landlord in 1850. Apparently, when police raided the premises, it was said that all four of the beds in the house were in use by well known prostitutes and their customers. Poole was fined £5 for 'failing to maintain good order in his house'. Poole and his wife were said to have once kept a brothel in nearby Hawley Croft. It has not been possible to pinpoint the exact position of this public house. It was presumably in Snow Lane and that is all we know.

The Britannia Inn, Worksop Road.
This inn was very possibly built around the turn of the 17th century, but long before it became an inn, it was two workers' cottages. When Benjamin Huntsman, the inventor of the crucible steel making process, had his steelworks in Church Street, (now Worksop Road) he lived there from about 1772. On one of the gable ends of the building there are the date figures for 1772, and these are reputed to have been made by Huntsman himself

using his new crucible steel. The building was later, for a short time, a school and then, in 1876, became the inn, which is as it stands today.

The Travellers Inn, Attercliffe Road.
The Miller family had an association with this pub for almost a century. In the 1780s Thomas and John Miller combined running the pub with working as knife makers, a John Miller was landlord in the 1860s, also a pen and pocketknife maker (his brother George was landlord of the nearby Cutler's Arms). Later, Thomas Miller was landlord. In 1892, Mrs Astill took over and she was followed by members of her family.

The Bath Hotel, Victoria Street.
When in 1867, a local businessman, Charles Hoyland, leased the site on which the pub now stands to a builder, he insisted that the land should not be used 'for the business of inn-keeper, publican or beerhouse keeper'. It was, however, and The Bath Hotel is now a popular pub with many CAMRA supporters and has been voted a 'pub of the year'.

The Three Horseshoes Hotel, Norfolk Street.
This is one of the public houses which were destroyed by German bombs in December, 1940. As well as being an hotel, it was also an oyster bar.

The Seven Stars, Trippet Lane.
In 1787, Thomas Beet, the landlord of this pub, was the only maker of knives in Sheffield to have his own trade mark. These were known as 'spotted' knives. Other men combined running a public house with following a trade. A John Webster of Little Sheffield, was a cutler and pattern maker, he also owned a bowling green.

The King's Head, Attercliffe Road.
The building which now houses this pub is only small, but has an interesting pedigree. It was once a grocers and earthenware dealers shop run by Robert Jackson, who was the father of Samuel, born in 1839, one of the founders of the now world famous tool making firm of Spear & Jackson. In 1839, it became a chemists and druggists shop owned by John Appleton. He was there for twenty-eight years, followed by his son for twenty years. After it became a pub, it was kept from 1898 until 1908 by George Littlewood, he was famous as a long distance runner and is mentioned in more detail elsewhere. The pub was nicknamed 'The Champion's Rest'.

The Parrot, Button Lane.
This pub was one of the last buildings of the town in this direction before Sheffield Moor began. It closed in 1908.

The Shakespear(e), Gibralter Street.
The landlord at the beginning of the 19th century was Benjamin Beet. At this time, one of the main sources of fresh water for the town was Bower Spring, which ran near this public house. In October, 1824, the water course ran dry and Mr Beet was instructed by the Town Trustees to:

> . . . make such search for this water as in his judgement was best. After much labour and expense, they found it again to the joy of the whole neighbourhood. It was above three months quite dry and now runs as plentiful as ever.
>
> *Joseph Woolhouse, 1832*

In 1835, Messrs Warburton & Co's Brewery applied to 'take in and enclose' the spring. The result of this is not known.

Punch Bowl public houses, Bridge Street and Coulston Street.
In 1787, William Potts was described in the town directory as a victualler of Colston Croft and in 1797, as of 20 Bridge Street. What the pub's name was then is not known, but under a later landlord, James Smith, it was known as the Punch Bowl. There was another Punch Bowl at the corner of Spring Street and Coulston Street and this pub was described as 'notorious'. It was kept, at one time, by Alfred 'Spotty' Milner.

The Greyhound, Gibralter Street.
Open in 1796, it was kept in about 1830 by John Hinchcliffe, an acting Constable of Sheffield. This pub was, at that time, the last building of the town in that direction, after that it was all fields and gardens. Mr Hinchcliffe also owned a large bowling green on a site where an Ebenezer Chapel was later built. The street was thus named Bowling Green Street.

The Ball Inn, Hawley Croft.
This pub, which closed in 1896, is mentioned in historical accounts as 'a good stone house built in this street.' It was empty for many years with the reputation of being haunted. It bore the date 1721 and in 1722 is believed to have been the residence of John Smith, who was the Master Cutler in that year. It later became The Ball Inn kept by Jonathan Beardshaw, he was followed by Thomas (Squire) Bright. Mr Bright was one of the twelve men listed as 'gentlemen' in the town directory of 1787 and it is possible that he was descended from the Bright family who had connections with Carbrook Hall, Attercliffe. He was also a rate collector.

The Cleeckham (or Cleckham) Inn, Cornish Place.
Cornish Place was off Cornish Street and has now gone. The actual position of this pub is not known and apart from the fact that the landlord owned a bowling green, there is little other information about it.

The Well Run Dimple, Fargate.
This stood on the original site of Barker's Pool and was first mentioned in writings in 1567, although it is thought to have been much older. It was probably named after a racehorse.

Today's 'Trendy' Names.
In recent times, many pubs with perfectly good and traditional names, which have stood the test of years, have become 'trendy' and have been renamed with phoney, either 'olde worlde' or strange names. I hope this fashion dies out as quickly as it appeared! Here are a few examples of what the '20th Century Heritage Business' thinks a Sheffield pub should be called: Dempsey's Bar; The Tut & Shive, The Tap & Spile; The Boomerang;

The Cask & Cutler; The Frog & Parrot; The Brewing Trough; The But & Ben, The Newt & Chambers, The Jervis Lum and The Hogs Head. There are others—unfortunately!

The Pack Horse Inn, West Bar.

This was a large, square building and a popular pub. It was a well known venue for boxing tournaments and once had stable space for fifty horses. It was demolished around 1902 to allow for road widening.

Public Houses as Social Centres

With the rapid expansion of Sheffield in the 1850s, entertainment began to appear in many public houses. The largest of these pubs was the Surrey Theatre on West Bar, which had dancing and singing turns on a regular basis. The Surrey Vaults public house was on the opposite corner. The Surrey Theatre was built in 1851, but was destroyed by fire in 1865 and the ruins were left until 1880, when the Vestry Offices were built on the site. A false fire alarm on September 13th, 1858, caused the deaths of five people—four were crushed to death in the panic and a fifth died when he jumped from an upstairs window!

West Bar became the focus for the night life of the town. There was The Blue Boar at 26 West Bar; The Surrey at 86 West Bar; The Gaiety Palace at 100 West Bar and The Tankard on the opposite side at 115 West Bar. These houses all had permanent stages and put on regular entertainment. Other pubs were The London Apprentice on the corner of West Bar Green; The Alhambra on Union Street, (later also burnt down); The Yorkshire Stingo, named after a famous strong Yorkshire beer, at 50 Division Street; The Fleur de Lys at 66 Fargate; The Grand (Star), Spring Street and The Blue Pig at 22 Workhouse Lane, just off West Bar.

These were the leisure amenities for the working men of Sheffield. In the future, Working Men's Clubs would flourish, but in the 19th century these few pubs provided them with a night out and a temporary escape from the problems of living and working in the conditions of the time. It is easy to forget that there was not much else—no TV, cinema, radio or motor cars. Most people lived, worked and drank in the very small area of the town around their houses. They had little choice.

Clubs and Societies.

Public houses were the centres to which the workers with leisure time graduated and many of them formed themselves into mutually beneficial 'Sick and Dividing Clubs' based at particular pubs. The object of these clubs was to help members should they fall ill and be unable to work. In those days, the general rule was no work, no money! Trade unions were still illegal and the welfare state was many years in the future.

The highlight of the year for these clubs, also known as Friendly Societies, was usually the Society Feast. These were marked more 'by rude plenty and good fellowship, than by delicacy of feeding and refinement of accessories'. In other words it was a rough and ready blowout with plenty to eat and drink!

By no means every pub was the haunt of villains and rogues. The town was well supplied with pubs which, though humble in appearance and accommodation, were conducted by a highly respectable class of men. They were proud of the good reputation of their inns and taverns which were conducted 'whole heartedly in the interests and welfare of their customers'.

Many of these houses had a distinctive class of customer and certain pubs, as happens today, would be a favourite meeting place for certain groups or trades. They were like social clubs and became the birthplace of the Friendly Societies and Unions. Some public houses were well known for the kind of club which met there.

The Q in the Corner, later known as The Shrewsbury, in Paradise Square, was the haunt most favoured by the theatrical profession and they formed the first Buffalo Lodge in Sheffield. The pub was renowned for its blind fiddlers and its most well known landlord was Samuel Goodlad.

Some Sick and Dividing Clubs have left records:

The Revolution Sick Society was started by Benjamin Crofts at the Crown and Cushion in Sycamore Street on 4th May 1789. In those days of uncertainty, a strongbox or iron chest was considered a safer depository for the club's cash than a bank, several of which had gone bankrupt in the town. One of the largest, owned by Nicholas Broadbent, collapsed in 1782. Mr Broadbent's house still stands at No. 3 Hartshead and is known as the Old Banker's House.

The monthly contribution to the Revolution Sick Society was at first 1/4d. 1/2d of this money went into the box and the remainder went into the kitty to pay for beer (1d a pint in those days). Candidates for membership had to be aged between twenty-one and thirty-one and the initial membership fee was 2/6d. Sick pay was ten shillings a week for the first twelve weeks and five shillings a week until the member was able to return to work. The Society held its annual feast every November 5th and charged a two shillings entrance fee. This club was very prosperous and had to limit its membership to two hundred men. In 1804, the Society moved its headquarters (probably much to the dismay of the landlord) to the King's Head and then in 1809 to the George. It was finally wound up in 1892 when there were twenty-three surviving members. Each of these received a final pay off of £2-16-0.

The Rodney Society founded in 1782, was based at the Rose & Crown in High Street. Also founded in 1782 was **The Norfolk Society** at the White Bear in High Street.

The Rawson Society started up at the Theatre Tavern on Arundel Street in 1782, moved to the Victoria in the High Street and then, in 1828, to the Three Tuns in Orchard Street with the aid of a generous donation from a Miss Rawson of Wardsend in memory of her brother, Thomas Rawson, who died in 1826. The Rawsons were a well known brewing family, with premises in the Pond Street area. Miss Rawson chose the age of her brother, who was 78 years old when he died, as the maximum number for membership of the society. Members reaching that age were entitled to an annuity of twenty pounds. The number of members in 1900 was fifty-two, which was a fair representation of the average membership since the 1850s.

John Beardshaw started **The Beardshaw Funding Society** in 1783 at the Cock in Hollis Croft and then continued it at The Ball, Hawley Croft. This pub is thought to have once been the residence of John Smith, Master Cutler in 1722 and an ancestor of the Reverend Joseph Hunter, the historian. The society was then removed by his descendent, Jonathan Beardshaw, to the Victoria in High Street and renamed **The Victoria Club Funding Society**.

The Royal Jubilee Friendly Society was started in 1809 at the Black Rock in Castle Street and in 1822 moved to the George Inn, Market Place. Later it was run for many years from the Black Swan on Snig Hill with John Crich as the landlord.
The Fitzwilliam Friendly Society was established in April 1822 at the Black Rock in Castle Street, which was kept then by John Fordham. It began with one hundred members and new members were limited to two a year.

These Sick Clubs and Friendly Societies were a way by which workers could join together and make for themselves some small provision for the sometimes bleak future.

There was one club which was slightly different from the others. In the 1880s a Sick and Dividing club, which met at the Blue Bell Inn, Worksop Road, Attercliffe was known as **The Stupid Club**. Its object appeared to be to satisfy the members' needs to argue amongst themselves on almost any topic under the sun. These arguments often ended in brawls. Funds paid into the club were used mostly to buy drink, that was the Dividing part; the Sick part was never drawn, because one of the rules of the club stated that before being ill, a member had to give a fortnight's notice! The Spill Major, also chairman of the club, sat nearest the fire and his main task was to light a wooden spill and pass it to whichever member required a light for his pipe. He was also supposed to keep order amongst the members which, judging from the 'stupidity' of the members, must have been a hopeless task . . . or so the story goes!

Landlords as Constables.
Mr Hinchcliffe, landlord of The Greyhound, Gibralter Street, was the only constable in the town in 1812. The next constable was Mr Waterfall, nick-named 'long foot', who was landlord of The Leg of Mutton and Trimmings, Smithfield. Thomas Smith was the constable in 1818. He was landlord of The Royal Oak, King Street. The debtors jail was next door to The Royal Oak and Mr Smith was the jailer. When this jail was closed and an old ware-house in Scotland Street, known as The Edinburgh Castle, was converted to a debtors gaol, Mr Smith gave up his public house and became its gaoler full time. Possibly it was a more lucrative position.

Odds and Ends.
There were two beerhouses which had no signs over the door. One was on the corner of Finlay Street/Hammond Street and was kept for a time by a Mrs Walker. It later became known as The Royal Albion. The other was No. 21 Meadow Street on the corner of Upper Allan Street. In 1883 it was kept by James Wood and in the early part of this century, it was known as 'The Widow's Hut' as it was a popular meeting place for local women. The land-lord during that period was James Dawes.

The Marshall Tavern, Pye Bank, was a tiny establishment and was named by the locals, 'The Bacon Box'. In the 19th century, a large amount of bacon and ham was imported from the continent and this used to be packed in large wooden boxes which were much prized for use as garden sheds and pigeon lofts—hence this small pub's nickname.

The Bull's Head, Dun Street, reputed to have been one of the roughest public houses in the town, was known by the locals as 'The Devil's Kitchen'. Dun Street is a small street in length, had no houses on it, but three public houses. This pub has been closed for many years, but the buildings have recently been refurbished. On the outside of the facade at the front is a rare advertisement for Old Albion Ales.

In 1802, freak high winds caused great damage to roofs in the town and 2,000lbs of lead were stripped from the roof of The Tontine Hotel, Haymarket. During that year, a temperature of -29° Fahrenheit was record-ed which killed all the vegetation in the area.

After The Tontine Hotel was pulled down, some of the materials from the old buildings were used to build a residential hotel and dining rooms known as Steer's Hotel. This was later converted into a suite of offices known as Tontine Chambers. Steer's Hotel was on the corner of Dixon Lane, off Haymarket.

A list of the streets and alleys which made up the original town of Sheffield in about 1770: Priorgate (part of High Street); Fargate; Pepper Alley (Norfolk Row); Norfolk Street; Coal Pit Lane (Cambridge Street); Burgess

Street; West Bar (with many lanes leading off). Less important were Balm Green; Castle Hill (off Waingate); Hollis Croft; Red Croft; The Underwater (off Bridge Street); Broad Lane; Church Street; Irish Cross (top of Snig Hill); Scargill Croft; Townhead Street; Bullstake (Haymarket); Dixon Lane; Jehu Lane (Commercial Street); Shude Hill; Waingate; Campo Lane; Millsands; Snig Hill; Water Lane; Castle Folds (or Foulds); Figtree Lane; Newhall Street (Bridge Street); The Isle (Bridge Street); West Bar Green; Castle Green; Hartshead; Pudding Lane (King Street); The Ponds (Pond Street); Castle Head; Ratten Row; Truelove's Gutter (Castle Street).

Here are a few facts about the brewing industry in Yorkshire, taken from the *Yorkshire Post* in the early 1990s: four million pints of beer are brewed every day. This is over 13% of the total beer production in the UK; there are 65 different brands of beer which are brewed solely in Yorkshire, 1 in 3 of these are cask conditioned beers.

All this beer adds up to an excise duty present to the Chancellor of the Exchequer of £260 million, or £750,000 per day from Yorkshire alone! The reason for this huge sum is simple—next to Ireland, this country has the highest taxed beer in Europe. Add VAT and the price of a pint is increased by about 50%. That is why this country drinks 21% of the beer brewed in Europe—and pays 55% of the total tax paid on beer in Europe!

On the Outskirts, Some Interesting Pubs and Pub Stories

Places like Handsworth, Owlerton and Norton are today considered to be merely part of the Sheffield metropolitan area, but in the 18th and 19th centuries these were small, independent villages. They had a separate lifestyle and many of the population only rarely, if ever, ventured into Sheffield town.

Indeed, it was said of one old man whose name was Jimmy Larder, that the nearest he had ever been to Sheffield was when he once visited Millhouses! Jimmy's job was to drive the one-horse omnibus from Dore & Totley railway station to Totley. That, it appears, was as far as he wanted to travel. This was in the early 1920s!

Here are a few tales about some of the pubs in these villages:

The Nailmaker's Arms, Norton.

One of the oldest public houses in South Yorkshire is The Nailmaker's Arms. It stands in Blackmoor Road, Norton, and takes its name from the local cottage industry of nailmaking. It was built in 1627 and although the inn has suffered at the hands of the brewery, has been over-renovated and no longer has the appearance of an ancient inn, it is still in business. Once, at the rear of the house, there was an old brewery building where the landlord made his own beer. This was a common practice before breweries increased in size and began to own strings of public houses themselves.

The Bagshawe Arms, Norton.

Once this was a fine country inn, but now it has been 'modernised' and spoilt. The building was formerly a farmhouse belonging to the Bagshawe family and some of the original farm buildings are still standing at the rear of the inn. It was enlarged in 1829 and, for some time during the 19th century, one of these outbuildings was used, every second Wednesday of the month, as the local Petty Sessions Court. In 1844, John Thomas, who was a local writer and poet, stopped for a meal at the inn. He later wrote a glowing, if rather flowery account, of the pig's chap, eggs and beer on which he had supped.

The Bowling Green Inn, Psalter Lane.

Off Cherrytree Road, Psalter Lane, stand the only two remaining houses which were once part of the hamlet of Cherrytree. One of these houses is called Roadside Cottage but was once known as Cherrytree House. This was built in 1635 and was converted into an inn called The Bowling Green

Inn. Thomas Jenkinson, who was also a maker of hammers, was the landlord. At the rear of the property were extensive gardens and these were known as the Cherrytree Hill Bowling Club and Tea Gardens. Although there is no evidence to support the story, and it does sound rather far fetched, it has been said that there was once an underground ballroom beneath the gardens, which was lit by a large number of Chinese lanterns. When Mr Jenkinson died in 1841, the building became derelict and was owned by a number of people before it was restored and now it makes a pleasant private dwelling house.

The Stag Hotel, Psalter Lane.

In the later 17th century, there used to be a decrepit beerhouse at the top of the now named Cemetery Road. It was in the possession of the Reverend Alexander MacKenzie. He demolished the old building and built a new one in Psalter Lane to replace it which opened in 1805. This was a shrewd move as this was the old turnpike road and the passing coaches brought in plenty of business. The name is taken from a stag on the MacKenzie family crest. The building has now been demolished and a new hotel built to the rear of the site. There used to be a MacKenzie Tavern at 189 Cemetery Road, but whether this was the original beerhouse is not known.

The Fleur de Lis, Totley.

The original public house on this site was thought to have been about 250 years old when it was demolished in 1933 and the present Fleur de Lis was built. There used to be a small cattle market held weekly at the front of the public house and at the rear was an animal pinfold. The name possibly comes from the heraldic iris on the coat of arms of the Barker family who lived at Totley Hall or it could be from the arms of King Edward III, who was king of both England and France.

The Cross Scythes, Totley.

Parts of the buildings which make up this attractive pub are considered to be at least 300 years old. It was first opened as a pub by a local farmer and scythe-maker, Samuel Hopkinson, in buildings rented from a well known local man, George Greaves. Mr Hopkinson hoped to take advantage of the increased traffic passing the building due to the opening of the new toll road. For a scythe-maker, the name, The Cross Scythes, was a natural choice!

Later landlords included Thomas Fisher, about 1836; John Thorpe, about 1846, who altered the name to Ye Old Cross Scythes; John Wagstaff; Job Green, until 1868 and Thomas Bown in 1872. In 1885, a Grimesthorpe haulage contractor, Michael Cottam, began a bus service which ran between The Cross Scythes and the new Dore & Totley railway station.

The Crown Inn, Hillfoot, Totley.
The buildings of this pub are about 300 years old. It is known to have been run by Dorothy Dalton in 1813. She was a tenant of Lord Middleton, then the Lord of the Manor of Totley. She was born in the village in about 1791 and the pub was later run by her son, Thomas, who was also a firebrick maker.

The Cross Daggers, Woodhouse.
Almost all the medieval buildings, farms and workers' cottages have been demolished in the area this century to make way for a modern housing estate. However, The Cross Daggers, the base of the market cross and the village stocks have been preserved.

The Old Heavygate Inn, Matlock Road, Walkley.
This inn was built in 1696 and in 1896, as part of the celebrations to mark the 200th anniversary of the pub, a whole sheep was roasted in the inn yard by the landlord and all passers-by, on that day, were given a slice of the roast meat and a free drink. It would have been a busy road!

The Rising Sun, Ecclesall.

This public house must date from at least 1786, because the landlord is mentioned on a gravestone inscription to be found in Ecclesall Woods. It stands above the grave of a wood collier, or charcoal burner, who was burned to death in his hut in that year. It reads:

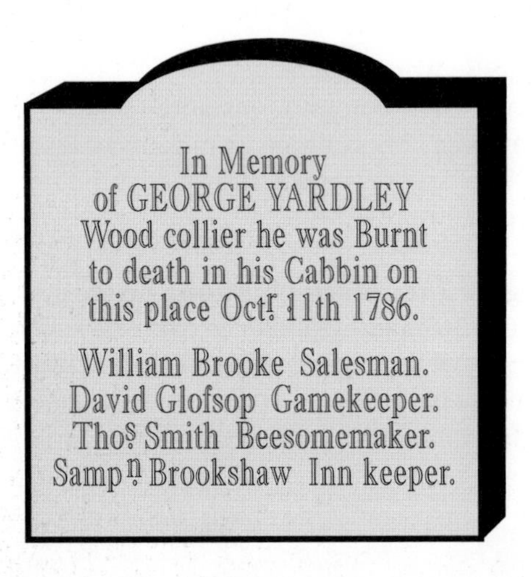

Sampson Brookshaw is known to have combined inn keeping with 'making common pocket and pen knives'. Beesomes were a type of broom or long handled brush made from bundles of thin twigs. They are still around today, but spelt besom—very good for shifting leaves!

The Norfolk Arms, Ringinglow Road.

In April 1876, quite a stir was created by a hoax started by one apparently news-starved journalist and compounded by a second. One of them, hoping no doubt to increase the sales of his newspaper, spread a rumour round Sheffield by means of a poster. It read: 'Horrible Murder at Ringinglow'! Soon, determined to get in on the act, a rival journalist issued a poster which read: 'Body Found'! This sensational news caused many people to trudge all the way out to Ringinglow, being as morbid about death as people are today, and after wandering around the area for hours finding nothing, they presumably finished up drinking and comparing notes in The Norfolk Arms. Mr Garratt was the landlord at the time and he, if few others, did well out of the hoax murder. If the two journalists and the landlord hatched up the plot between them, it was never disclosed. It makes a good story, anyway!

The Old Horns Inn, High Bradfield.

Although the crime did not take place there, The Old Horns played a part in a crime which has become known as The Kirkedge Murder.

In March 1782, a man named Francis Fearn, who was a local workshy waster and drunkard, decided that he needed to make some fast money. He worked out a plan. In those days of common poverty, not many people owned a watch or a clock and it was a common thing for public houses to run a 'watch and clock club'. These clubs had a number of members, each of whom paid in a fixed contribution each week. As the money mounted up, each member in turn was able to buy a time-piece of his choice.

Fearn decided that he could convince a local watchmaker, Nathan Andrews, that such a club was planned at The Old Horns. He spoke to Mr Andrews and they arranged to meet and walk together to High Bradfield; Fearn hoping that the watchmaker would be carrying a good load of samples and cash. They met on the following Monday afternoon and set off on the long walk to The Old Horns. That was the last time that Nathan Andrews was seen alive!

Mr Andrew's wife became worried when he had not returned on Tuesday morning and informed the Town Constable of her fears. A search was made and on the Tuesday evening, 19th March, Mr Andrew's dead and blood soaked body was discovered by a man named John Hudson at Kirkedge. His throat had been cut!

The constables knew that both men had set out together on the Monday afternoon and went to Sims Croft, where Francis Fearn had lodgings. They caught him in bed and after searching him discovered a watch known to have belonged to Mr Andrews.

Fearn confessed and was held in Sheffield Jail for four months before being taken to York to stand trial at the Assizes on July 13th 1782. It was a 'cut and dried' case and Fearn was not even allowed to speak in his own defence. The Baron of the Exchequer, Sir James Eyre, sentenced him to death.

Two days later, Fearn was taken into the prison yard by the executioner. He was put on a horse-drawn cart and the rope arranged around his neck. His last act was one of surprising bravado. He took off his shoes and threw them into the eagerly awaiting crowd, saying, 'That's made him a liar. He said I'd die wi' mi boots on and I've proved him wrong'! He is believed to have been referring to one of his many former employers.

When the driver of the cart forced the horse forward, Francis Fearn swung into space. It was said later that he 'died hard'!

His corpse was returned to Sheffield and hung in chains on Loxley Common, where it remained as a grim warning to others for fifteen years or more. It was said that he 'fell from his irons on Christmas Day, 1797'. The gibbet post, for which a man named Thomas Holdsworth was paid fifteen shillings to make and carry to Loxley, was taken down in 1810 and the wood used as either building materials or as a footbridge over the River Loxley. Probably the only useful thing that Francis Fearn ever had anything to do with!

Certain people did, however, prosper from the murder of Mr Andrews—a bill dated 30th July, 1782 claims 'the sum of £14-19-00 on prosecuting Francis Fearne [sic] for the murder of Nathan Andrews. Paid to Mr Wheats'!

Sportsman's Inn, Crosspool.

The former Sheffield Wednesday and England footballer, full back Ernest Blenkinsop, kept this house for several years. He played over 400 games for Wednesday and was capped 26 times for England. He also played for Liverpool.

Peacock Hotel, Owler Bar.

The landlord of this pub, from 1888 until his death in 1903, was a well known hay and straw dealer, William Hutchinson Broughton. He was formerly the landlord of the Punch Bowl, South Street, Moor. His hay and straw business was in Pond Street.

Cross Keys, Handsworth.

This pub is unique in being probably the only licenced premises to be inside the curtilage of a churchyard. The church is St Mary's, which is at the rear of the pub buildings. The pub was formerly the church house used by the chaplains and lay clerks. It was used as a school between about 1600 and 1800 and was then sold for £43, before becoming a public house in later years. It is said to have had a secret passage (another?) which led to the now demolished Handsworth Hall. This was probably to allow Roman Catholic priests an escape route during the religious upsets of the period. Both the church and the pub buildings were erected by William de Lovetot in 1250.

Wadsley Jack, Rural Lane, Wadsley.

The name of this public house comes from the name of a fictional character created in a book written by Reuben Hallam and published in 1866. Hallam was born in December, 1818 and died in November, 1908 aged almost 90. At one time he kept the Shoulder of Mutton in Bradwell and later the Horse & Jockey (formerly the White Hart) at Tideswell. He wrote the stories about 'Wadsley Jack', which were humorous tales about the antics and adventures of an itinerant knife grinder. These were serialised in the *Telegraph*.

The Big Tree, Chesterfield Road.

Up until about 1935, this pub was known as The Mason's Arms. The original 'big tree' was fatally damaged many years ago when a circus elephant, which was tied to the tree, tore off the main branch. After the tree died, it was replaced by another in 1935 and the pub took its name from that. The original tree is said to have sheltered John Wesley when he visited Woodseats and preached to the villagers. Also, Francis Chantrey is said to have sat in its shade whilst producing wood carvings. At the time of writing, yet another replacement tree has arrived, so it will be a fair number of years before the Big Tree really lives up to its name again.

The present building was erected in 1901 and beneath its carpets there are mosaics depicting the masons' trade and there are masons signs on the gable ends facing the road.

Old Buildings, New Pubs

A number of no-doubt excellent public houses, which are situated in the area covered by this book, have been purposely left out. The reason is simply that they are new pubs in new buildings and as such have little, if any, historical background or attraction. They are usually, although such pubs as the Penny Black are not, situated in or around new housing developments. There are, however, exceptions:

Yates Wine Lodge.
This pub, situated on the corner of Division Street and Carver Street, is very new, built in 1993, and the building and interior are of modern design. In fifty years or so, it will have mellowed and if it is allowed to, could become one of the landmark pubs in Sheffield.

The Saddle.
This West Street pub is also very new. It has been built next to the original Saddle public house which was a very popular small pub dating from at least 1825. The New Saddle is more of a wine bar than a public house, but deserves mention if only because of the effort expended by the owners to maintain a pub on that site.

Barkers.
Sited on the corner of Holly Lane and West Street. The building is again very modern, but it is built to last and attractively designed. It houses a combination of pub, restaurant and 'night spot'. It has been expensively built to cater for the modern customer, no pensioners will linger over a pint in this bar. If the owners can resist the urge to constantly alter the decor to keep up with modern 'fashions', then it could develop into a very well known meeting place.

Four pubs are worthy of mention for the simple reason that they have put down roots in notable old buildings.

Probably the oldest building is the Grade II Listed, Globe Works on Penistone Road. This interesting warren of small workshops and businesses was only saved from a council demolition order thanks to the determined efforts of far sighted local people. It is Dickensian in appearance and the pub on the ground floor is called the **Rattener's Rest**, conjuring up memories, for some people, of a period of violent industrial unrest which took place in Sheffield during the 19th Century.

A two-tier public house set-up with the **Dickens** on the upper floors and **Le Metro** in the basement, has been developed from an old Georgian school building in Carver Street. This building was erected in 1812, as it says on a large square plaque, 'by subscription'. It is architecturally plain and symmetrical as is the style of Georgian buildings and its conversion into licenced premises possibly saved it from dereliction or even demolition.

The old cathedral building, now called the **Gladstone**, in St James Street, was at one time, I believe, either a church school or living quarters for the clergy. It has obvious 'churchy' influences in its design with huge pointed and leaded windows and some fine stone carvings. It finally became a public house in the early 1990s following much narrow-minded wrangling over planning permissions, having stood, forlorn and neglected for a number of years. It may now be a haunt of the demon drink, but at least it is kept in good repair!

The final building of note is that of the former registry offices opposite the central libraries in Surrey Street. It has an interesting frieze of old masonic symbols along the front of the building and also above the entrance door. The pub is called—the **Surrey**. Above it there is a health studio called—the Fringe! Enough said.

Bibliography

The following is a list of publications which were consulted during the compilation of this book:

The Sheffield Gang Wars, J.P. Bean.

A Popular History of Sheffield, J. Edward Vickers.

Crime in Sheffield, J.P. Bean.

Old Sheffield Town, J. Edward Vickers.

The Inn Explorer's Guide, Frank Bottomley.

Quality Pays—The Story of Joshua Tetley and Son, Clifford Lackey.

Old Sheffield, Its Streets, People and Stories, J. Edward Vickers.

Aspects of Local History, Dennis Benson.

Grinders and Buffers, Herbert Housley.

Illustrated Guide to Sheffield and Neighbourhood, published by Pawson and Brailsford.

How They Lived in Old Ecclesall, Mary M. Bramhall.

History of Langsett and a Few More Stocksbridge Stirrings, Jack Branston.

The Ancient Village of Hereseige, Hathersage, Tom D. Tomlinson.

Fabric of the Past—Some Listed Buildings in South Yorkshire, published by Barnsley Council.

Scrapbook of N.E. Sheffield and S. Yorks, No 3, published by The Earl Marshal and Tinsley Adult Education Centre's Local History Groups.

Drawings of Historical Totley, Brian Edwards.

A Century of Sheffield 1835–1935 (Folio's 1, 2 and 4), David Robins.

Wincobank and Blackburn—A History of the Lower Blackburn Valley, C Wilson.

The Prince of Pleasure and His Regency, J.B. Priestley.

Sheffield, Its Story and Its Achievements, Mary Walton.

Pubs and People Around Sheffield, Roy Davey.

Sheffield 200 Years Ago, Joseph Woolhouse.

A Second Helping of Peter Harvey's Sheffield, Peter Harvey.

A Third Helping of Peter Harvey's Sheffield, Peter Harvey.

Drunkenness in Sheffield, G.L. Saunders.

The Story of Paradise Square, published by Sheffield City Libraries.

Bygone Breweries of Sheffield, Dave Parry, Don Parry and Alan Walker.

Before and After Bramall Lane, Keith Farnsworth.

Sheffield's East Enders, Keith Farnsworth

Innwards, published by S.H. Ward & Co. Ltd.

The Story of Old Attercliffe, G.R. Vine.

Bought of…, compiled by Mary Chesworth.

Strange Sheffield, David Clarke & Rob Wilson.

Sheffield Since 1900, Peter Harvey.

Sheffield in the Eighteenth Century, R.E. Leader.

Reminiscences of Old Sheffield, R.E. Leader.

Mottershaw's Sheffield, Pauline Shearstone.

Also consulted were many editions of both White's and Kelly's Sheffield Directories and newspaper cuttings relating to the Sheffield Papers of The Hunter's Society.

Many thanks are extended to the staff of Sheffield's Local Studies Library for allowing me the use of their excellent research facilities and for their personal assistance.

I should also like to thank Sheffield City Libraries for extending to me their permission to reproduce photographs from their extensive collection and for supplying the facilities which made this possible.

Photographs

The Royal Standard, St Mary's Road, 1833–still open

The Mill Tavern, Earsham Street, formerly The Albion, The Golden Perch, still open

The Corner Pin, Carlisle Street East, popular workman's pub, open 1864–still open

The Alexandra Hotel, Carlisle Street East, open1865–closed 1974, finally demolished 1995

Horse Parade, Rutland Road, circa 1903

Farmyard Vaults, Scotland Street, closed 1898

Neepsend Tavern, Neepsend Lane, 1839–1974; now a sauna suite

Don Brewery, demolished 1995; the sign has been preserved and set into a wall beside the new road

SHEFFIELD

ROYAL VICTORIA HOTEL

Proprietress - MRS. GEORGE MEYER.

Honoured by the presence of their Royal Highnesses the PRINCE AND PRINCESS OF WALES on the occasion of their visit to this town.

FIRST-CLASS HOUSE,

Replete with every modern comfort, adjoining the Victoria Station, with which it is connected by a covered way.

HOTEL

SHEFFIELD.

First-Class Commercial & Family Hotel.

PRIVATE ROOMS. BATHS. SMOKE AND BILLIARD SALOON.

CABS, HANSOMS, WEDDING & PARTY CARRIAGES.

Four-Horse Coaches leave the Door daily during the Summer for Chatsworth, Baslow, and other places of interest.

The Black Swan, Pond Street, open 1825

Lady's Bridge and the Elephant & Castle

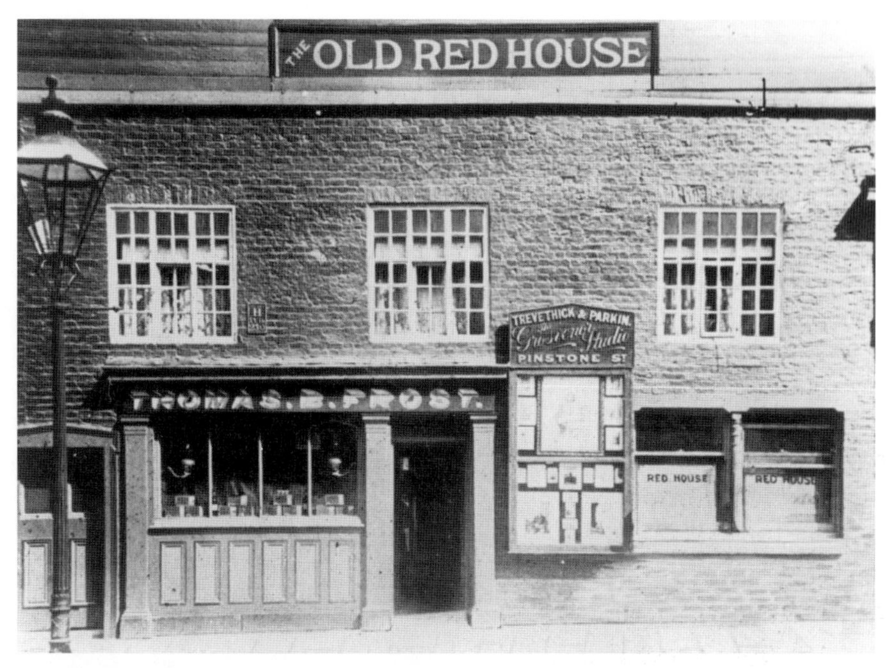

The Old Red House, Fargate, 1780–1917

The Bee Hive, West Street, 1825–still open, although completely rebuilt

The Robin Hood, Attercliffe Road

The Red Lion, Penistone Road, open 1835

The Red Lion, London Road, still open

The Broadfield Hotel, Abbeydale Road, still open

GEORGE INN AND POST OFFICE HOTEL,
(OPPOSITE THE POST OFFICE,)
MARKET PLACE, SHEFFIELD.

COMMERCIAL AND FAMILY HOTEL,
THOMAS HARTSHORN, Proprietor.

HOT & COLD BATHS.
HANSOM'S CABS and OMNIBUSES to and from the Manchester, Great Northern, and Midland Railway Stations.
BILLIARDS, &c.

DEVONSHIRE ARMS,
(NEAR THE CRIMEAN MONUMENT,)
SOUTH - STREET, SHEFFIELD MOOR,
(LATE JOHN CADMAN.)

WILLIAM STACEY,
In returning thanks to his numerous friends for the patronage he has received since taking to the business of the above Hotel, begs to inform them that he has always in stock a choice selection of WINES and SPIRITS purchased direct from the best markets.

HOME BREWED ALE, BOTTLED PORTER, & BITTER BEERS.
GOOD STABLING.

York Family & Commercial Hotel,

BROOMHILL,  **SHEFFIELD,**

JOSEPH HIELD, PROPRIETOR.

J.H. takes the present opportunity of returning his sincere thanks to the numerous Friends who have so kindly and liberally honoured him with their support during his occupation of the above Hotel.

The York Hotel is situated in a healthy locality, about twenty minutes' ride from the Railway Stations, and will be found to possess all the comforts of a private home. It has an excellent Commercial Room, Smoking Room, cheerful Sitting Rooms, and Comfortable Bed Rooms. The strictest attention is paid to cleanliness.

The Proprietor hopes to secure a continuance of the patronage and recommendation of his Friends, and begs to say that every article he supplies is of the best description, and on the most reasonable terms.

OMNIBUSES ARE CONSTANTLY RUNNING TO AND FROM THE TOWN.
A CAB STAND ADJOINING.

THE

WHARNCLIFFE,

KING-ST., SHEFFIELD.

The Proprietors respectfully announce completion of alterations, with a view to the further requirements and comfort of the Public.

THE ARRANGEMENTS IN

THE BUFFET

Now offer selections of PORTS and SHERRIES of the Finest Quality, drawn from the Wood, and supplied in Dock Glasses, at very moderate prices.

THE NEW

SMOKING, READING AND WRITING ROOM,

On the Ground Floor, is abundantly provided with DAILY and WEEKLY JOURNALS, and has a CIGAR CABINET, containing over Twenty Brands of the Finest Havana Tobacco. Coffee instantly served at any hour. Entrance through the Hall.

THE RESTAURANT,

Replete with every convenience, affords great facilities to Families, Residents, Commercial Gentlemen, and other Visitors to the Town.

THE HOTEL ACCOMMODATION

Is of a first-class character, and Guests are assured that nothing is spared to promote their comfort and satisfaction.

WM. H. GARSIDE, Manager.

The Upperthorpe Hotel, Upperthorpe Road

The Carlton, Attercliffe Road, open 1845–still open

The Ball, Upwell Street, open 1830–still open

The Yellow Lion Hotel, Haymarket, 1787–1926

The Globe Works, Penistone Road, Rattener's Rest pub on ground floor

The Anglers Rest, New George Street which became Boston Street, open 1841

The Abbey, Abbey Lane photographed in 1922 during extension work

Pomona Hotel, Ecclesall Road, rebuilt 1980s, still open

NEWARK & SHEFFIELD
BREWERIES COMPANY LIMITED,
BREWERS
OF
INVALID STOUT,
Mild Ales
AND
Bitter Beers.
ALSO
IMPORTERS & BONDERS
OF
FOREIGN WINES & SPIRITS,
Registered Offices:—
Scotland Street Brewery,
SHEFFIELD.

ESTABLISHED 1865.

TELEPHONE No. 2265.

HOOSON BROTHERS,
Pale Ale, Mild and Bitter Beer Brewers,
PARK BREWERY,
SHEFFIELD.

Sole Brewers of the
"Portland Beer."

Awarded Diploma at the Brewers' Exhibition, London, 1907, for the Excellence of their Beers.

JAMES HAYNES,
PALE MILD
ALE AND PORTER
Brewer and Bottler,
Crown Brewery,
SHEFFIELD.

W. H. BIRKS & Co.
ARE PREPARED TO SUPPLY THE
FINEST ALES
To Private Families,
At 1s., 1s. 1d., 1s. 2d., 1s. 4d., and 1s. 6d. per Gall.

LADY'S BRIDGE BREWERY,
BRIDGE STREET.

Telephone No. 764.

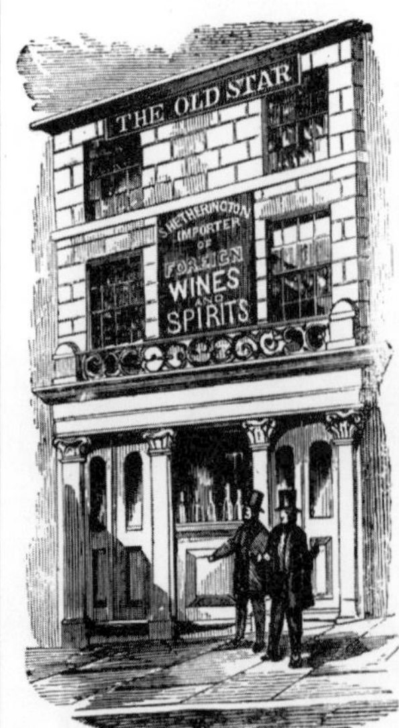

THE
OLD STAR
WHOLESALE & RETAIL
WINE AND SPIRIT
VAULTS
AND
BOTTLED
Ale and Porter
STORES,
(Next Fisher Holmes and Co's Warehouse,)
TOP OF OLD HAYMARKET
SHEFFIELD,
S. HETHERINGTON
(Late Partner at Old No. 12,)
PROPRIETOR.

Public House Lists and Maps

The following pages contain as near as possible a full list of all the public houses and alehouses that have ever existed in the area covered by this book.

To make things easier for the reader, the area has been split up into small sections, each of which has it's own list of public houses and a map. If it has been possible to find out the opening and closing dates of an individual pub, then this has been included in the information supplied, along with any name change over the years. Also given is a number which corresponds with the position number on the appropriate map.

The maps have been based on turn of the century publications with occasional alterations where this has appeared to be necessary.

Over the years, many street numbers have been altered and also on occasion, the actual position of a pub has altered. The location given on the map will be either the actual position of the pub or the latest one that has been found.

Major street alterations:

Coal Pit(t) Lane became Cambridge Street
South Street, Moor became The Moor
Pudding Lane became King Street
Church Lane became Church Street
Market Street became Fitzalan Square
New George Street became Boston Street
Church Street, Attercliffe became Worksop Road

Button Lane as well as other streets have
disappeared and many names have been altered.

Some of the public houses feature on more than one list/map, but the total number of individual public houses which appear in the book is in excess of 1400.

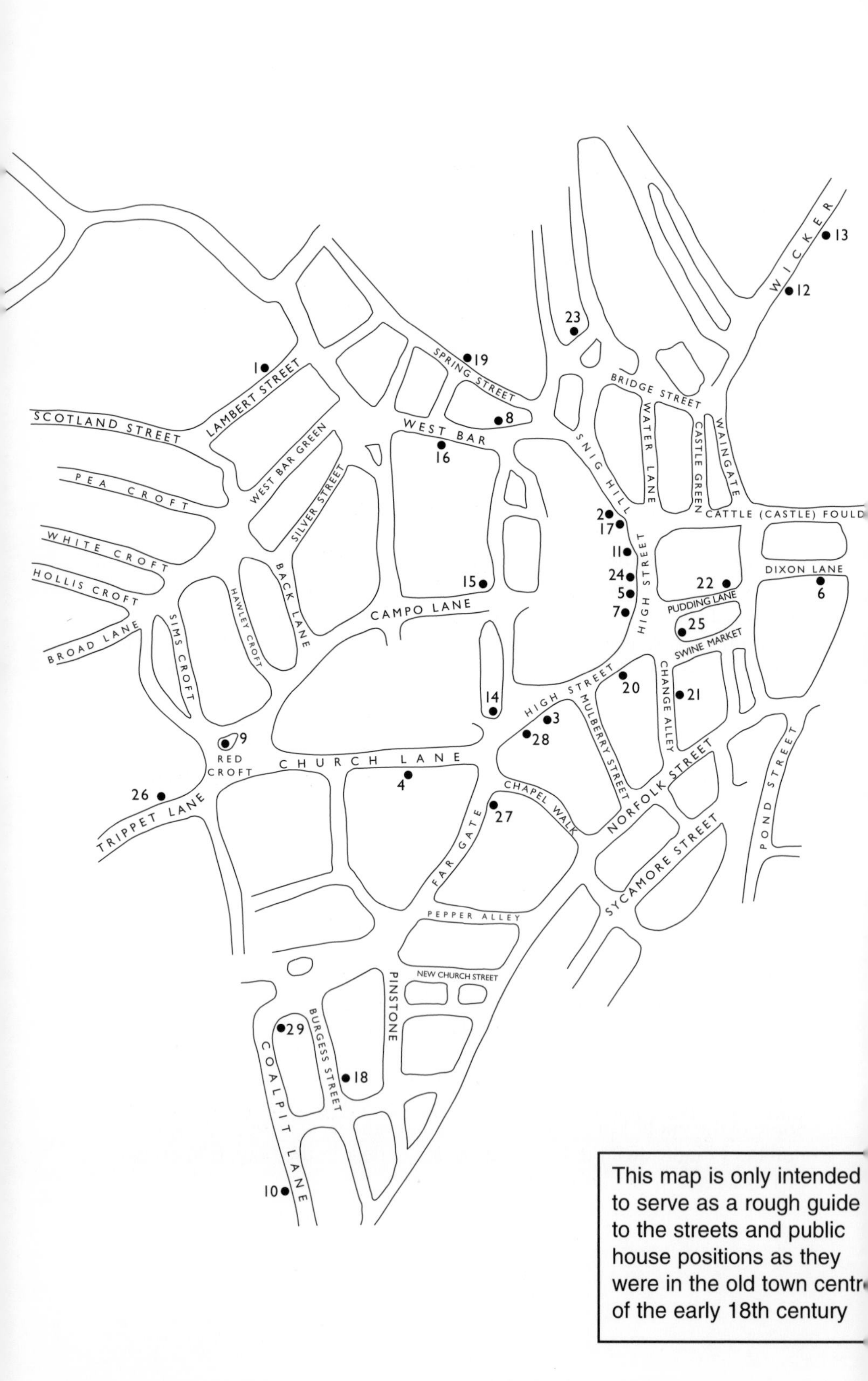

This map is only intended to serve as a rough guide to the streets and public house positions as they were in the old town centre of the early 18th century

Map 1

1 African Prince, Lambert St (1774–1833)
2 Angel, Angel St (1657—bombed 1940)
3 Bay Childers, High St (now Church St) (open 1825)
4 Bird in Hand, Church Lane (open 1761)
5 Blackamoor Head (became Grey Horse 1787), High St (1675–1917)
6 Blue Ball, Dixon Lane (or Castle Foulds) (open 1774)
7 Blue Bell (once Old Blue Bell, now Cavell's), High St (open 1825)
8 Blue Boar, 26 West Bar (open 1774)
9 Brown Cow, Red Croft (open 1774)
10 Chequers (also known as The Old Cow), Coal Pit Lane (now Cambridge St) (open 1825)
11 Cock, High St (1686–1752)
12 Cock, Wicker (open 1825)
13 Crown and Cushion (became The Bull & Oak), Wicker (1774—still open)
14 Crown Inn, High St (now Church St) (1710–1772)
15 Crown Inn, Campo Lane (1796–1903)
16 Fountain, West Bar (open 1774)
17 George Inn, High St (1781–1899)
18 Globe, Burgess St (open 1774)
19 Golden Ball, Spring St (open 1774)
20 Horse and Cat (formerly Bay Childers, Bay Horse, Queen Victoria, finally Westminster), High St (1774—bombed 1940)
21 King's Head (Old King's Head), Change Alley (1572—bombed 1940)
22 Norfolk Arms, Pudding Lane (open 1742)
23 Pear Tree (or Palm Tree), Millsands (open 1774)
24 Rose and Crown, High St (1675–1812)
25 Rose and Crown, Market Place (open 1774)
26 Seven Stars, Trippet Lane (later Pinfold St) (open 1787)
27 Spread Eagle, Fargate (1794–1896)
28 White Bear, High St (now Church St) (1780–1900)
29 Yellow Lion (became Cambridge Arms), Coal Pit Lane (now Cambridge St) (open 1736)

Note: The following pub was known to be in this area though the actual location is unknown:

Reindeer, Castle Foulds

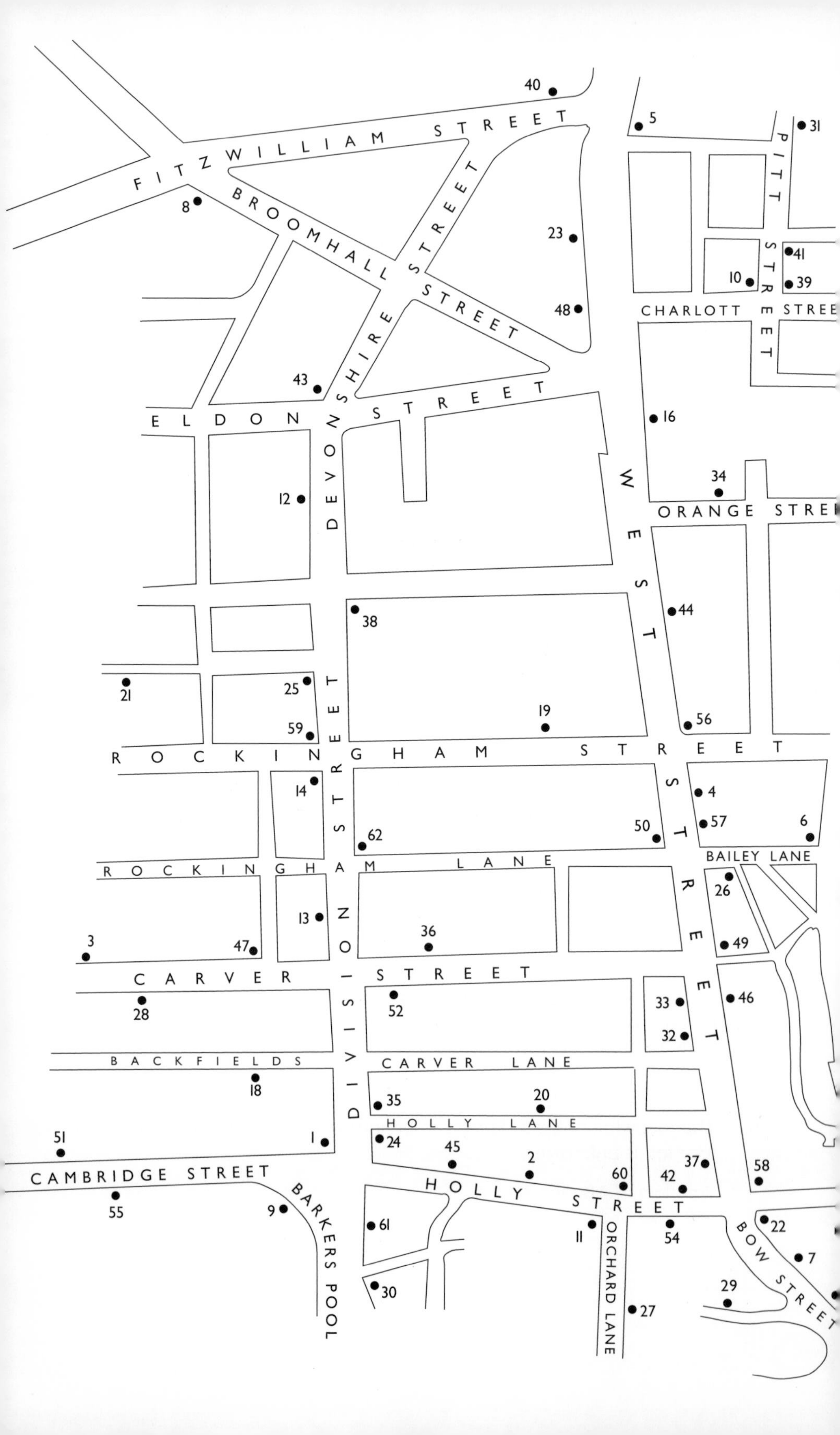
FITZWILLIAM STREET
BROOMHALL STREET
DEVONSHIRE STREET
ELDON
STREET
CHARLOTT
STREE
PITT STREET
WEST STREET
ORANGE STRE
ROCKINGHAM STREET
ROCKINGHAM LANE
BAILEY LANE
CARVER STREET
DIVISION STREET
BACKFIELDS
CARVER LANE
HOLLY LANE
HOLLY STREET
CAMBRIDGE STREET
BARKERS POOL
ORCHARD LANE
BOW STREET
40
5
31
8
23
41
10
39
48
43
16
12
34
44
38
21
25
59
19
56
14
4
57
6
50
62
26
13
36
49
3
47
28
33
52
46
32
18
35
20
51
1
24
45
2
37
60
42
58
55
9
61
11
54
22
7
29
30
27

Map 2

1 Albert (formerly Union), 2 Coal Pit Lane (1797–1988)
2 Amateur's Rest,17 Holly St
3 Ball (Charity Boy), 86 Carver St (1825–1903)
4 Barton Vaults,118 West St
5 Beehive, now The Foundry & Firkin, 200 West St (1825—still open)
6 Black Boy, 29 Bailey Lane (1850–1910)
7 Blue Boar, 26 Bow St
8 Broomhall House, 49 Broomhall St
9 Cambridge Arms (formerly The Yellow Lion), 1 Coal Pit Lane (open 1736)
10 Charlotte Tavern, 17 Charlotte St
11 Crown, 24 Holly St (1796–1810)
12 David and Goliath, 111 Devonshire St (open 1841)
13 Dolphin Hotel, 37 Division St (1845–1895)
14 Forester's Inn, 57 Division St (still open)
15 Greyhound, 66 Holly St
16 Hallamshire,182 West St (still open)
17 Hen and Chickens, 18 Bow St
18 Huntsman's Rest, 9 Backfields
19 John Bull,126 Rockingham St
20 Jolly Bacchus, Holly Lane
21 King's Head, 29 Canning St (open 1825)
22 King William (possibly also King William IV), 1 Holly St (1833–1898)
23 Mail Coach (formerly The Commercial, now Scruffy Murphy's), 149 West St (1800—still open)
24 Manchester, 4 Division St
25 Mansfield Hotel, 73 Division St
26 Milton Arms, 4 Bailey Lane (open 1833)
27 Mountain Deer, 14 Orchard Lane
28 Napoleon, 85 Carver St (1833–1921)
29 Norfolk Arms, 18 Sands Paviers (open 1833)
30 Norfolk Hotel, 98 Barkers Pool (closed 1898)
31 Odd Fellow's Arms, 38 Pitt St
32 Odd Fellow's Rest, 53 West St (1835–1893)
33 Old Raven, 61 West St (closed 1903)
34 Orange Tree Tavern, 7 Orange St
35 Original John Bull, 6 Division St
36 Pheasant, 40 Carver St (1833–1898)
37 Pheasant, 37 West St (closed 1893)

38 Prince of Wales (now The Frog & Parrot), 94 Division St (still open)
39 Prince of Wales, 19 Charlotte St
40 Raven (then The Hornblower, now O'Hagan's), 12 Fitzwilliam St (still open)
41 Red Deer Inn, 18 Pitt St (1825—still open)
42 Red Lion (now The Old Red Lion), 35 Holly St (1825—still open)
43 Reindeer, 139 Devonshire St (open 1841)
44 Rising Sun, 146 West St (closed 1903)
45 Rose and Crown, 9 Holly St (open 1825)
46 Royal, 86 West St (1833–1893)
47 Royal George, 60 Carver St (1833–1970)
48 Royal Mail, 131 West St (closed 1893)
49 Saddle, 96 West St (1825—closed 1992, re-opened adjoining as Saddle Wine Bar, 1993)
50 Salutation, 85 West St (closed 1893)
51 Sportsman, 20 Coal Pit Lane (still open)
52 Stag, 45 Carver St (1825–1898)
53 Star,15 Orange St
54 Three Merry Smiths, 55 Holly St
55 Wellington Tavern, 21 Coal Pit Lane (open 1833)
56 West Street Hotel, 128 West St (still open)
57 West Street Vaults, 112 West St (closed 1893)
58 Wharncliffe Arms (formerly Manchester; William McReady), 42 West St (open 1787)
59 White Lion, 61 Division St
60 White Lion, 25 Holly St (open 1796)
61 White Lion, 116 Barker's Pool (1796–c1920)
62 Yorkshire Stingo, 50 Division St (open 1833)

Note: Coal Pit(t) Lane became Cambridge Street

The Mail Coach Inn now known as Scruffy Murphy's

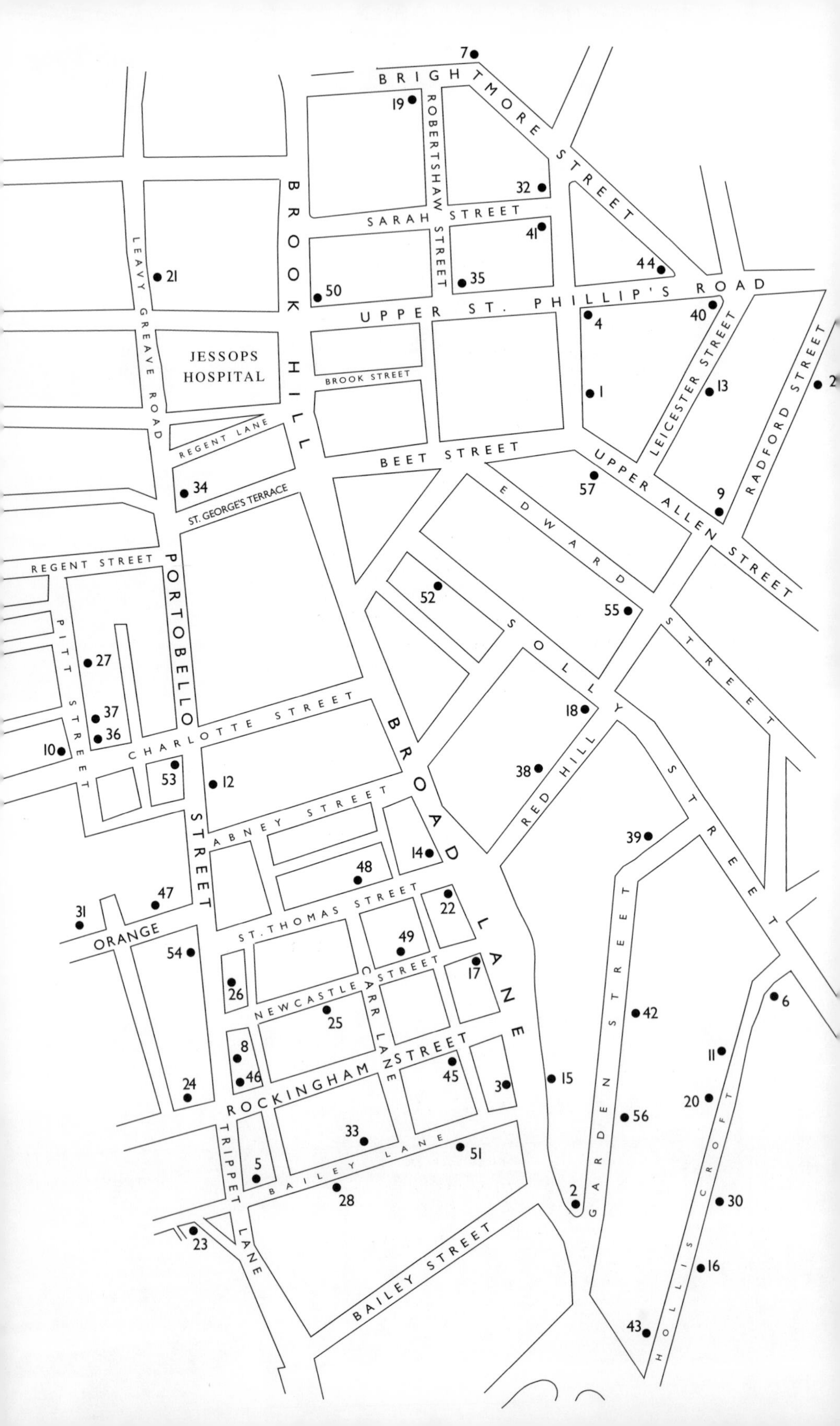
BRIGHTMORE STREET
ROBERTSHAW STREET
SARAH STREET
BROOK HILL
LEAVY GREAVE ROAD
JESSOPS HOSPITAL
UPPER ST. PHILLIP'S ROAD
BROOK STREET
REGENT LANE
BEET STREET
LEICESTER STREET
RADFORD STREET
UPPER ALLEN STREET
ST. GEORGE'S TERRACE
REGENT STREET
PORTOBELLO
EDWARD
SOLLY
PITT STREET
CHARLOTTE STREET
BROAD
RED HILL
STREET
ABNEY STREET
ORANGE
ST. THOMAS STREET
LANE
NEWCASTLE STREET
CARR LANE
GARDEN STREET
ROCKINGHAM STREET
TRIPPET LANE
BAILEY LANE
BAILEY STREET
HOLLIS CROFT

Map 3

1 Albion, 4 Mitchell St (open 1835)
2 Ball Inn, 44 Broad Lane (1825–1906)
3 Barrel Inn (became Fagan's), 69 Broad Lane (1825—still open)
4 Bay Horse, 46 Upper St. Phillips Rd (open 1845)
5 Black Boy, 29 Bailey Lane (1850–1910)
6 Black Bull, 94 Hollis Croft (1825–1900)
7 Brightmore Tavern, 23 Brightmore St
8 Britannia (or Old Britannia), 122 Portobello St
9 Brown Cow, 1 Radford St
10 Charlotte Tavern, 17 Charlotte St
11 Cock, 59 Hollis Croft (1780–1901)
12 Dove and Rainbow, 172 Portobello St
13 Falcon Inn, 18 Leicester St
14 Florist, 119 Broad Lane (open 1839)
15 Fox and Duck, 50 Broad Lane (1825–1926)
16 Gate, 10 Hollis Croft (1833–1955)
17 George and Dragon, 93 Broad Lane (1825–1958)
18 Hope and Anchor, 223 Solly St
19 Imperial, 45 Robertshaw St
20 King's Arms, 51 Hollis Croft (1833–1898)
21 Leavey Greave Hotel, 26 Leavey Greave Rd
22 Live and Let Live (became The Britannia), 101 Broad Lane (open 1797)
23 Milton Arms, 4 Bailey Lane (open 1833)
24 New Britannia, 72 Rockingham St
25 Newcastle Arms, 35 Newcastle St (closed 1905)
26 Nimrod, 164 Portobello St
27 Odd Fellow's Arms, 38 Pitt St
28 Old House at Home, 42 Bailey Lane (1830–1922)
29 Old House at Home (became a social club), 34 Radford St (open 1796)
30 Orange Branch, 28 Hollis Croft (open 1825)
31 Orange Tree Tavern, 7 Orange St
32 Ostrich Inn, 39 Mitchell St
33 Pheasant, 51 Bailey Lane (1830–1902)
34 Portobello, 248 Portobello St
35 Prince Leopold, 37 Upper St Phillips Rd
36 Prince of Wales, 19 Charlotte St
37 Red Deer, 18 Pitt St (1825—still open)
38 Red Hill Tavern, 33 Red Hill (open1796)
39 Red Place Tavern, 91 Garden St (1833–1910)
40 Rocket Inn, 106 Upper St Phillips Rd (1830–1920)
41 Rose and Crown, 52 Sarah St

42 Royal Exchange, 64 Garden St
43 Royal Oak, 11 Hollis Croft (1825—still open)
44 Salutation, 85 Upper St Phillips Rd (closed 1965)
45 Scarborough Arms, 13 Rockingham St
46 Sovereign Inn, 70 Rockingham St
47 Star, 15 Orange St
48 Tuscan Tavern, 17 St Thomas St
49 Union Tavern, 14 Newcastle St (1833–1905)
50 Victoria, 1 Upper St Phillips Rd
51 Wheatsheaf, 74 Bailey Lane (1833–1904)
52 White Horse, 275 Solly St (open 1833)
53 White Swan, 36 Charlotte St (closed 1905)
54 Willow Tree, 147 Portobello St
55 Woodman, 137 Edward St (open 1824)
56 Woodman's Hut, 46 Garden St (1825–1900)
57 Woolsack, 277 Upper Allen St

Note: The following pub was known to be in this area though the actual location is unknown:

Harrow, Broad Lane (open 1774)

Still standing after at least 170 years

DEVONSHIRE STREET
DEVONSHIRE LANE
CHESTER STREET
WELLINGTON STREET
TRAFALGAR STREET
ROCKINGHAM STREET
FITZWILLIAM STREET
ELDON STREET
BOWDON STREET
BROOMHALL STREET
THOMAS STREET
HEADFORD STREET
BATH STREET
EGERTON STREET
CLARENCE STREET
MILTON STREET
HODGSON STREET
MOORE STREET
YOUNG STREET
GREEN STREET
BISHOP STREET
BRIDGEFIELD ROAD
CLARENCE LANE
BUTTON LANE
SOUTH STREET
ELLIN STREET
ELDON STREET BREWERY

Map 4

1 Albert Inn, 113 Broomhall St (1835–1992)
2 Alexandra, 111 Eldon St (1833–1956)
3 Alma Hotel, Trafalgar St
4 Anvil Maker's Arms, 119 Young St (closed 1917)
5 Baker's Arms, 127 Clarence St (open 1825)
6 Ball Inn, 182 Young St (1835–1905)
7 Barley Mow, 99 Broomhall St (open 1833)
8 Bath Hotel, 139 Broomhall St (closed 1968)
9 Bay Horse, 143 Milton St (1825–1910)
10 Brewery House, 79 Button Lane (1774–1910)
11 British Lion, 38 Thomas St (closed 1910)
12 Broomhall House, 49 Broomhall St
13 Broomhall Tavern, 105 Broomhall St (1833–1964)
14 Brunswick, 54 Thomas St (closed 1964)
15 Butcher's Arms, 61 Bath St
16 Canterbury Hotel, 29 Egerton St (1833–1910)
17 Chandos, 217 Rockingham St (open 1825)
18 Chester Castle, 62 Eldon St
19 Clarence Hotel, 109 Clarence St (1833–1925)
20 Crown and Anchor, 218 Fitzwilliam St
21 Cup, 52 Button Lane (open 1825)
22 Derby, 53 Egerton St (closed 1910)
23 Derby Hotel, 25 Lawson St
24 Devonshire Arms, 51 Eldon St (closed 1917)
25 Dog and Gun, 102 Button Lane (1825–1917)
26 Dog and Gun, 122 Trafalgar St (1830–1910)
27 Dog and Gun, 18 Headford St (1833–1962)
28 Eagle (or Black Eagle), 80 Wellington St
29 Economical Hotel, 130 Eldon St
30 Egerton Hotel, 138 Fitzwilliam St
31 Exchange, 53 Eldon St
32 Exchange, 89 Thomas St (closed 1910)
33 Fitzwilliam Hotel, 72 Fitzwilliam St
34 Forester's Arms, 91 Headford St (closed 1917)
35 Grey Horse, 55 Chester St
36 Hammer and Anvil, 152 South St, Moor (1825–1917)
37 Hare and Hounds, 108 Clarence St (closed 1910)
38 Hodgson Arms, 49 Hodgson St (1860–1970)
39 Industry, 67 Fitzwilliam St
40 Industry Inn, 147 Young St (closed 1917)

41 King and Miller, 60 Chester St
42 Lincoln City Arms, 114 Clarence St (1845–1963)
43 Milton Arms, 66 Thomas St (1825–1964)
44 Noah's Ark, 140 Tudor St (closed 1910)
45 Norfolk Arms, 85 Clarence St (1841–1968)
46 Odd Fellow's Rest, 94 Button Lane (1830–1908)
47 Oxford House, 131 Moore St
48 Paragon Hotel, 131 Thomas St
49 Peacock, 200 Fitzwilliam St
50 Pilot, 2 Green St
51 Princess Hotel, 199 Fitzwilliam St
52 Princess Royal, 72 Trafalgar St
53 Prince of Wales, 49 Egerton St (1833–1910)
54 Punch Bowl, 140 South St, Moor (1825–1938)
55 Ram Inn, 272 Rockingham St
56 Reindeer, 139 Devonshire St (open 1841)
57 Royal Oak, 91 Milton St
58 Scarborough Arms, 104 Milton St (1830–1963)
59 Sportsman, 125 Thomas St (1825–1963)
60 Sportsman's Cottage, 74 Button Lane (1825–1908)
61 Victoria Hotel, 22 Thomas St
62 Vine, 7 Hodgson St
63 Washington, 79 Fitzwilliam St (still open)
64 Wellington Arms, 90 Wellington St
65 Wentworth Arms, 262 Rockingham St (open 1833)
66 Wentworth House, 78 Button Lane (1825–1917)
67 Woodman, 166 South St, Moor (open 1833)
68 Young Street Tavern, 162 Young St

THE WASHINGTON

SCOTLAND STREET
PEA CROFT
WHITE CROFT
HOLLIS CROFT
WESTBAR GREEN
QUEEN STREET
SILVER STREET
WORKHOUSE CROFT
PARADISE STREET
PARADISE SQUARE
SILVER STREET HEAD
LEE CROFT
HAWLEY CROFT
SCHOOL CROFT
SIMS CROFT
RADFORD ROW
BROAD LANE
TOWNHEAD STREET
CAMPO LANE
ST. JAMES' STREET
CHURCH STREET
BAILEY STREET
BAILEY LANE
PINFOLD STREET
TRIPPET LANE
LEOPOLD STREET

Map 5

1 Ancient Pineapple, 3 Radford Row (1797–1896)
2 Ball Inn, 44 Broad Lane (1825–1906)
3 Ball, 20 Hawley Croft (1780–1901)
4 Ball (formerly The Golden Ball), 26 Campo Lane (open 1824)
5 Ball, 28 Townhead St (1825–1900)
6 Balloon Tavern, 83 Trippet Lane
7 Bay Horse, 53 West Bar Green (1825–1926)
8 Black Boy, 29 Bailey Lane (1850–1910)
9 Blue Bell, 72 Silver Street Head (closed 1903)
10 Boot and Shoe, 79 Campo Lane (1845–1905)
11 Brown Cow, 1 Broad Lane (open 1833)
12 Brown Cow (or Old Brown Cow), 27 Trippet Lane (open 1889)
13 Burn's Head Tavern (became The Canterbury Inn), 10 Townhead St (1825–1900)
14 Butcher's Arms, 27 Townhead St (1825–1900)
15 Canterbury Hall Hotel, 19 Pinfold St (1833–1897)
16 Clarence Hotel, 109 Paradise St (1833–1925)
17 Clarence Hotel, 1 Paradise Sq
18 Clarender Hotel, 1 Paradise St
19 Clown and Monkey, Paradise Sq
20 Cock Inn, 11 Paradise Sq (1825–1900)
21 Cock and Bottle (also known as The Eagle Tavern), 46 Hawley Croft (1825–1896)
22 Cross Daggers, 52 West Bar Green (1797—1926)
23 Crown, 52 Silver Street Head (closed 1903)
24 Crown, 54 Campo Lane (1796–1903)
25 Crown and Cushion, 23 Broad Lane (open 1841)
26 Crystal Palace, 52 Townhead St (1797–1898)
27 Dog and Partridge, 56 Trippet Lane (open 1797—still open)
28 Druid Tavern, 37 Bailey St (1833–1900)
29 Duke of Clarence, 15 Radford Row (1797–1900)
30 Eagle Tavern, 75 Queen St (1825–1898)
31 Flying Dutchman, 33 Silver Street Head (closed 1896)
32 Fountain, 4 Pinfold St (open 1833)
33 Fox and Duck (or Old Fox & Duck), 50 Broad Lane (1825–1926)
34 Gardener's Rest, 55 Townhead St (closed 1900)
35 Gate, 10 Hollis Croft (1833–1955)
36 Golden Ball, 6 Campo Lane (rebuilt after 1900,resited 1968—still open)
37 Grapes, 80 Trippet Lane (1825—still open)
38 Green Seedlings, 57 Bailey St (1825–1902)
39 Greyhound Tavern, 3 Pinfold St (open 1796)

40 Horse and Jockey, 10 Broad Lane (closed 1900)
41 Lamb, 6 Radford Row (closed 1896)
42 Lincolnshire Arms, 26 Broad Lane (closed 1902)
43 Little Tankard, 11 West Bar Green (1825–1893)
44 Live and Let Live, 36 Hawley Croft (closed 1903)
45 London Apprentice, 1 West Bar Green (1797–1896)
46 Mason's Arms, 43 Campo Lane (1797–1905)
47 Moseley's Arms (formerly Rose Inn), 81 West Bar (1849—still open)
48 Nelson, 78 Trippet Lane (open 1841)
49 New Tankard, 41 Sims Croft (1825–1900)
50 Norfolk, Sims Croft (open 1797)
51 Number One, 49 Silver St (closed 1903)
52 Number Two, 63 Silver St (closed 1903)
53 Odd Fellow's Arms, 25 Silver St (1833–1893)
54 Old House at Home, 42 Bailey Lane (1830–1922)
55 Old Oak Tree, 13 Silver St (closed 1903)
56 Paradise Inn, 36 Campo Lane
57 Paradise Street Vaults, 20 Paradise St
58 Pheasant, 51 Bailey Lane (1830–1902)
59 Potter's Arms, 20 Workhouse Croft
60 Printer's Arms, 76 Queen St (1833–1917)
61 Punch Bowl, 50 Silver Street Head (1825–1903)
62 Q in the Corner (later known as The Shrewsbury Hotel), 17 Paradise Square (open 1825)
63 Queen's Head, Campo Lane (open 1796)
64 Queen Street Hotel, 57 Queen St (1774–1920)
65 Rawson's Arms, 85 Tenter St (1833–1896)
66 Red House, Lee Croft (closed 1893)
67 Red Lion, 89 Trippet Lane (1833–1930)
68 Reindeer, Hawley Lane (1833–1905)
69 Reuben's (or Rubens) Head, 63 Campo Lane (1825–1905)
70 Rose and Crown, 65 Queen St (1797–1898)
71 St. George's Tavern, 35 Broad Lane (1825–1921)
72 Seven Stars, 36 Pinfold St (open 1787)
73 Smithy Door Tavern, 26 Hawley Croft (1833–1893)
74 Social Tavern, 38 Bailey St (1833–1902)
75 Spread Eagle (or Eagle Tavern), 39 West Bar Green (1797–1903)
76 Star, 16 Silver St (open 1752)
77 Three Tuns, 39 Silver Street Head (1825—still open)
78 Vulcan, 51 Hawley Croft (open 1833)
79 Union, 61 Silver Street Head (1833–1903)
80 Union, 50 Hawley Croft (open 1830)

81 Virginia Vaults, 64/66 Queen St (closed 1917)
82 Warm Hearth Stone, 1 Town Head St (1790–1896)
83 We Three Loggerheads Inn, 30 Hawley Croft (1830–1889)
84 Wheatsheaf, 46 Sims Croft
85 Wheatsheaf, 74 Bailey Lane (1833–1904)
86 White Lion, 30 Bailey St
87 White Lion, 37 West Bar Green (1796–1903)
88 Windsor Castle, 50 School Croft (1797–1907)
89 Windsor Castle, 21 Silver St (1833–1896)
90 Yorkshire Clown, 24 Paradise Square (1830–1893)

Note: The following pubs were known to be in this area though the actual location is unknown:

Cup, Campo Lane (open 1872)
White Horse, Gregory Row, Gregory Row no longer exists

A popular live music pub

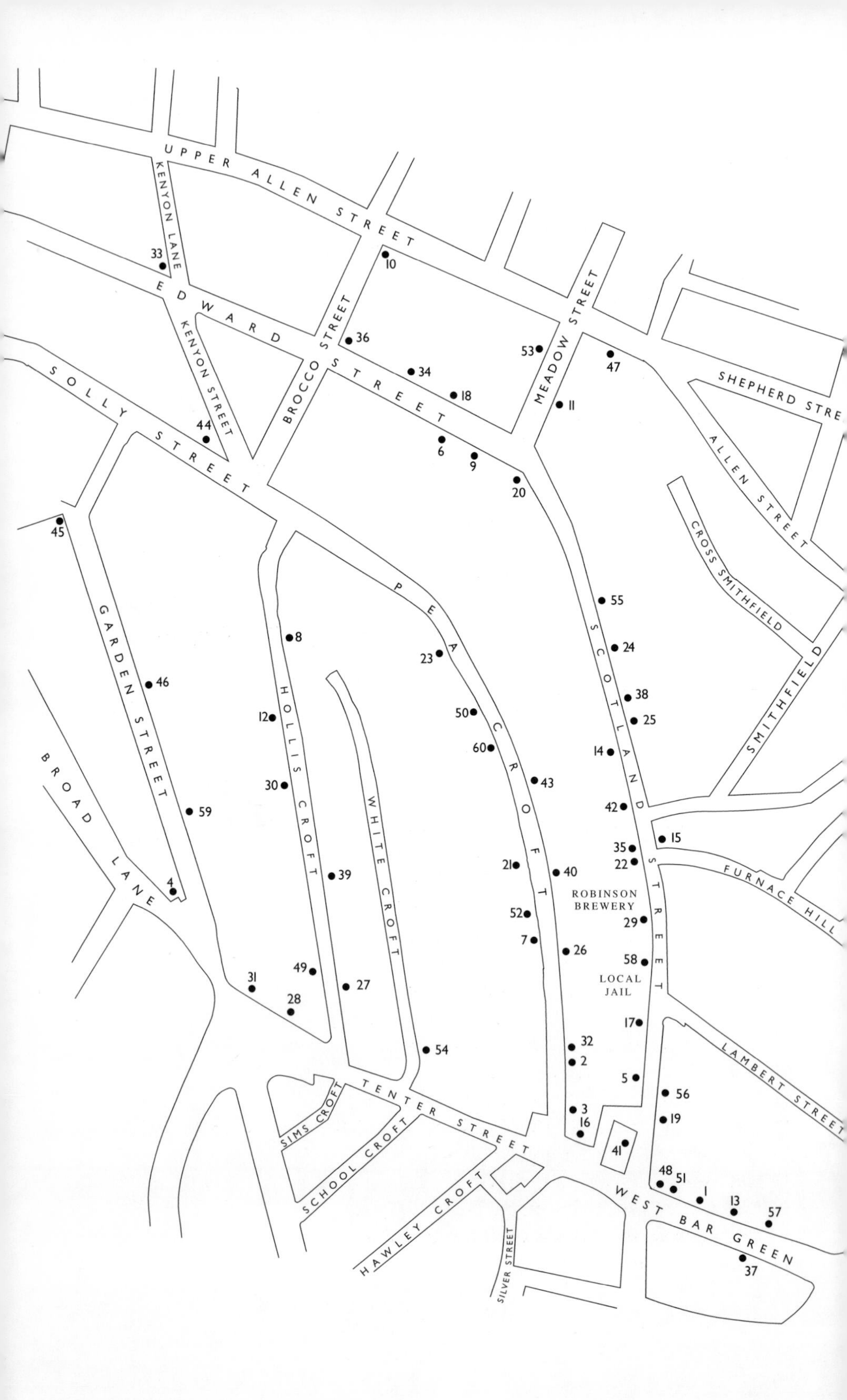
UPPER ALLEN STREET
KENYON LANE
EDWARD STREET
KENYON STREET
BROCCO STREET
MEADOW STREET
SHEPHERD STRE
ALLEN STREET
CROSS SMITHFIELD
SMITHFIELD
SOLLY STREET
GARDEN STREET
BROAD LANE
PEA CROFT
HOLLIS CROFT
WHITE CROFT
SCOTLAND STREET
FURNACE HILL
ROBINSON BREWERY
LOCAL JAIL
LAMBERT STREET
TENTER STREET
SIMS CROFT
SCHOOL CROFT
HAWLEY CROFT
SILVER STREET
WEST BAR GREEN

Map 6

1 American Stores, 36 West Bar Green (closed 1893)
2 Anchor, 20 Pea Croft (1833–1900)
3 Ball (also known as The Ring O' Bells), 8 Pea Croft (open 1797)
4 Ball Inn, 44 Broad Lane (1825–1906)
5 Ball, 17 Scotland St (Grindle Gate) (open 1797)
6 Barrel, 31 Edward St (1786–1906)
7 Barrel (or Old Barrel), 75 Pea Croft (1825–1900)
8 Black Bull, 74 Hollis Croft (1825–1900)
9 Black Horse, 17 Edward St (1796–1906)
10 Brocco Hotel, 167 Upper Allan St
11 Chequers (or Old Chequers Inn), 4 Meadow St (open 1825)
12 Cock, 59 Hollis Croft (1780–1901)
13 Corporation Arms, 24 West Bar Green
14 Crabtree, 121 Scotland St (1833–1902)
15 Crooked Billet, 62 Scotland St
16 Cross Daggers, 52 West Bar Green (1797–1926)
17 Crown (now R&B's Uptown Bar), 35 Scotland St (1797—still open)
18 Cutler's Arms, 66 Edward St
19 Evening Gun, 8 Scotland St (open 1797)
20 Fair Trades Hotel, 137 Scotland St
21 Falcon, 65 Pea Croft (open 1825)
22 Farmyard Vaults, 102 Scotland St (closed 1898)
23 Filesmith's Arms, 91 Pea Croft (1825–1898)
24 Filesmith's Arms, 128 Scotland St (closed 1902)
25 Fortunes of War, 112 Scotland St (open 1825)
26 French Horn, 34 Pea Croft (1797–1900)
27 Gate (or Old Gate), 10 Hollis Croft (1833–1955)
28 Horse and Jockey, 10 Broad Lane (closed 1900)
29 Hussar, 51 Scotland St (built 1816–1927)
30 King's Arms, 51 Hollis Croft (1833–1898)
31 Lincolnshire Arms, 26 Broad Lane (closed 1902)
32 Lion and Lamb, 22 Pea Croft (closed 1900)
33 Manor Castle Inn, 82 Edward St
34 Nottingham Castle, 72 Edward St (open 1833)
35 Old Hussar (known as The Travellers Inn), 67 Scotland St (1816–1927)
36 Old Lincoln Castle, 24 Brocco St
37 Old Tankard, 17 West Bar Green
38 Old Turk's Head, 108 Scotland St (1825–1902)
39 Orange Branch, 28 Hollis Croft (open 1825)
40 Paul Pry, 64 Pea Croft (open 1833)

41 Pie House, 5 Scotland St
42 Queen's Hotel (or The Queen), 85 Scotland St (1797—still open)
43 Ram, 82 Pea Croft (open 1830)
44 Red House, 168 Solly St (open 1796—still open)
45 Red Place Tavern, 91 Garden St (1833–1910)
46 Royal Exchange, 64 Garden St
47 Royal Oak, 89 Upper Allen St (1825–1933)
48 Royal Oak, 44 West Bar Green (open 1797)
49 Royal Oak, 11 Hollis Croft (1825—still open)
50 Stag, 83 Pea Croft
51 Standard, 38 West Bar Green
52 Star (or Old Star), 38 Pea Croft
53 Star Inn, 11 Meadow St (1797–1917)
54 Star Inn, 8 White Croft (open 1825)
55 Turk's Head (or New Turk's Head), 118 Scotland St (1825–1910)
56 Union, 14 Scotland St (open 1797)
57 White Lion, 12 West Bar Green (1796–1903)
58 Wine Vaults, 47 Scotland St
59 Woodman's Hut, 46 Garden St (1825–1900)
60 Yorkshire Cricketers, 79 Pea Croft (1833–1895)

Note: The following pub was known to be in this area though the actual location is unknown:

Ball, Solly St (closed 1910)

A typical workman's corner pub

WARD STREET
GIBRALTAR STREET
SHALESMOOR
MOOR FIELDS
TRINITY STREET
SNOW LANE
QUEENS ROW
BLUE BOY STREET
SMITHFIELD
CROSS SMITHFIELD
JOBSON PLACE
JOBSON ROAD
ROSCOE ROAD
HENRY STREET
MALINDA STREET
SUDBURY STREET
HOYLE STREET
MATTHEW STREET
DONCASTER STREET
ELLIS STREET
SHEPHERD STREET
ALLEN STREET
BURNT TREE LANE
MEADOW STREET
MORPETH STREET
BONVILLE STREET
CRAVEN STREET
UPPER ALLAN STREET
BROCCO STREET
WELL MEADOW STREET
DOVER STREET
NETHERTHORPE STREET

Map 7

1 Acorn, 204 Shalesmoor (1825–1960)
2 Alhambra, 78 Meadow St (closed 1922)
3 Angler's Rest, 15 Snow Lane (1833–1910)
4 Beehive, 7 Bowling Green St (closed 1925)
5 Blue Boy (or Original Blue Boy), 41 Shepherd St (1833–1948)
6 Blue Boy, 9 Blue Boy St (1833–1910)
7 Bull's Head, 29 Cross Smithfield St (1797–1925)
8 Burnt Tree Tavern, 83 Hoyle St
9 Butcher's Arms, 276 Shalesmoor
10 Chequers, 4 Meadow St (open 1825)
11 Corner Pin, 80 Allen St (1833–1900)
12 Corn Mill Inn (or Old Club Mill Inn), 20 Smithfield (1825–1930)
13 Crown Inn, 23 Blue Boy St (1835–1938)
14 Eagle Tavern, 26 Shepherd St (closed 1910)
15 Eagle and Child, 28 Smithfield (1833–1917)
16 Earl Grey, 226 Moorfields (open 1833)
17 Ellis Street Tavern (also known as The Gardener's Rest), 21 Ellis St
18 Filesmith's Arms, 40 Trinity St (open 1797)
19 Free Trades Inn, 66 Allen St
20 Greyhound, 185 Gibralter St (open 1796)
21 Havana Hotel, 57 Meadow St
22 Haylock Inn (or Havelock Inn), 104 Upper Allen St
23 Life Guardsman, 262 Moorfields
25 Meadow Street Hotel (now The Meadow), 110 Meadow St (still open)
26 Milton's Head, 29 Allen St (1825–1958)
27 Morpeth Arms, 108 Upper Allen St (1833–1960)
28 Nag's Head, 273 Shalesmoor (1833—still open)
29 New Brunswick, 86 Upper Allen St (1833–1950)
30 Norfolk Arms, 39 Shepherd St (1833–1930)
31 Old Half Moon Inn, 64 Allen St (1845–1910)
32 Palatine Hotel, 54 Malinda St
33 Peacock, 11 Hoyle St
34 Pheasant, 9 Hoyle St (open 1833)
35 Prince of Wales, 271 Shalesmoor (open 1882)
36 Prince of Wales, 67 Meadow St
37 Raglan Inn, Meadow St
38 Red Lion, 202 Shalesmoor (1833–1917)
39 Red Lion, 15 Smithfields (open 1825)
40 Reform Tavern, 41 Smithfields (1833–1925)
41 Reuben's Head, 16 Shepherd St (open 1830)

42 Rising Sun, 38 Matthew St
43 Rosco Arms, 65 Hoyle St (1833–1917)
44 Royal Oak, 89 Upper Allen St (1825–1933)
45 Royal Oak, 16 Allen St (1833–1930)
46 Sawmaker's Arms, 40 Burnt Tree Lane
47 Sheffield Arms, 42 Meadow St (1818–1948)
48 Ship, 284 Shalesmoor (1833—still open)
49 Star Inn, 11 Meadow St (1797–1917)
50 Talbot Inn, 40 Hoyle St
51 White Hart, 64 Doncaster St
52 White Horse, 65 Malinda St
53 Widow's Hut, 21 Meadow St

Note: The following pub was known to be in this area though the actual location is unknown:

Snow Lane Tap, Snow Lane

AVANA · HOTEL
WINDSOR
ALE · AND · STOUTS
FRED BUNTING
BEER
BILLIARDS
WARDS The Meadow
WARDS
The Meadow
HOT & COLD
FOOD
WARDS
The Meadow
SHEFFIELD

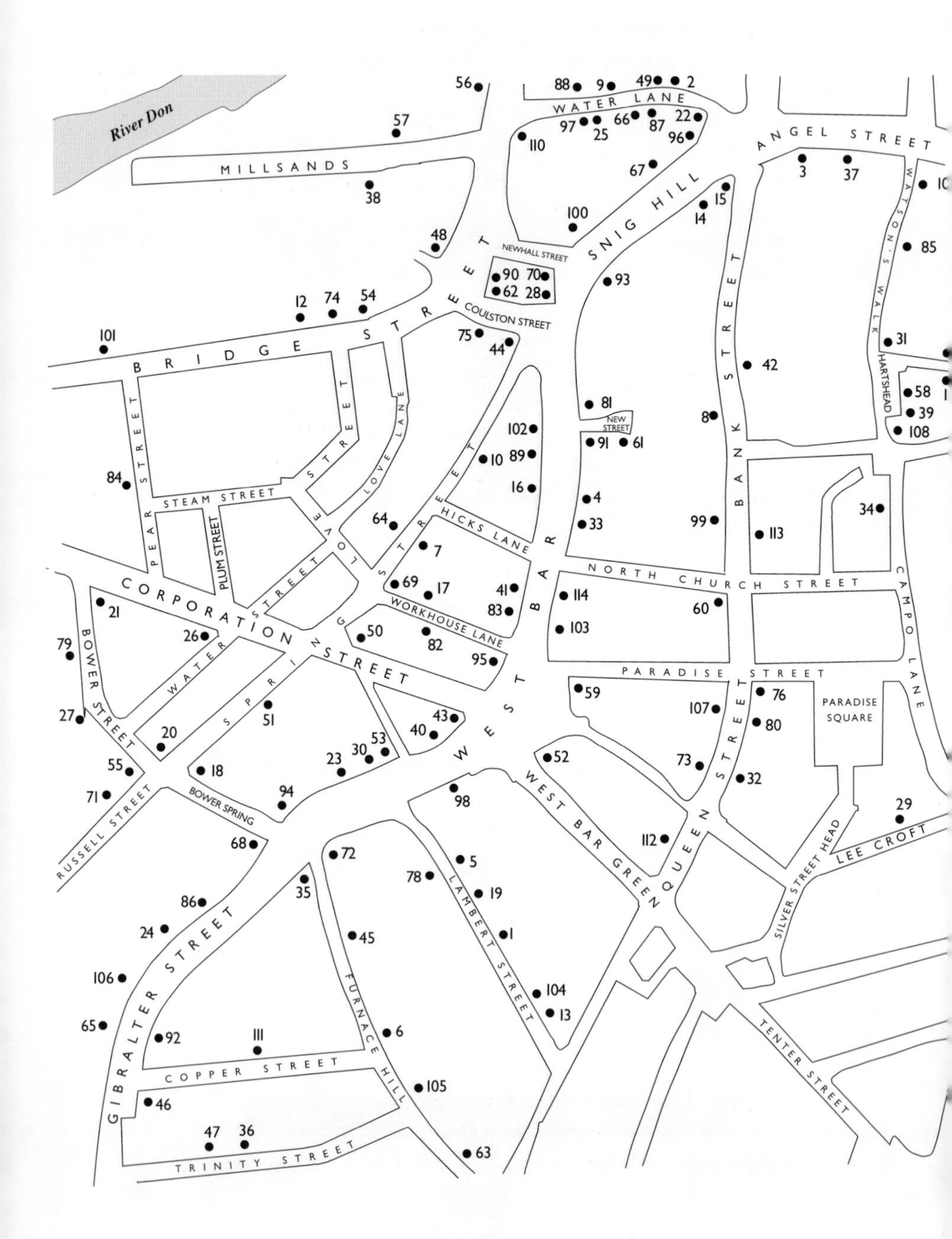
River Don
MILLSANDS
WATER LANE
ANGEL STREET
SNIG HILL
NEWHALL STREET
COULSTON STREET
BRIDGE STREET
WATSON'S WALK
HARTSHEAD
BANK STREET
NEW STREET
PEAR STREET
STEAM STREET
PLUM STREET
LOVE LANE
LOVE STREET
HICKS LANE
NORTH CHURCH STREET
CAMPO LANE
CORPORATION STREET
WORKHOUSE LANE
SPRING STREET
WATER STREET
BOWER STREET
WEST BAR
PARADISE STREET
PARADISE SQUARE
QUEEN STREET
WEST BAR GREEN
BOWER SPRING
RUSSELL STREET
SILVER STREET HEAD
LEE CROFT
LAMBERT STREET
FURNACE HILL
GIBRALTER STREET
COPPER STREET
TRINITY STREET
TENTER STREET

Map 8

1 Albion Tavern, 26 Lambert St (closed 1896)
2 All Nations, 18 Water Lane (1797–1895)
3 Angel, 15 Angel St (1657—bombed 1940)
4 Australian Arms, 49 West Bar (1825–1893)
5 Ball, 50 Lambert St (1796–1825)
6 Ball (also known as The Golden Ball), 46 Furnace Hill (1797–1920)
7 Ball, 27 Spring St (1797–1903)
8 Bank Street Hotel, 24 Bank St (1857–1900)
9 Barrel, 36 Water Lane (1796–1898)
10 Beehive, 23 Spring St (open 1833)
11 Beeswing, 46 Hartshead (1797–1905)
12 Bird in Hand, 82 Bridge St (open 1833)
13 Birmingham Arms,18 Lambert St (1833–1900)
14 Black Lion (or Old Black Lion), 3 Snig Hill (1833–1920)
15 Black Swan (Mucky Duck), 1 Snig Hill (1774—still open)
16 Blue Boar, 26 West Bar (1825–1958)
17 Blue Pig, 22 Workhouse Lane (open 1833)
18 Bower Spring Tap, 2 Bower Spring
19 Canine Inn, 34 Lambert St (1825–1896)
20 Canning Tavern,2 Bower St (open 1833)
21 Carlton, 17 Corporation St (open 1830)
22 Castle Inn, 1 Water Lane (open 1825)
23 Clock Maker's Arms, 122 West Bar (1833–1893)
24 Coach and Horses, 156 Gibralter St (1833–1908
25 Coach and Horses, 37 Water lane (1833–1898)
26 Corporation Hotel, 37 Corporation St
27 Cross Keys, 9 Bower St (open 1825)
28 Crown, 6 West Bar Green (open 1833)
29 Crown Inn, Lee Croft (open 1726)
30 Dog and Partridge, 112 West Bar (1833–1893)
31 Dove and Rainbow (now Tut & Shive), 25 Hartshead (1782, rebuilt adjoining—still open)
32 Eagle Tavern, 75 Queen St (1825–1898)
33 Eagle Vaults, 51 West Bar (closed 1905)
34 East Parade Hotel, 2 Campo Lane
35 Farrier's Arms, 145 Gibralter St (1833–1900)
36 Filesmith's Arms, 40 Trinity St (open 1797)
37 Fleur de Lys (or Three Fleur de Lys), 7 Angel St (1796—bombed 1940)
38 Forge Tavern, Millsands
39 Freemason's Arms, 8 Hartshead (1796–1893)
40 Gaiety Palace,100 West Bar

41 George, 56 West Bar (open 1833)
42 George and Dragon, 17 Bank St (open 1889)
43 George and Dragon (or Old George & Dragon), 96 West Bar (open 1825)
44 Grand Concert Hall, 2 Spring St
45 Grapes Tavern, 74 Furnace Hill (1832–1920)
46 Greyhound, 185 Gibralter St (open 1796)
47 Hare and Hounds (or Old Hare & Hounds), 51 Trinity St (open 1825)
48 Horse and Garter, 32 Bridge St (open 1833)
49 Horse and Garter, 24 Water Lane (open 1830)
50 Industry Inn, Corporation St
51 London Apprentice, 77 Spring St (open 1833)
52 London Apprentice, 1 West Bar Green (1797–1896)
53 London House, 112 West Bar (closed 1905)
54 Lord Raglan Inn, 50 Bridge St
55 Marquis Of Waterford, 2 Russell St
56 Mason's Arms, 18 Bridge St (1797–1898)
57 Millsands Tavern, 12 Millsands
58 Montgomery Tavern, 12 Hartshead (1852–1893)
59 Moseley's Arms (formerly The Rose Inn), 81 West Bar (1849—still open)
60 Murray's Arms, 13 Queen St (open 1797)
61 Nelson Inn, 13 New St, West Bar (open 1824)
62 Nottingham House Hotel, 13 Bridge St
63 Odd Fellow's Arms, 26 Furnace Hill (1833–1893)
64 Old Bird in Hand, 28 Spring St (open 1796)
65 Old Cherry Tree, 186 Gibralter St (open 1825)
66 Old House at Home, 33 Water Lane (1797–1898)
67 Old Market Inn, Snig Hill (1797–1898)
68 Old Star, Gibralter St
69 Pack Horse Inn, 2 West Bar (1825–1902)
71 Pheasant, 8 Russell St
72 Prince of Wales, 143 Gibralter St (1833–1902)
73 Printer's Arms (or Painter's Arms), 76 Queen St (1833–1917)
74 Punch Bowl, 35 Bridge St (open 1825)
75 Punch Bowl, 12 Coulson St (open 1797)
76 Queen Street Hotel (or Queen's Hotel), 57 Queen St (1774–1920)
77 Red Lion, 39 Hartshead (1755–1903)
78 Red Lion, 51 Lambert St (open 1839)
79 Rifle Tavern, 15 Bower St
80 Rose andCrown, 65 Queen St (1797–1898)
81 Rose and Crown, 31 West Bar (1797–1903)
82 Rose Inn, 41 Work House Lane (1787–1849)

83 Royal George, 60 West Bar (closed 1893)
84 Royal Oak, 6 Pear St
85 Shades, 20 Watson's Walk (1797—bombed 1940)
86 Shakespeare, 146 Gibralter St (1833—still open)
87 Ship, 31 Water Lane (1796–1898)
88 Soldier's Return, 42 Water Lane (1797–1896)
89 Sportsman, 20 West Bar (1797–1893)
90 Sportsman, 33 Bridge St (1825–1898)
91 Sportsman's Inn, 41 West Bar
92 Star Inn, 181 Gibralter St (open1833)
93 Strong Arm, 1 West Bar (open 1796)
94 Sun, 134 West Bar (open 1833)
95 Surrey Vaults (or Hotel), 86 West Bar
96 Swan Hotel, 2 Snig Hill (open 1797)
97 Talbot Arms, 39 Water Lane (1833–1895)
98 Tankard, 115 West Bar (closed 1896)
99 Three Cranes, 46 Queen St (1825—still open)
100 Three Travellers Inn, 82 Snig Hill (open 1825)
101 Three Tuns, 128 Bridge St
102 Tramway Hotel, 16 West Bar (closed 1893)
103 Turf Tavern, 77 West Bar
104 Union, 16 Lambert St
105 Union, 38 Furnace Hill (open 1825)
106 Victoria, 170 Gibralter St
107 Virginia Vaults, 64/66 Queen St (closed 1917)
108 Vine Tavern, 4 Hartshead (closed 1893)
109 Waterloo Tavern (also known as The Turf Tavern), 26 Watson's Walk (1774–1906)
110 Wheatsheaf, 11 Bridge St
111 White Horse, 34 Copper St (open 1833)
112 White Lion, 86 Queen St (1825–1903)
113 White Lion, 37 Queen St
114 White Swan, 75 West Bar (1797–1903)

Note: The following pubs were known to be in this area though the actual location is unknown:

Crown and Thistle, Irish Cross (bottom of Snig Hill) (1780–1901)
French Horn, Hartshead (1780–1901)
Travellers, Snig Hill (open c.1780)
Vine Tavern, Furnace Hill (open 1825)
Whiley's Saloon, Hartshead (open 1825)

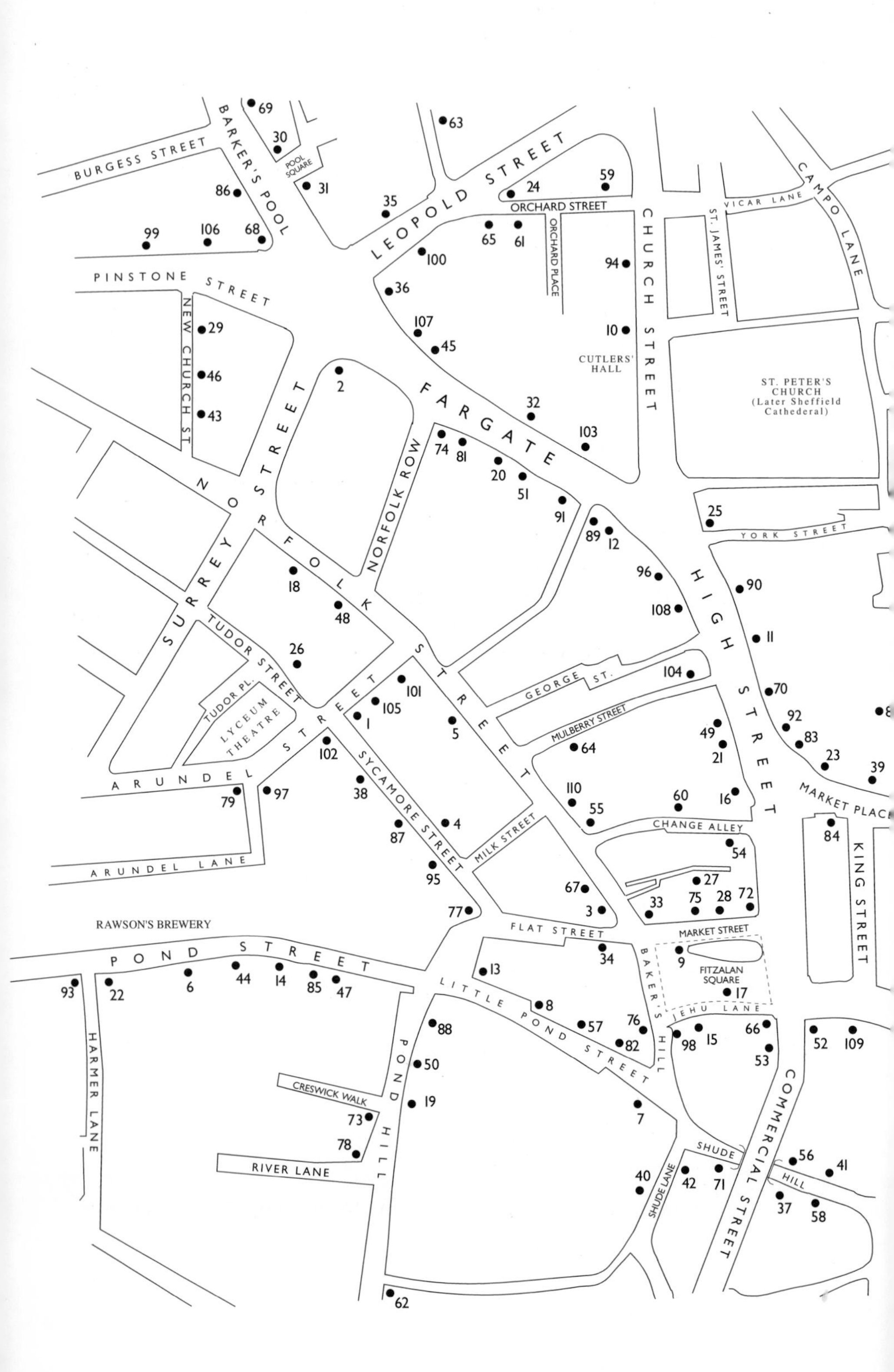

BURGESS STREET
BARKER'S POOL
POOL SQUARE
LEOPOLD STREET
ORCHARD STREET
ORCHARD PLACE
CHURCH STREET
VICAR LANE
ST. JAMES' STREET
CAMPO LANE
PINSTONE STREET
NEW CHURCH ST
CUTLERS' HALL
ST. PETER'S CHURCH (Later Sheffield Cathederal)
FARGATE
NORFOLK ROW
NORFOLK STREET
SURREY STREET
YORK STREET
HIGH STREET
TUDOR STREET
TUDOR PL.
LYCEUM THEATRE
GEORGE ST.
MULBERRY STREET
ARUNDEL STREET
SYCAMORE STREET
MILK STREET
CHANGE ALLEY
MARKET PLACE
KING STREET
ARUNDEL LANE
RAWSON'S BREWERY
FLAT STREET
MARKET STREET
FITZALAN SQUARE
JEHU LANE
BAKER'S HILL
POND STREET
LITTLE POND STREET
HARMER LANE
POND HILL
CRESWICK WALK
RIVER LANE
SHUDE LANE
SHUDE HILL
COMMERCIAL STREET

Map 9

1 Adelphi, 13 Arundel St/Sycamore St (demolished 1969)
2 Albany Hotel, Fargate/Surrey St (temperance hotel at one time, now bank) (open 1889)
3 Ball, 3 Norfolk St (1833–1900)
4 Balloon Tavern, 21 Sycamore St (1835–1900)
5 Bank Tavern, 65 Norfolk St (closed 1900)
6 Barrel, 103 Pond St (1825–1930)
7 Barrel, 40 Little Pond St
8 Beehive, 13 Little Pond St (closed 1910)
9 Bell, Market St (site moved to other side of Fitzalan Sq before 1890) (1796–1974)
10 Bird in Hand, Church St (open 1761)
11 Blackamoors Head, 25 High St (1718–1787, became The Grey Horse, closed 1917)
12 Black Swan, 3 Fargate (open 1797)
13 Black Swan, 1 Little Pond St (open 1825)
14 Blue Ball, (or Blue Bell) 91 Pond St (1833–1910)
15 Blue Bell, 13 Jehu Lane (open 1825)
16 Bodega (George or George & Dragon until 1904), High St (1774—bombed 1940)
17 Bricklayer's Arms, 8 Jehu Lane (open 1796)
18 Brown Bear, 109 Norfolk St (1825—still open)
19 Brushmaker's Arms (or Tavern), 31 Pond Hill (1825–1917)
20 Chequers, Fargate (open 1833)
21 Clarence, 56 High St (1825–1900)
22 Clarence Hotel, 133 Pond St (1825–1905)
23 Cock (later The Star, then The Carlton [1901], High St (1686–1753)
24 Compass Inn, 28 Orchard St (closed 1910)
25 Crown, 1 High St (1710–1772)
26 Crown and Cushion, 9 Tudor St (open 1789)
27 Cross Daggers, Cross Daggers Yard, High St (1825–1968)
28 Cup, 4 Market St (1825–1910)
29 Cutler's Arms, 7 New Church St (open 1833)
30 Cutler's Arms, 86 Fargate (closed 1883)
31 Cutler's Inn, 84 Fargate (1797–1883)
32 Cutler's Arms, 38 Fargate (1825–1910)
33 Elephant, 2 Norfolk St (1825–1968)
34 Falcon, 15 Flat St
35 Filesmith's Arms, 66 Leopold St
36 Fleur de Lis, 66 Fargate (open 1797)
37 French Horn, 7 Shude Hill (open 1796)

38 Garrick Hotel, 6 Sycamore St (1834–1917)
39 George Inn, 19 Market Place (1774–1910)
40 Golden Ball (also known as The Ball), 39 Forge or Shude Lane (open 1796)
41 Golden Lion, 2 Shude Hill (1833–1895)
42 Golden Lion, 3 Forge Lane
43 Grapes, 11 New Church St (1830–1896)
44 Grapes, 95 Pond St (1796–1924)
45 Green Dragon, 42 Fargate (1825–1926)
46 Green Man, 9 New Church St (1823–1890)
47 Greyhound, 77 Pond St (1796–1930)
48 Hay's Spirit Vaults (now Hay's Art Gallery), 97 Norfolk St (open 1797)
49 Horse & Cat (became The Westminster), 48 High St (open 1774—bombed 1940)
50 Horse & Jockey (also known as The Lyceum Hotel), 19 Pond Hill (open 1797)
51 King's Arms, 17 Fargate (1797–1898)
52 King's Arms, 2 Haymarket (1797–1898)
53 King's Arms, 12 Commercial St (1825–1973)
54 King's Head, 1 Change Alley (1772—bombed 1940)
55 King & Miller, 16 Norfolk St (1825–1908)
56 Lion & Lamb, 6 Shude Hill (open1833)
57 Little Tankard (or The Tankard), 29 Little Pond St (open 1825)
58 Mason's Arms, 3 Shude Hill (1833–1900)
59 Mermaid, 6 Orchard St (open 1825)
60 Mitre Tavern, 32 Change Alley (closed 1929)
61 Mitre, 27 Orchard St (1825–1910)
62 Moulder's Arms, Pond Hill
63 Mountain Deer, 14 Orchard Lane
64 Mulberry Tavern, 2 Mulberry St (1825—still open, rebuilt in 1980's)
65 Museum, 25 Orchard St (1797–1988, rebuilt, reopened as The Orchard, then The Brewing Trough, now The Hogshead, still open)
66 Nag's Head, Jeho Lane (open 1790)
67 Norfolk Arms, 5 Norfolk St (1825–1900)
68 Norfolk Arms, 73 Fargate (closed 1898)
69 Norfolk Hotel, 98 Barker's Pool (closed 1898)
70 Old Blue Bell, now Cavell's, 31 High St (open 1710—still open, rebuilt)
71 Old English Gentleman, 34 Shude Hill (1796–1917)
72 Old London Mart, Market St (1892—bombed 1940, rebuilt 1959 as The Marples, still open)
73 Old Queen's Head, Pond Hill (1851—rebuilt 1993, still open)
74 Old Red House, 35 Fargate (1780–1917)
75 Old Star, 6 Market St

76 Palace Inn, Bakers Hill (open 1833)
77 Prince of Wales, 38 Sycamore St (1825–1898)
78 Queen Hotel, River Lane (open 1890)
79 Raglan Inn, Arundel St
80 Red Lion, off Market Place (open 1755)
81 Rodney Arms, 33 Fargate (1825–1898)
82 Rose Tavern, 39 Little Pond St (1833–1900)
83 Rose and Crown, 37 High St (1675–1812)
84 Rose and Crown, Market Place (1692–1776)
85 Royal Oak, 83 Pond St (1796–1930)
86 Scarborough Arms, 79 Fargate (1797–1890)
87 Shakespeare (or Shakespeare & Crown), 16 Sycamore St (open 1840)
88 Sir Francis Burnett, 5 Pond Hill (1825–1910)
89 Sportsmans Group, 5 Fargate
90 Spread Eagle, 19 High St (1833–1890)
91 Spread Eagle, 9 Fargate (1794–1896)
92 Star Hotel, 35 High St (1797–1900)
93 Station Inn, 147 Pond St (1796–1910)
94 Stone House, 19 Church St (1790—still open)
95 Sycamore Tree, 24 Sycamore St (1833–1917)
96 Thatched House Tavern, 2 High St (closed 1928)
97 Theatre Tavern, 37 Arundel St (open 1774)
98 Three Horseshoes, Jehu Lane (bombed 1940)
99 Three Stags Heads, 24 Pinstone St (1825–1898)
100 Three Tuns (or Old Three Tuns), 55 Leopold St (1825–1987)
101 Tudor Tavern, 5 Arundel St (open 1833)
102 Turf Tavern, 15 Arundel St
103 Union, 18 Fargate (closed 1910)
104 Victoria (or Queen Victoria), 40 Mulberry St (1796–1900)
105 Waggon and Horses, 13 Arundel St (open 1825)
106 Waterloo Tavern, 18 Pinstone St (1796–1898)
107 Well Run Dimple, 58 Fargate (built 1793–1896)
108 White Bear, 10 High St (1780–1900)
109 Yellow Lion, 12 Haymarket (closed 1928)
110 Yeomanry Hotel, 32 Norfolk St (1833–1896)

Note 1: Part of Fargate became Barkers Pool

Note 2: The following pubs were known to be in this area though the actual location is unknown:

Carlton, High St (open 1901)
Crooked Billet, Crooked Billet Yard, off High St (open 1794)
Golden Cross, High St (open 1771)
Mitre, Fargate (1780–1901)
Owl (also known as Shout 'em Downs or The Hullet), Norfolk St (1780–1901)

BALM GREEN
BARKERS POOL
DIVISION STREET
CARVER
ROCKINGHAM
BACKFIELDS
CAMBRIDGE STREET
BURGESS STREET
CROSS BURGESS STREET
CHARLES STREET
PINSTONE STREET
WELLINGTON STREET
ROCKINGHAM LANE
ROCKINGHAM STREET
EMPIRE PALACE
UNION STREET
MOOR HEAD
FURNIVAL STREET
MOORHEAD BREWERY
MOOR
PORTER STREET
UNION LANE
MATILDA STREET
BUTTON LANE
SOUTH STREE BREWERY
UNION

Map 10

1 Albert (formerly Union), 2 Coal Pit Lane (1797–1980)
2 Alhambra, 1–17 Union St (destroyed by fire 1882, rebuilt as Phoenix, 1910)
3 Angel (formerly Crown & Anchor until 1902), 14 Button Lane (1825–1956)
4 Athol Hotel, 9 Charles St
5 Ball (Charity Boy or Old Ball Inn), 86 Carver St (1825–1903)
6 Barleycorn, 38 Coal Pit Lane (1795–1988)
7 Barrel, 64 Pinstone St (open 1790)
8 Bay Horse, 40 South Street, Moor (open 1833)
9 Bethel Arms, Backfields (open 1835)
10 Black Swan, 21 Burgess St (1825–1898)
11 Blue Boar, 16 Cross Burgess St
12 Boot and Shoe, 52 Pinstone St (1833–1898)
13 Bull's Head, 2 Matilda St
14 Cambridge Arms, 73 Coal Pit Lane (open 1833)
15 Ceylon Hotel, 16 Wellington St (1833–1917)
16 Chandos, 217 Rockingham St (open 1825)
17 Chequers (Old Cow), 64 Coal Pit Lane (open 1825)
18 Commercial Hotel, 18 Button Lane (1797–1908)
19 Commercial Inn, 34 Button Lane
20 Crown Inn, 21 Pinstone St (1796–1898)
21 Cup, 52 Button Lane (open 1825)
22 Cutler's Arms, 86 Fargate (closed1883)
23 Cutler's Inn, 84 Fargate (1797–1883)
24 Devonshire Arms, 23 South St, Moor (1825—bombed 1940)
25 Dog and Gun, 108 Carver St (open 1797)
26 Dog and Partridge, 53 Coal Pit Lane (open 1825)
27 Dolphin Hotel, 37 Division St (1845–1895)
28 Empire Music Hall, 16 Charles St
29 Fisherman's Tavern, 100 Backfields
30 Forester's Inn, 57 Division St (still open)
31 Golden Ball, 30 Burgess St (open 1797)
32 Grapes, 1 South St, Moor
33 Huntsman's Rest, 9 Backfields
34 Jolly Grinders, 8 Porter St (1833–1896)
35 London House, 25 Pinstone St (1796–1898)
36 Manchester 4 Division St
37 Millstone, 12 Cross Burgess St (open 1833)
38 Milton Arms (Miner's Arms), 272 Rockingham St (closed 1963)

39 Monument Tavern, 35 Button Lane
40 Napoleon, 85 Carver St (1833–1921)
41 Nelson (now The Hind), Moorhead (rebuilt 1963)
42 Norfolk Arms, 73 Fargate (closed1898)
43 Norfolk Hotel, 98 Barker's Pool (closed 1898)
44 Old Cricket Players, 69 Coal Pit Lane (open 1825)
45 Original John Bull, 6 Division St
46 Oxford Blue, 15 Burgess St (1825–1898)
47 Parrot Inn, 9 Button Lane (1833–1908)
48 Pheasant, 40 Carver St (1833–1898)
49 Presser's Arms, 20 Burgess St (1797–1927)
50 Portland Arms, 184 Rockingham St
51 Red Lion (also known as Nell's Bar), 52 Coal Pit Lane (open 1796)
52 Reform Tavern, 76 Coal Pit Lane (open 1796)
53 Reuben's Head, 43 Burgess St (closed 1898)
54 Rockingham Arms,194 Rockingham St (open 1825)
55 Royal George, 60 Carver St (1833–1970)
56 Scarbrough Arms, 79 Fargate (1797–1890)
57 Sportsman, 28 South Street, Moor (open 1833)
58 Sportsman, 20 Coal Pit Lane (still open)
59 Stag, 45 Carver St (1825–1898)
60 Steelmelter's Tavern, 107 Carver St (closed 1898)
61 Three Horseshoes Hotel & Oyster Bar, 72 Norfolk St (bombed1940)
62 Three Pigeons, 20 Button Lane (1787–1908)
63 Three Pigeons, 117 Carver St (open 1825)
64 Three Stag's Heads, 24 Pinstone St (1825–1898)
65 Turner's Arms, 4 Burgess St (1833–1898)
66 Waterloo Tavern, 18 Pinstone St (1796–1898)
67 Wellington Tavern, 21 Coal Pit Lane (open 1833)
68 Wentworth Arms, 262 Rockingham St (open 1833)
69 Wheatsheaf, 21 Button Lane (1833–1920)
70 White Lion, 61 Division St
71 White Lion, 110 Barker's Pool (1796–c1920)
72 Yellow Lion (became the Cambridge Arms), 1 Coal Pit Lane (open 1736)
73 Yorkshire Man (became The Yorkshireman's Arms), 31 Burgess St (1796—still open)

Note 1: Coal Pit(t) Lane became Cambridge Street
Note 2: The following pubs were known to be in this area though the actual location is unknown:

Blacksmith's Cottage, Button Lane (open 1874, building dated 1705)
Three Stags, Carver St (open 1814)

The Albert was demolished in 1980, it is now a car park

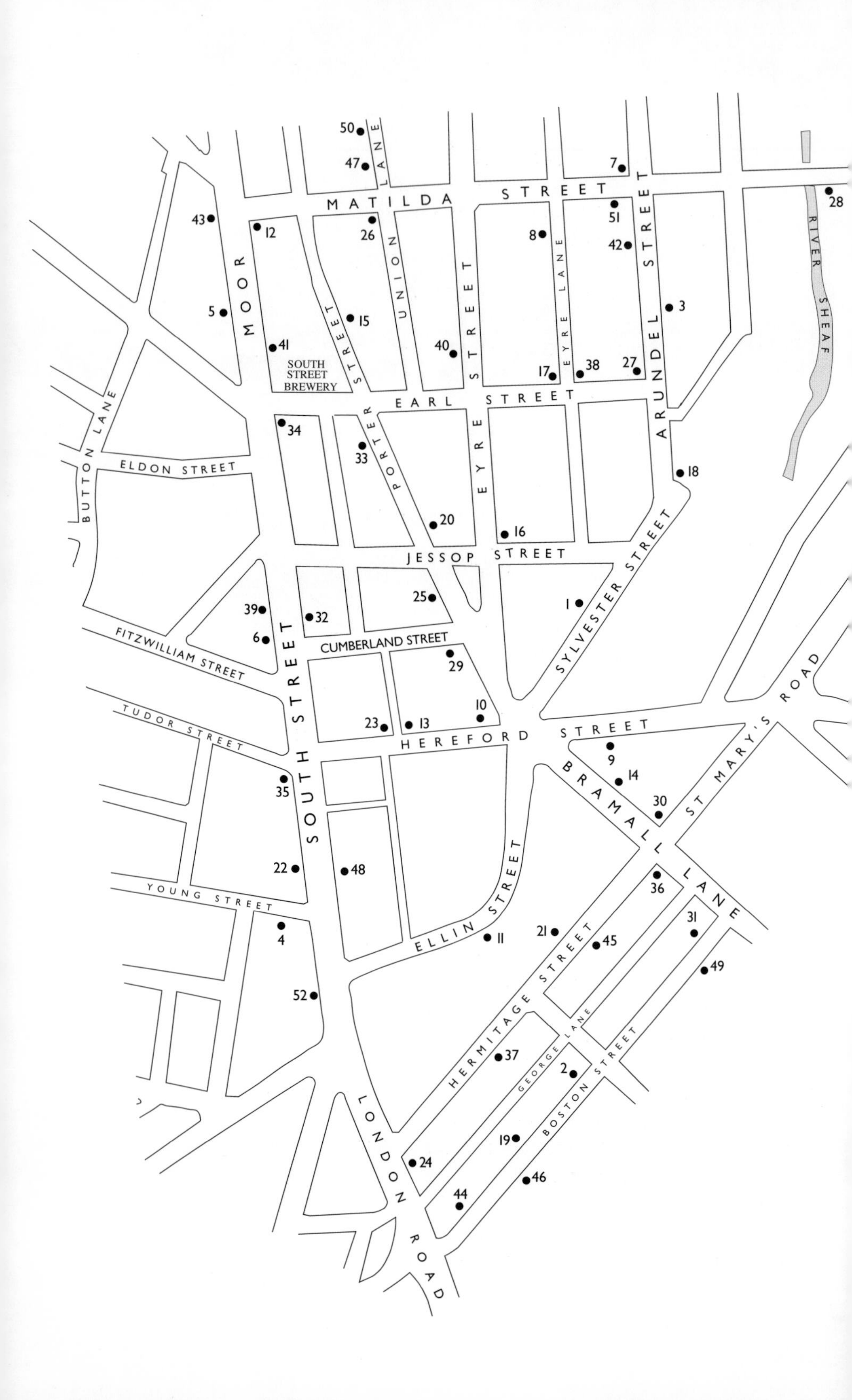
MATILDA STREET
LANE
UNION STREET
MOOR
SOUTH STREET BREWERY
EYRE STREET
EYRE LANE
ARUNDEL STREET
RIVER SHEAF
EARL STREET
PORTER STREET
BUTTON LANE
ELDON STREET
JESSOP STREET
CUMBERLAND STREET
FITZWILLIAM STREET
SYLVESTER STREET
TUDOR STREET
SOUTH STREET
HEREFORD STREET
BRAMALL LANE
ST MARY'S ROAD
YOUNG STREET
ELLIN STREET
HERMITAGE STREET
GEORGE LANE
BOSTON STREET
LONDON ROAD
1
2
3
4
5
6
7
8
9
10
11
12
13
14
15
16
17
18
19
20
21
22
23
24
25
26
27
28
29
30
31
32
33
34
35
36
37
38
39
40
41
42
43
44
45
46
47
48
49
50
51
52

Map 11

1 Albion, 12 Sylvester St (1851–1926)
2 Angler's Rest, 46 New George St (open1841)
3 Arundel Castle, 257 Arundel St (1833–1926)
4 Ball, 182 Young St (1835–1905)
5 Bay Horse, 40 South Street, Moor (open 1833)
6 Bazaar, 116 South St, Moor (open 1833)
7 Birmingham Arms, 79 Matilda St
8 Blademaker's Arms (or Brickmaker's Arms), 92 Eyre Lane
9 Bricklayer's Arms, 66 Hereford St (closed 1968)
10 Bridge Inn, 47 Hereford St
11 Brunswick Inn, 16 Ellin St
12 Bull's Head, 2 Matilda St
13 Carpenter's Arms, 19 Hereford St
14 Chantrey Arms, 11 Bramall Lane (open 1880)
15 Clock, 41 Porter St (1833–1922)
16 Consort, 215 Eyre St (1825–1903)
17 Crimea Tavern, 63 Earl St (1841–1903)
18 Gas Tank Tavern, 293 Arundel St (1833–1901)
19 George Hotel, 52 New George St
20 Globe, 107 Porter St
21 Greyhound Tavern, 38 Hermitage St
22 Hammer & Anvil, 152 South Street, Moor (1825–1917)
23 Hereford Arms, 17 Hereford St
24 Hermitage, 11 London Rd (open 1832 as Harvey's Tavern, then The Hermitage, now Harvey's Bar, still open)
25 Industry, 118 Porter St (1833–1920)
26 Livery Stables, 32 Union Lane
27 Lord Nelson, 166 Arundel St (still open)
28 Matilda Tavern, 100 Matilda St (1825—still open)
29 Moorfoot Tavern, Cumberland St
30 Norfolk Arms, 1 St Mary's Rd
31 Old Mill Tavern, 4 New George St (1833–1900)
32 Pheasant, 123 South Street, Moor
33 Porter Cottage, 66 Porter St (1825–1905)
34 Pump Tavern, 79 South Street, Moor (1825—still open)
35 Punch Bowl, 140 South Street, Moor (open 1825)
36 Queen Adelaide, 32 Bramall Lane (open 1835)
37 Rising Sun, 67 Hermitage St
38 Royal Hotel, 106 Eyre Lane (open 1928)
39 Sheffield Moor,114 South Street, Moor
40 Sir Admiral Lyons, 176 Eyre St (1833–1908)

41 South Street Hotel, 71 South Street, Moor
42 Sportsman Inn, 140 Arundel St
43 Sportsman, 28 South Street, Moor (open 1833)
44 Spring Tavern, 74 New George St
45 Star of Lemont, 29 Hermitage St
46 Talbot, 51 New George St
47 Three Legs, 30 Union Lane
48 Traveller's Rest, 135 South Street, Moor
49 Umpire, 9 New George St
50 Union Tavern, 24 Union Lane
51 White Horse, 76 Matilda St
52 Woodman, 166 South Street, Moor (open 1833)

Note 1: South Street, Moor became The Moor
Note 2: New George Street became Boston Street

Both these old pubs have long been demolished

LYCEUM THEATRE
SURREY STREET
ARUNDEL STREET
POND STREET
RAWSON'S POND BREWERY
HARMER LANE
SHEAF STREET
MIDLAND STATION
ARUNDEL LANE
NORFOLK LANE
HOWARD STREET
EYRE STREET BREWERY
EYRE STREET
PATERNOSTER ROW
POND STREET
TURNER STREET
CROSS TURNER STREET
CHARLES STREET
SUFFOLK ROAD
FORNHAM STREET
LEADMILL ROAD
UNION LANE
EYRE LANE
ARUNDEL STREET
BROWN STREET
FURNIVAL STREET
LEADMILL STREET
SIDNEY STREET
MATILDA LANE
MATILDA STREET
BRITTAIN STREET
ST MARY'S ROAD
SHELF STR
MATILDA STREET

Map 12

1 Arundel Cottage, 49 Arundel Lane (1841–1917)
2 Ball, 72 Howard St (open 1845)
3 Ball, 60 Charles St (open 1825)
4 Barrel, 103 Pond St (1825–1930)
5 Barrel, 8 Charles St
6 Ben Lomond (formerly City Arms), 23 Eyre St (1833–1908)
7 Birmingham Arms, 79 Matilda St
8 Black Horse, 64 Howard St (1825–1902)
9 Brave Old Oak, 58 Charles St
10 Brewer's Arms, 26 Eyre St
11 Bridge Inn, 219 Pond St (1796–1900)
12 Britain (Brittain) Arms, 120 Matilda St (1830–1970)
13 Carter's Rest, 123 Matilda St (open 1830)
14 Clarence Hotel, 133 Pond St (1825–1905)
15 Columbia Tavern, 10 Fornham St
16 Cossack, 45 Howard St (1833, became The But & Ben, 1995—still open)
17 Cup, 19 Paternoster Row
18 Elephant and Castle, 117 Arundel St
19 Empire Canteen (or Music Hall, Rifleman's Canteen),16 Charles St
20 Filesmith's Arms, 61 Charles St (1833–1901)
21 Forester's Arms, 45 Eyre St
22 Globe Inn, 54 Howard St (1797—still open)
23 Golden Ball, 203 Pond St (1825—1900)
24 Grinder's Rest, 43 Charles Lane
25 Howard Arms, 5 Suffolk Rd
26 Howard Hotel, 2 Howard St (still open)
27 Lamb (also known as The Golden Ball), 31 Howard St (1825–1903)
28 Matilda Tavern, 100 Matilda St (open 1825)
29 Midland, 18 Turner St
30 Midland Station Hotel, Pond St
31 Miner's Arms, 198 Arundel St
32 Minerva (now Yorkshire Grey), Charles St (1833—still open)
33 Montgomery Hotel, 225 St Mary's Rd
34 Norfolk Arms, 2 Suffolk Rd (still open)
35 Old Mill Dam, 29 Brit(t)ain St (1841–1941)
36 Red Lion, 103 Eyre St
37 Red Lion, 109 Charles St (1825—still open)
38 Rodley Inn (or Rodney Inn), 97 Leadmill Rd
39 Rodney Inn, 46 Leadmill Rd
40 Roebuck (now The Newt & Chambers), 1 Charles St (1790—still open)
41 Rose and Crown, 21 Paternoster Row (open 1825)

42 Royal Standard, 156 St Mary's Rd (1833—still open)
43 Rutland Arms, 86 Brown St (1833—still open)
44 Sportsman's Inn, 4 Paternoster Row
45 Stag Inn, Pond St
46 Station Inn, 147 Pond St (1796–1910)
47 Suffolk Hotel, 24 Turner St
48 Swan With Two Necks, 28 Furnival St (open 1825)
49 Talbot Commercial Hotel, 71 Arundel St
50 Theatre Tavern, 49 Arundel St (open 1774)
51 True Briton, 61 Brown St
52 Truro Tavern, 189 St Mary's Rd
53 Turner's Arms, Brown St
54 Wheatsheaf, 81 Eyre Lane

Note : The following pub was known to be in this area though the actual location is unknown:

Sheaf Tavern, Sheaf St (1825–1900)

Now known as The But & Ben

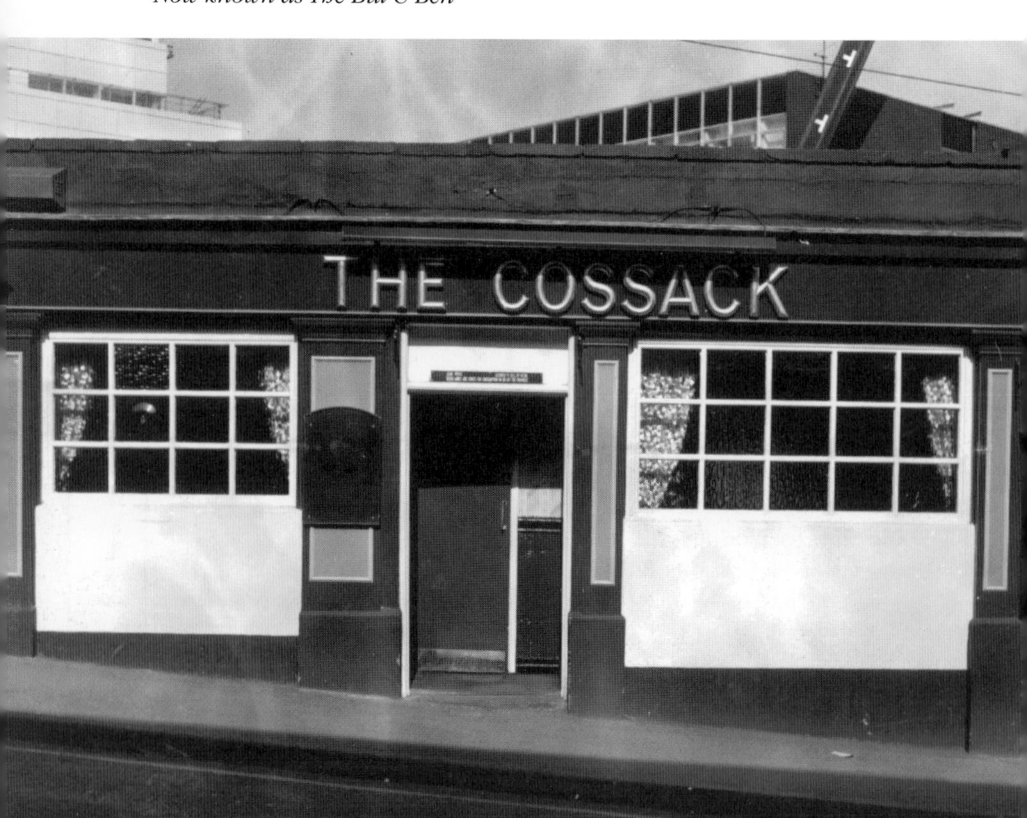

Once known as The Roebuk it has been a pub since at least 1790

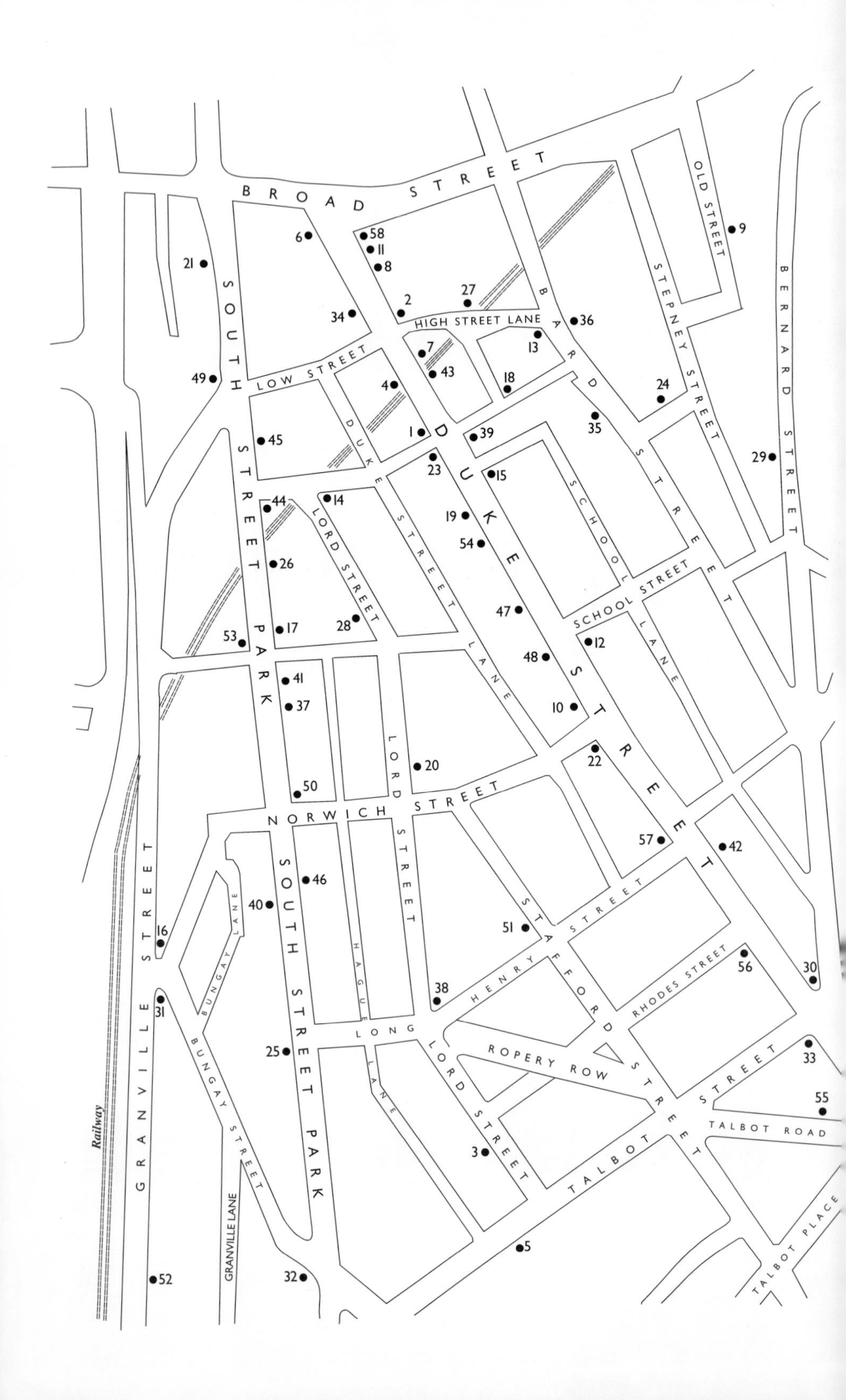

BROAD STREET
OLD STREET
STEPNEY STREET
BERNARD STREET
HIGH STREET LANE
BARD STREET
SOUTH STREET PARK
LOW STREET
DUKE STREET
DUKE STREET LANE
LORD STREET
SCHOOL STREET
SCHOOL LANE
NORWICH STREET
LORD STREET
SOUTH STREET PARK
HAGUE
LONG
LANE
LORD STREET
STAFFORD STREET
HENRY STREET
RHODES STREET
ROPERY ROW
TALBOT STREET
TALBOT ROAD
TALBOT PLACE
GRANVILLE STREET
BUNGAY LANE
BUNGAY STREET
GRANVILLE LANE
Railway
1
2
3
4
5
6
7
8
9
10
11
12
13
14
15
16
17
18
19
20
21
22
23
24
25
26
27
28
29
30
31
32
33
34
35
36
37
38
39
40
41
42
43
44
45
46
47
48
49
50
51
52
53
54
55
56
57
58

Map 13

1 Alma Cottage, 56 Duke St (1845–1917)
2 Ball, 31 Duke St (1824–1900)
3 Barrel,134 Lord St (open 1845)
4 Barrel, 36 Duke St (1830–1902)
5 Black Darling, 75 Talbot St (open 1833)
6 Bull's Head, 2 Duke St (1825–1902)
7 Collier's Arms (Park Tavern), 37 Duke St (1833–1902)
8 Crown Inn, 13 Duke St (1825–1902)
9 Crown & Cushion, 21 Old St (open 1825)
10 Cup, 120 Duke St (closed 1900)
11 Duke Inn, 7 Duke St (1833–1902)
12 Eagle Tavern, 117 Duke St (closed 1900)
13 Feathers, 46 High St Lane (open 1833)
14 Filesmith's Arms, 1 Lord St
15 Golden Ball, 63 Duke St (1839–1902)
16 Granville Inn, 89 Granville St
17 Green Dragon, 71 South Street, Park (1833–1910)
18 Grey Horse, 15 Crown Alley
19 Hare and Hounds, 72 Duke St (closed 1910)
20 Lord Ratcliffe Arms, 95 Lord St (1833–1904)
21 Mason's Arms, 14 South Street, Park (closed 1900)
22 Mason's Arms,130 Duke St (1833–1900)
23 Mason's Arms, 58 Duke St
24 Miner's Rest (or Arms), 7 East St
25 Monument Tavern, 190 South Street, Park (closed 1921)
26 Monument Tavern, 61 South Street, Park (closed 1922)
27 Moulder's Return, 7 High Street Lane (1833–1901)
28 Napier Hotel, 28 Lord St (open 1833)
29 New Inn, 48 Bernard St (open 1833)
30 New Inn, 183 Duke St
31 Norfolk Arms, 91 Granville St
32 Norfolk Tap (or Hotel), 224 South Street, Park
33 Odd Fellow's Arms, 202 Duke St
34 Old Crown, 8 Duke St (closed 1903)
35 Old Feathers Inn, 46 Bard St
36 Old Park Gate, 41 Bard St
37 Oxford Hotel, 83 South Street, Park (closed 1930)
38 Peter's Hotel, 121 Lord St
39 Plumper's Inn, 49 Duke St (closed 1921)
40 Prince of Wales, 116 South Street, Park (closed 1910)
41 Prince of Wales, 73 South Street, Park
42 Red Lion, 145 Duke St (1825—still open)

43 Reformers, 39 Duke St (1833–1902)
44 Reindeer, 39 South Street, Park (1830–1934)
45 Rising Sun, 45 South St, Park (closed 1910)
46 Reuben's Head, 117 South Street, Park (1833–1904)
47 Robin Hood, 86 Duke St (1825–1950)
48 Shepherd Inn, 118 Duke St (1830–1910)
49 Shrewsbury Tavern, 26 South Street, Park (1825–1920)
50 Shrewsbury Hotel, 109 South Street, Park (1830–1934)
51 Stafford Arms, 30 Stafford St
52 Station Inn, Granville St
53 Sun, 78 South Street, Park (closed 1959)
54 Swan Tavern, 74 Duke St (1833–1902)
55 Talbot Inn, 19 Talbot Rd (closed 1976)
56 Town Arms, 166 Duke St (1839–1902)
57 Weighhouse Inn, 168 Duke St (1839–1902)
58 Ye Old English Samson, 1 Duke St

The Red Lion Duke Street

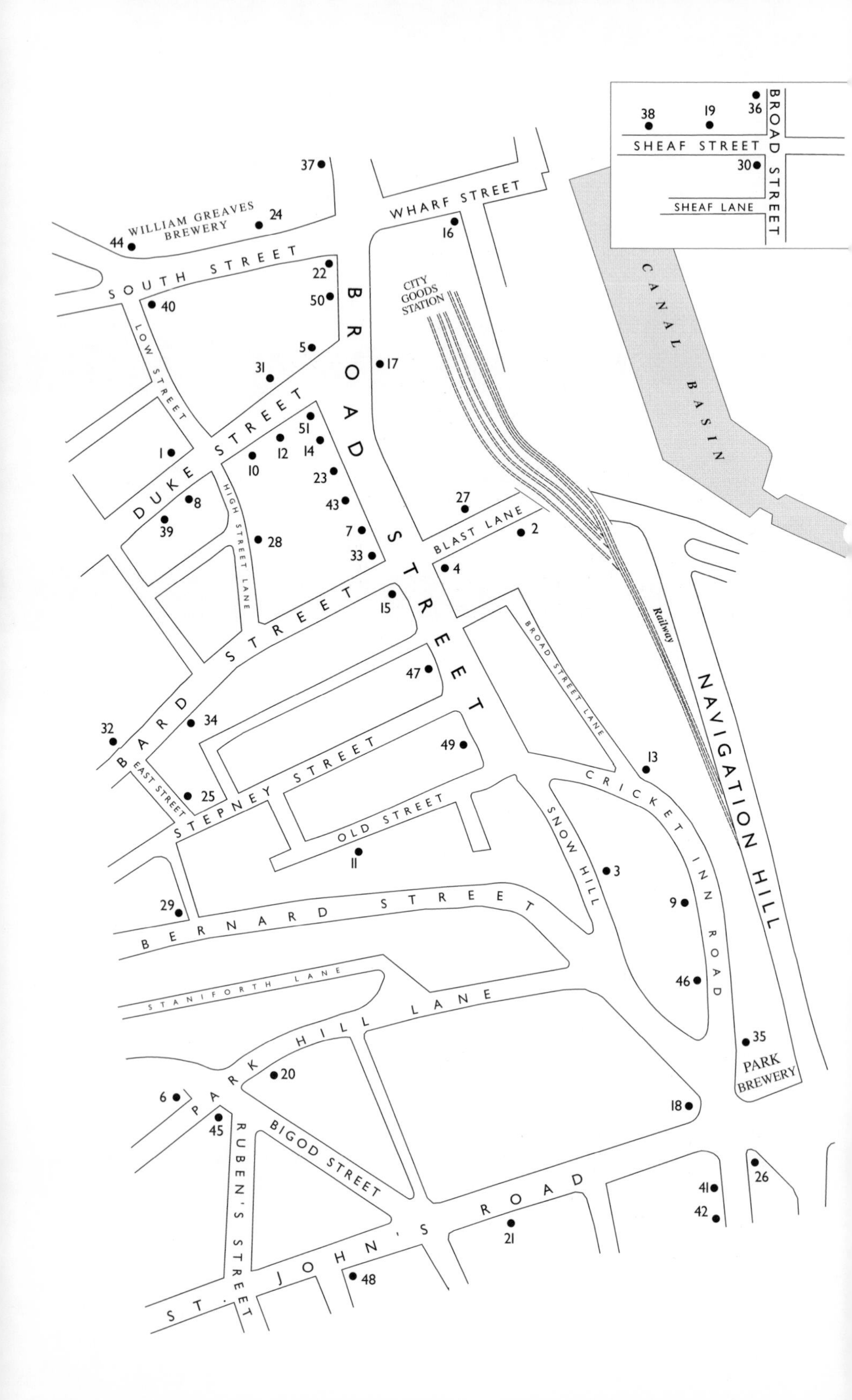

WILLIAM GREAVES BREWERY
SOUTH STREET
WHARF STREET
BROAD STREET
CITY GOODS STATION
LOW STREET
DUKE STREET
HIGH STREET LANE
BLAST LANE
BROAD STREET LANE
Railway
NAVIGATION HILL
CANAL BASIN
SHEAF STREET
SHEAF LANE
BARD STREET
EAST STREET
STEPNEY STREET
OLD STREET
SNOW HILL
CRICKET INN ROAD
BERNARD STREET
STANIFORTH LANE
PARK HILL LANE
PARK BREWERY
BIGOD STREET
RUBEN'S STREET
ST. JOHN'S ROAD

Map 14

1 Barrel, 36 Duke St (1830–1902)
2 Basin Tavern, 36 Blast Lane
3 Bay Tree, 23 Snow Hill
4 Blue Ball (or Ball Inn), 67 Broad St (open 1833)
5 Bull's Head, 2 Duke St (1825–1902)
6 Chequers, 68 Weigh Lane (open 1825)
7 Cock, 76 Broad St (1833–1910)
8 Collier's Arms (Park Tavern), 37 Duke St (1833–1902)
9 Cricket Inn, 20 Cricket Inn Rd (closed 1993)
10 Crown Inn, 13 Duke St (1825–1902)
11 Crown and Cushion, 21 Old St (open 1825)
12 Duke Inn, 7 Duke St (1833–1902)
13 Durham Ox, 15 Cricket Inn Rd (closed 1993)
14 Globe, 52 Broad St (1825–1902)
15 Golden Cock, 82 Broad St
16 Golden Fleece, 12 Wharf St (open 1839)
17 Green Man, 23 Broad St (1825–1902)
18 Haigh Tree Inn, 1 Bernard Rd (open 1825)
19 Horse and Jockey, 14 Sheaf St (1825–1900)
20 Hospital Tavern, 13 Park Hill Lane (open 1833)
21 Hyde Park (cricket ground inn), St John's Rd
22 Industry, 34 Broad St (1797–1972)
23 Lord Nelson, 60 Broad St
24 Mason's Arms, 14 South Street, Park (closed 1900)
25 Miner's Rest (or Arms), 7 East St
26 Miner's Rest (or Arms), 61 Cricket Inn Rd
27 Miner's Tavern, Blast Lane
28 Moulder's Return,7 High Street Lane (1833–1901)
29 New Inn, 48 Bernard St (open 1833)
30 New Market Hotel, 20 Broad St (1825–1972)
31 Old Crown, 8 Duke St (closed 1903)
32 Old Feathers Inn, 46 Bard St
33 Old Harrow, 80 Broad St (open 1825)
34 Old Park Gate, 41 Bard St
35 Park Inn, 51 Cricket Inn Rd
36 Pheasant, 10 Broad St (1797–1910)
37 Plough, 28 Broad St
38 Queen's Head, 20 Sheaf St
39 Reformer's, 39 Duke St (1833–1902)
40 Reindeer, 39 South Street, Park (1830–1934)

41 Rose Cottage, 70 Cricket Inn Rd
42 Royal George, 94 Cricket Inn Rd
43 Shrewsbury Arms, 74 Broad St (1797–1902)
44 Shrewsbury Tavern, 26 South St, Park (1825–1920)
45 Sportsman Inn, 45 Park Hill Lane
46 Talbot Arms (or Inn), 50 Cricket Inn Rd
47 Tankard and Punchbowl, 94 Broad St (1825–1910)
48 Target, 75 St Johns Rd
49 Traveller's Rest, 106 Broad St (closed 1902)
50 Vine Tavern, 38 Broad St (1833–1910)
51 Ye Old English Sampson, 1 Duke St

The Cricket

Boarded up and awaiting demolition

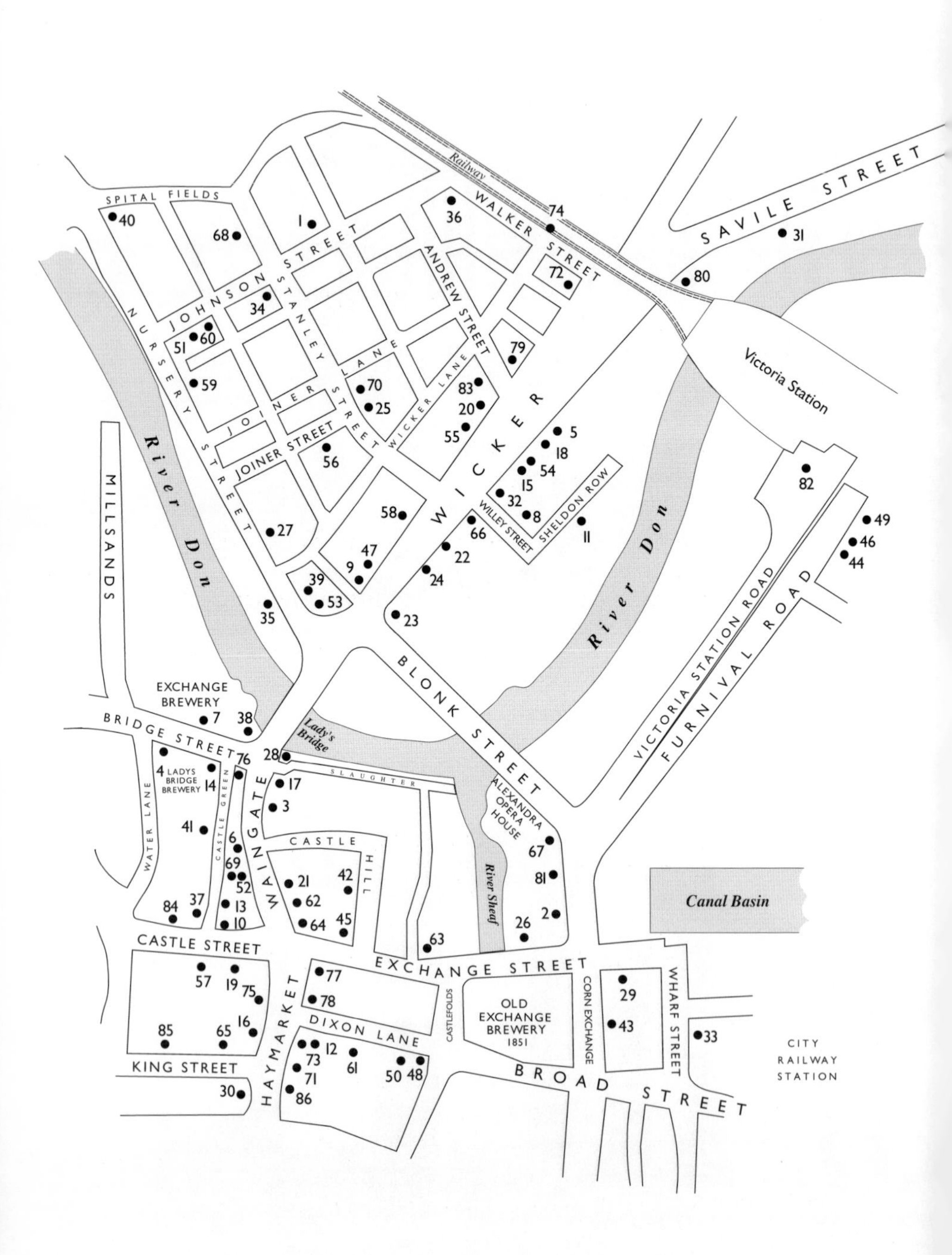

SPITAL FIELDS
JOHNSON STREET
WALKER STREET
SAVILE STREET
Railway
ANDREW STREET
STANLEY STREET
NURSERY STREET
JOINER LANE
JOINER STREET
WICKER LANE
WICKER
WILLEY STREET
SHELDON ROW
Victoria Station
River Don
MILLSANDS
EXCHANGE BREWERY
BRIDGE STREET
Lady's Bridge
BLONK STREET
VICTORIA STATION ROAD
FURNIVAL ROAD
LADYS BRIDGE BREWERY
WATER LANE
CASTLE GREEN
WAINGATE
SLAUGHTER
CASTLE HILL
ALEXANDRA OPERA HOUSE
River Sheaf
Canal Basin
CASTLE STREET
EXCHANGE STREET
HAYMARKET
DIXON LANE
CASTLEFOLDS
OLD EXCHANGE BREWERY 1851
CORN EXCHANGE
WHARF STREET
KING STREET
BROAD STREET
CITY RAILWAY STATION

Map 15

1 Albion, 35 Johnson St (1839–1924)
2 Alexandra Hotel, 37 Furnival Rd
3 Anvil, 24 Waingate (1828–1926)
4 Artillery Man, 7 Bridge St (open 1833)
5 Ball, 64 Wicker
6 Barrel, 9 Waingate (1833–1898)
7 Bay Childers, 4 Bridge St (open 1825)
8 Bay Horse, 9 Willey St
9 Big Gun (or Great Gun), 7 Wicker (1796—still open)
10 Black Rock, 17 Castle St (1797–1921)
11 Blacksmith's Arms, 10 Sheldon Row
12 Board, 6 Dixon Lane (open 1833)
13 Boston Castle, 6 Castle Green (1797–1898)
14 Bridge Inn, 5 Bridge St (open 1797)
15 Brown Cow, 56 Wicker (still open)
16 Brunswick, 15 Haymarket (closed 1975)
17 Bull and Mouth (became Tap & Spile), 30 Waingate (1790, rebuilt 1928—still open)
18 Bull and Oak (formerly Assembly House, Crown & Cushion), 62 Wicker (1715—still open)
19 Cannon Spirit Vaults (now The Cannon), 30 Castle St (1774—still open)
20 Chequers, 61 Wicker (1825–1900)
21 Coach and Horses, 16 Waingate (1825–1895)
22 Cock, 26 Wicker (open 1825)
23 Corner Pin, 14 Wicker (1815–1917)
24 Crown Inn, 24 Wicker (open 1774)
25 Crown and Anchor, 18 Stanley St (open 1830)
26 Durham Ox, 51 Exchange St
27 Dusty Miller, 24 Nursery St (open 1833)
28 Elephant & Castle, Lady's Bridge
29 Exchange (Maunche Hotel), 40 Exchange St (open 1833, rebuilt, 1881, demolished 1964)
30 Fitzalan Vaults, Haymarket (1786–1930)
31 George Inn, 20 Savile St (closed 1920)
32 Golden Ball (or The Ball), 52 Wicker (open 1890)
33 Golden Fleece, 12 Wharf St (open 1839)
34 Harlequin (formerly Harlequin & Clown), 26 Johnson St (1839—still open)
35 Hare & Hounds, 27 Nursery St (1893—still open)
36 Harp Tavern, 33 Walker St
37 Hen and Chickens (or Old hen & Chickens), 3 Castle Green (open 1851—still open)

38 Lady's Bridge (formerly Brewer on the Bridge, Brewery Tap) 2 Bridge St (closed 1993)
39 Lion (or Black Lion) Hotel, 4 Nursery St (closed 1980's—became boarding house)
40 Manchester Hotel (formerly Manchester Railway Hotel), 108 Nursery St (still open)
41 Mason's Arms, 17 Castle Green (open 1833)
42 Navigation House, 9 Castle Hill (1833–1897)
43 Neptune Inn, 22 Corn Exchange (open 1839)
44 New Bull & Oak, 26 Furnival Rd (open 1833)
45 New Market Inn, 13 Exchange St (1833–1921)
46 New Market Inn (Station Inn), 28 Furnival Rd
47 New White Lion, 23 Wicker (1825–1991, became shop)
48 Norfolk Arms, 26 Dixon Lane (1833—still open)
49 Norfolk House, 38 Furnival Rd
50 Norfolk Vaults, Dixon Lane
51 Nursery Tavern, 8 Johnson St (open 1833)
52 Old White Hart, 7 Waingate (1756–1898)
53 Old White Lion, 3 Wicker
54 Orange Branch, 56 Wicker (1787–1900)
55 Punch Bowl, 57 Wicker
56 Queen's Bays, 16 Joiner St
57 Queen's Head Inn (or Old Queen's Head), 14 Castle St (1797–1921)
58 Railway, 31 Wicker (1833–1900)
59 Railway Inn, 70 Nursery St (open 1833)
60 Red Lion, 18 Johnson St (open 1825)
61 Rock Tavern, 20 Dixon Lane (1796–1972)
62 Rose & Crown (The Britannia), 12 Waingate (1765–1926)
63 Rotherham House, 27 Exchange St (open 1797)
64 Royal Hotel (formerly The Reindeer, built 1779), 24 Waingate (1797–1928)
65 Royal Oak, 29 King St (1774—bombed 1940)
66 Sir John Falstaff, 48 Wicker (1825–1910)
67 Smithfield Hotel, 29 Furnival Rd
68 Spitalfields, 57 Stanley St (open 1833)
69 Stag Inn, 14 Castle Green (1841–1898)
70 Stanley Street Tavern, 24 Stanley St (open 1833)
71 Star, 26 Haymarket (open 1780)
72 Station Inn, 86 Wicker (still open)
73 Steer's Hotel, Haymarket
74 Sun Inn, 12 Walker St (open 1833)
75 Sun Tavern(became Old No. 12, 1833), 27 Haymarket (1790–1955)

76 Three Whitesmiths, 1 Bridge St (1825–1898)
77 Tontine Hotel, Haymarket (1786–1850)
78 Tontine Tap, Haymarket (1786–1850)
79 Viaduct Inn, 79 Wicker (still open)
80 Victoria Arches Tavern (changed to The Cricket Ball Inn, 1914), 2 Savile St (closed 1918)
81 Victoria Hotel, 33 Furnival Rd
82 Victoria Station Hotel (Royal Victoria), Victoria Station Rd (still open)
83 Waterloo Tavern, 3 Andrew St (open 1833)
84 Waverley Hotel (or Imperial Hotel), Castle St
85 Wharncliffe Hotel, 13 King St (open after 1818 on site of old debtors prison)
86 Yellow Lion, 12 Haymarket (1787–1926)

Note : The following pubs were known to be in this area though the actual location is unknown:

Bull & Bitch (open c.1800)
Chandler's Arms, Bullstake (later Haymarket) (1780–1901)
Coach & Six, Haymarket (open 1808)
Cock, Castle Hill (open 1780)
Commercial Inn, Haymarket (open c1800)
Falstaff, Wicker (open c.1780)
Norfolk Arms, King St (open 1774)
Old Star Inn, possibly 6 Haymarket

Formerly The Harlequin and Clown

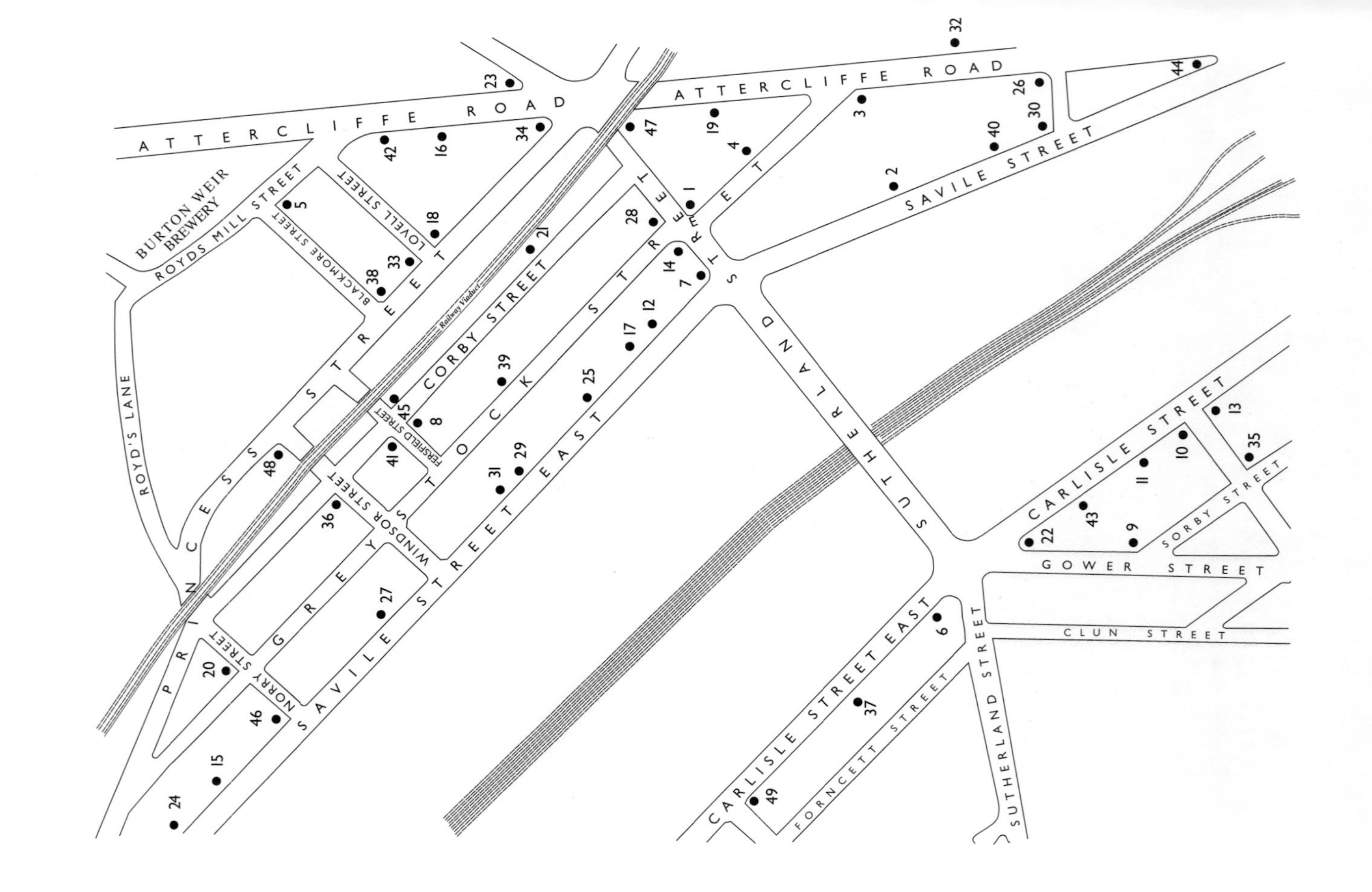
ATTERCLIFFE ROAD
BURTON WEIR BREWERY
ROYDS MILL STREET
ROYD'S LANE
PRINCESS STREET
BLACKMORE STREET
LOVELL STREET
Railway Viaduct
CORBY STREET
FERSFIELD STREET
STOCK STREET
WINDSOR STREET
GREY STREET
NORRY STREET
SAVILE STREET EAST
SAVILE STREET
SUTHERLAND STREET
CARLISLE STREET
SORBY STREET
GOWER STREET
CLUN STREET
CARLISLE STREET EAST
FORNCETT STREET
32
23
44
34
42
16
47
19
3
26
30
40
4
2
5
18
1
28
21
38
33
14
7
12
17
39
25
45
8
48
41
31
29
36
27
20
46
15
24
13
35
10
11
43
22
9
6
37
49

Map 16

1 Albert, 31 Sutherland St (1855—still open)
2 Atlas, 274 Savile St (1860–1920)
3 Bay Horse, 1 Greystock St (open 1860)
4 Birmingham Arms, 40 Greystock St (1860–1920)
5 Brewer's Inn, 46 Blackmore St (closed 1926)
6 Carlisle Street Hotel, 5 Carlisle Street East (1864—still open)
7 Cricket Ball Inn (formerly Victoria Arches Tavern), 2 Savile Street East (1860–1918)
8 Crown Inn, 107 Corby St (1860–1926)
9 Cup, 112 Sorby St (1866–1932)
10 Cyclops, 101 Carlisle St (1864–1922)
11 Fisherman's Inn, 115 Carlisle St (1862–1917)
12 George, 20 Savile Street East (closed 1920)
13 Grapes Inn, 99 Carlisle St (1862–1898)
14 Great Gun, 38 Greystock St (closed 1932)
15 Great Gun, 186 Savile Street East (1860–1920)
16 Halfway, 195 Attercliffe Rd (1870–1959)
17 Industry Inn, 24 Savile Street East (1860–1940)
18 Labour in Vain, 62 Princess St (closed 1920)
19 Local Fields Tavern, 151 Attercliffe Rd (1864–1932)
20 Lord Nelson, 184 Greystock Rd (open 1868)
21 Moulder's Arms, 25 Corby St (open 1868)
22 Norfolk Arms, 195 Carlisle St (1860—still open)
23 Norfolk Arms, 160 Attercliffe Rd (open 1831)
24 Norfolk Arms, 208 Savile Street East (open 1864)
25 Norfolk Arms, 56 Savile Street East (closed 1940)
26 Old King John, 35 Attercliffe Rd (1860–1926)
27 Perserverance, 108 Savile Street East (closed 1932)
28 Plumpers, 36 Sutherland St (closed 1989)
29 Prince of Wales, 82 Savile Steet East (1864–1920)
30 Prince of Wales (became billiard saloon), 240 Savile St (closed 1920)
31 Queen, 88 Savile Street East (closed 1920)
32 Queen, 20 Attercliffe Rd (closed 1930)
33 Railway Tavern, 64 Princess St (1864–1912)
34 Rawson's Arms, 161 Attercliffe Rd (1868–1941)
35 Rising Sun, 88 Sorby St (open 1879)
36 Rising Sun, 127 Corby St (1879–1917)
37 Rock Inn, 31 Carlisle Street East (1864–1932)
38 Roller's Tavern, 70 Princess St (closed 1926)
39 Royal George, 167 Greystock St (open 1870)
40 Royal Oak, 250 Savile St (1868–1956)

41 Royal Oak, 109 Corby St (closed 1920)
42 Royd's Inn, 213 Attercliffe Rd (1865–1940)
43 Sir Robert Peel, 157 Carlisle St (1862–1917)
44 Twelve O'Clock Inn, 1 Attercliffe Rd (open 1825)
45 Viaduct Inn, 108 Corby St (closed 1930)
46 Victoria, 136 Savile Street East
47 Weir Head Hotel, 1 Sutherland St (closed 1926)
48 Windsor Castle, 129 Princess St (closed 1932)
49 Woodman Inn, 87 Carlisle Street East (1864–1935)

TETLEY
NORFOLK ARMS HOTEL.
WINES.
SPIRITS.
TETLEY
TETLEY

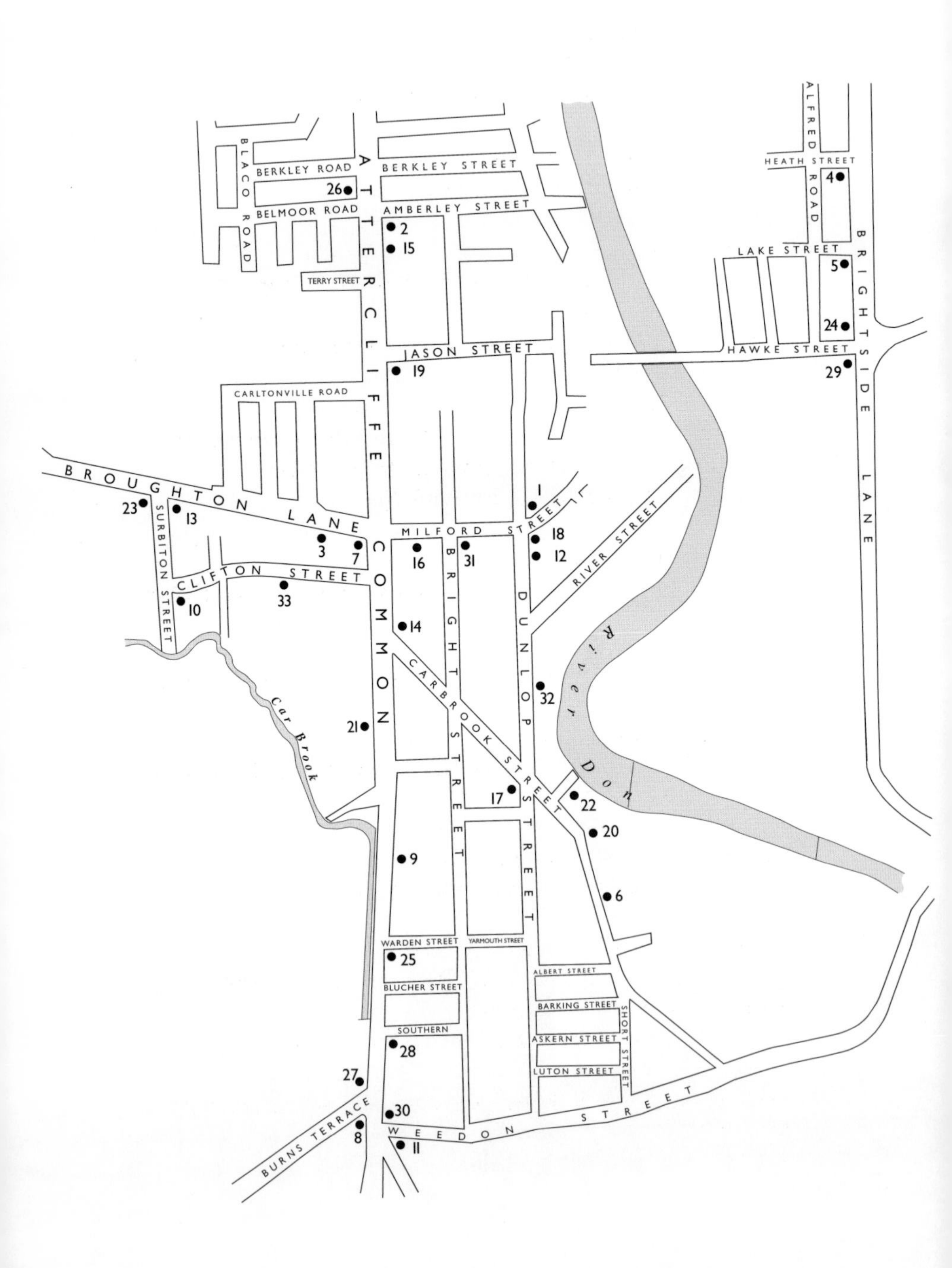
BERKLEY ROAD
BERKLEY STREET
BLACO ROAD
BELMOOR ROAD
AMBERLEY STREET
TERRY STREET
ATTERCLIFFE COMMON
JASON STREET
CARLTONVILLE ROAD
BROUGHTON LANE
SURBITON STREET
CLIFTON STREET
MILFORD STREET
BRIGHT STREET
DUNLOP STREET
CARBROOK STREET
RIVER STREET
River Don
Car Brook
HEATH STREET
ALFRED ROAD
LAKE STREET
HAWKE STREET
BRIGHTSIDE LANE
WARDEN STREET
YARMOUTH STREET
BLUCHER STREET
SOUTHERN
ALBERT STREET
BARKING STREET
ASKERN STREET
LUTON STREET
SHORT STREET
BURNS TERRACE
WEEDON STREET
1
2
3
4
5
6
7
8
9
10
11
12
13
14
15
16
17
18
19
20
21
22
23
24
25
26
27
28
29
30
31
32
33

Map 17

1 Alexandra, 91 Dunlop St
2 Amberley, 221 Attercliffe Common (1860–1961)
3 Bird in Hand, 49 Broughton Lane (open 1861)
4 Bird in Hand, 624 Brightside Lane
5 Blucher, 672 Brightside Lane (open 1860)
6 British Oak, 227 Carbrook St (open 1865)
7 Broughton, 1 Broughton Lane (open 1864)
8 Burn's Hotel, 12 Sheffield Rd
9 Carbrook Hall, 537 Attercliffe Common (1861—still open)
10 Clifton, 79 Clifton St (open 1774)
11 Commercial, 3 Sheffield Rd (1870–1994, re-opened 1995)
12 Dunlop Inn, Dunlop St
13 Enfield Arms, 95 Broughton Lane (1825—still open)
14 Excelsior, Attercliffe Common (closed 1993, buildings demolished)
15 Filesmith's Arms, 229 Attercliffe Common (1862–1961)
16 Fitzwilliam Hotel, 14 Milford St (closed 1926)
17 Industry, 206 Dunlop St
18 King's Head, 95 Dunlop St
19 Lambpool, 291 Attercliffe Common (1870–1988, building demolished 1993)
20 New Inn, 211 Carbrook St
21 Pheasant, 436 Attercliffe Common (demolished 1927, new pub built, still open)
22 Prince of Wales, Weir Head, off Carbrook St
23 Railway (then The Stadium, now The Noose & Gibbet), 97 Broughton Lane (still open)
24 River Don Inn, 712 Brightside Lane (open 1857)
25 Royal, 617 Attercliffe Common (open 1870)
26 Salutation, 126 Attercliffe Common (open 1870)
27 Tinsley Hotel, 2 Sheffield Rd
28 Union Inn, 651 Attercliffe Common (closed 1940)
29 Wellington (or Duke of Wellington), 720 Brightside Lane (still open)
30 Wellington, 683 Attercliffe Common
31 Wentworth House Hotel, 26 Milford St (1833—still open)
32 White Lion, 131 Dunlop St
33 Yellow Lion (possibly formerly The Arrow or Harrow), 59 Clifton St (open 1796)

MILNER ROAD
WORKSOP ROAD
BODMIN STREET
SHIRLAND LANE
BRITMALL STREET
OLD HALL ROAD
LEEDS ROAD
FELL RD
ATTERCLIFFE ROAD
NEWARK STREET
BROMPTON ROAD
CLAY STREET
LEIGH STREET
SWALLOW STREET
LIVERPOOL STREET
NEWHALL ROAD
RIVER DON
OLD COURSE OF RIVER DON
MILL DAM
DON ROAD
WINDMILL STREET
STAMFORD STREET
CASTOR ROAD
SANDERSON STREET
PAGET STREET
ALFRED ROAD
WOODBINE ROAD
STEVENSON ROA
BRIGHTSIDE LANE

Map 18

1 Albion, 694 Attercliffe Rd (1819–1920)
2 Barrel, (Coach & Horses, 1838), 756 Attercliffe Rd (open 1819)
3 Blue Bell, 120 Worksop Rd (open 1825)
4 Brickmaker's Arms, 21 Newhall Rd (open 1864)
5 Britannia, 24 Worksop Rd (1876—still open)
6 Cocked Hat, 75 Worksop Rd (still open)
7 Cutler's Arms, 74 Worksop Rd (still open)
8 Forge Inn, 95 Newhall Rd
9 Fox House, Shirland Lane (1870—still open)
10 Gate, 76 Attercliffe Rd (closed 1990)
11 George, 95 Worksop Rd
12 Golden Ball (formerly The New Inn), 838 Attercliffe Rd (1825–1985)
13 Greyhound, 822 Attercliffe Rd (1830—still open)
14 Hill Top Hotel, 69 Attercliffe Rd (1860–1961)
15 Junction, 354 Brightside Lane
16 King's Head, 709 Attercliffe Rd (1853—still open)
17 Licenced Victuallers, 480 Brightside Lane
18 Lodge Inn, 143 Newhall Rd (open 1870)
19 Mason's Arms, Attercliffe Rd (closed 1862)
20 Midland Hotel, 2 Alfred Rd (1870—still open)
21 Miner's Arms, 750 Attercliffe Rd
22 New Hall Tavern, Sanderson St
23 New Inn, 378 Brightside Lane (1858–1910)
24 Omnibus, 766 Attercliffe Rd
25 Pheasant, 170 Worksop Rd (open 1825)
26 Plough, 20 Milner Rd (open 1825)
27 Plough, 75 Worksop Rd (open 1825)
28 Queen's Head, 660 Attercliffe Rd (1825–1990)
29 Royal George, 498 Brightside Lane (open 1866)
30 Station Inn, 732 Attercliffe Rd (still open)
31 Steam Clock, 352 Brightside Lane (closed 1917)
32 Tramcar, 851 Attercliffe Rd (1868–1961)
33 Traveller's Inn, 784 Attercliffe Rd (1835—still open)
34 Vine Tavern, 49 Newhall Rd (closed 1902)
35 White Hart, 119 Worksop Rd (1825–1992)

Note: Church Street became Worksop Road

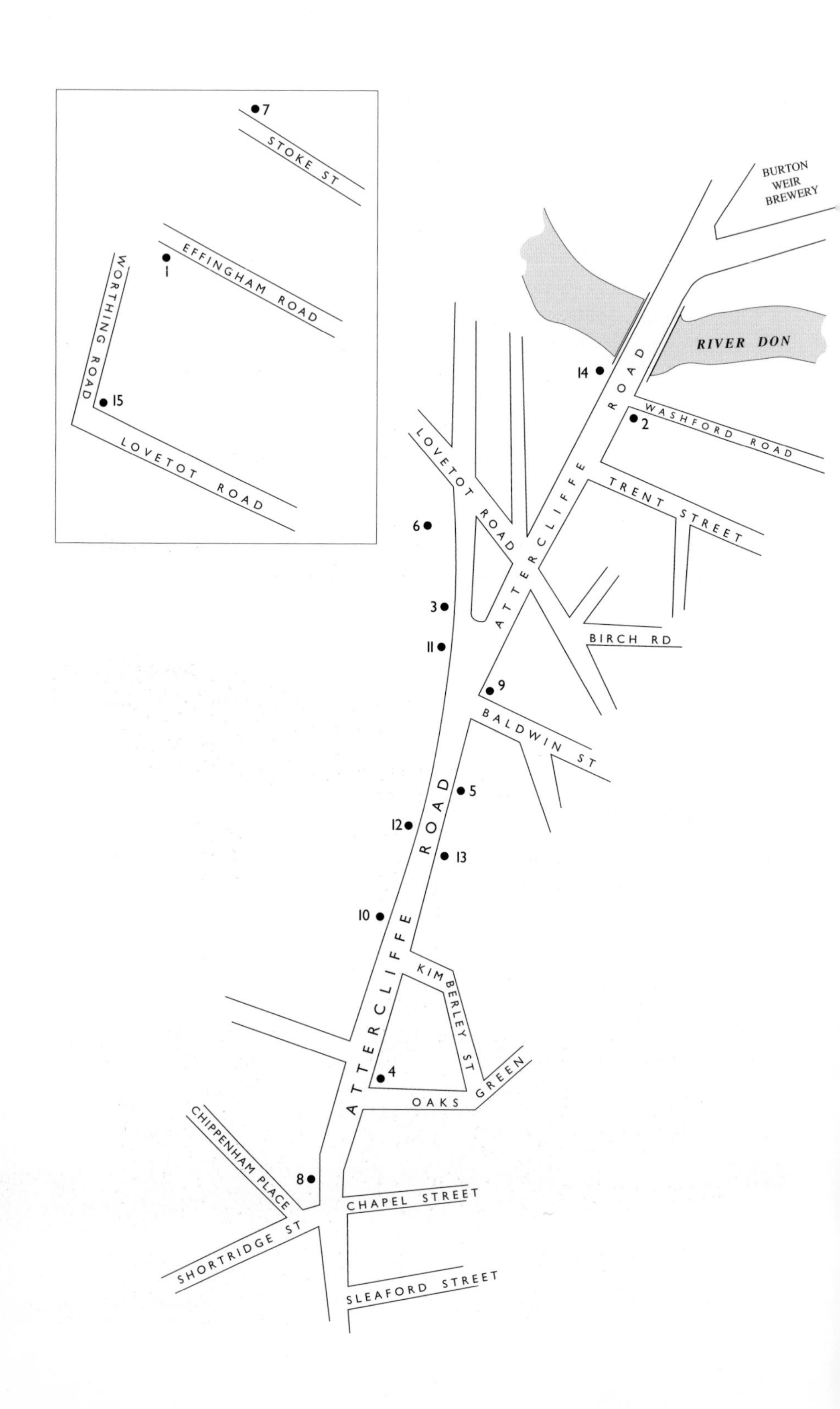

7
STOKE ST
EFFINGHAM ROAD
1
WORTHING ROAD
15
LOVETOT ROAD
BURTON
WEIR
BREWERY
RIVER DON
14
ROAD
WASHFORD ROAD
2
LOVETOT ROAD
ATTERCLIFFE
TRENT STREET
6
3
11
BIRCH RD
9
BALDWIN ST
5
ROAD
12
13
10
ATTERCLIFFE
KIMBERLEY ST
4
OAKS GREEN
CHIPPENHAM PLACE
8
CHAPEL STREET
SHORTRIDGE ST
SLEAFORD STREET

Map 19

1 Baltic Inn, 420 Effingham Rd (open 1833)
2 Bridge Inn, 387 Attercliffe Rd (1862—bombed 1940)
3 Burton Arms, 434 Attercliffe Rd (closed 1920)
4 Carlton, 563 Attercliffe Rd (1845—still open)
5 Dog & Partridge, 575 Attercliffe Rd (1865—still open)
6 Fleur de Lis, off Attercliffe Rd
7 Grey Horse, 25 Stoke St (open 1850)
8 Horse & Jockey, 638 Attercliffe Rd (still open)
9 Old Green Dragon, 469 Attercliffe Rd (open 1774—closed 1950's)
10 Robin Hood, 548 Attercliffe Rd (open 1900)
11 Royal Oak, 484 Attercliffe Rd (1870–1938)
12 Sportsman (formerly The Hope & Anchor), 504 Attercliffe Rd (1870—still open)
13 Victoria, 631 Attercliffe Rd (open 1841)
14 Washford Arms, 380 Attercliffe Rd (1850–1970's, became a chip shop)
15 Woodbourn (or Old Woodbourne Hotel), 2 Lovetot Rd

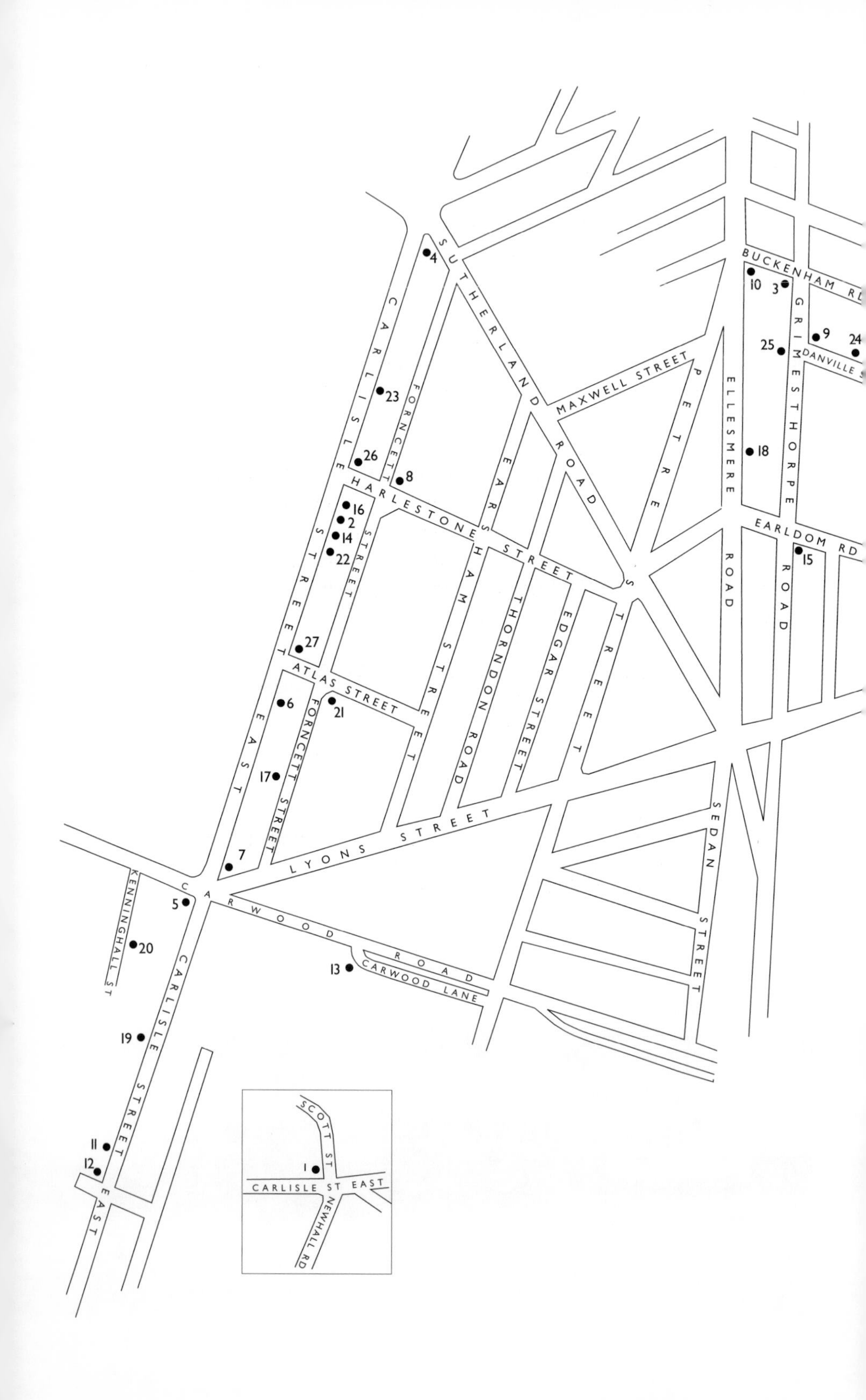
SUTHERLAND ROAD
MAXWELL STREET
PETRE
ELLESMERE ROAD
BUCKENHAM RD
GRIMESTHORPE ROAD
DANVILLE S
CARLISLE STREET EAST
FORNCETT
HARLESTONE STREET
EARSHAM STREET
EARLDOM RD
STREET
ATLAS STREET
FORNCETT STREET
THORNDON ROAD
EDGAR STREET
LYONS STREET
SEDAN STREET
CARWOOD ROAD
CARWOOD LANE
KENNINGHALL ST
CARLISLE STREET
EAST
SCOTT ST
CARLISLE ST EAST
NEWHALL RD

Map 20

1 Alexandra, 549 Carlisle Street East (1865–1974)
2 Atlas, 131 Carlisle Street East (1862–1922)
3 Buckenham Hotel, 62 Grimesthorpe Rd (1876–1976)
4 Carlisle Street Hotel, 5 Carlisle Street East (1864—still open)
5 Carwood, 8 Carlisle Street East (1864–1986)
6 Coach & Horses, 147 Carlisle Street East (1864–1936)
7 Corner Pin, 231 Carlisle Street East (1864—still open)
8 Crown Inn, 87 Forncett St (1865—still open)
9 Danville Hotel, 1 Danville St (1883–1925)
10 Ellesmere Hotel, 55 Ellesmere Rd (open 1865)
11 Engineers, 116 Carlisle Street East (1864–1916)
12 Fair Trades (or Free Trades), 118 Carlisle Street East (1864–1916)
13 Hallcar Tavern, 2 Carwood Lane (or Grove) (still open)
14 Little Atlas, 135 Carlisle Street East (1864–1922)
15 Normanton, 123 Grimesthorpe Rd (1879—still open)
16 Palmerstone Hotel, 129 Carlisle Street East (1864–1926)
17 Pedestrian Tavern, 238 Forncett St (closed 1922)
18 Public Gardens Inn, Ellesmere Rd
19 Railway Tavern, 46 Carlisle Street East (1864–1907)
20 Ram Inn, 15 Kenninghall St (1866–1914)
21 Red Lion, Forncett St (open1864)
22 Rifle Corps Hotel, 137 Carlisle Street East (1860–1958)
23 Rock, 51 Carlisle Street East (1864–1932)
24 Star Inn, 49 Danville St (1883–1960)
25 Tea Gardens (formerly The Gardeners Arms), 90 Grimesthorpe Rd (1850—still open)
26 Woodman Hotel, 87 Carlisle Street East (1864–1935)
27 Wrekin, 143 Carlisle Street East (1864–1936)

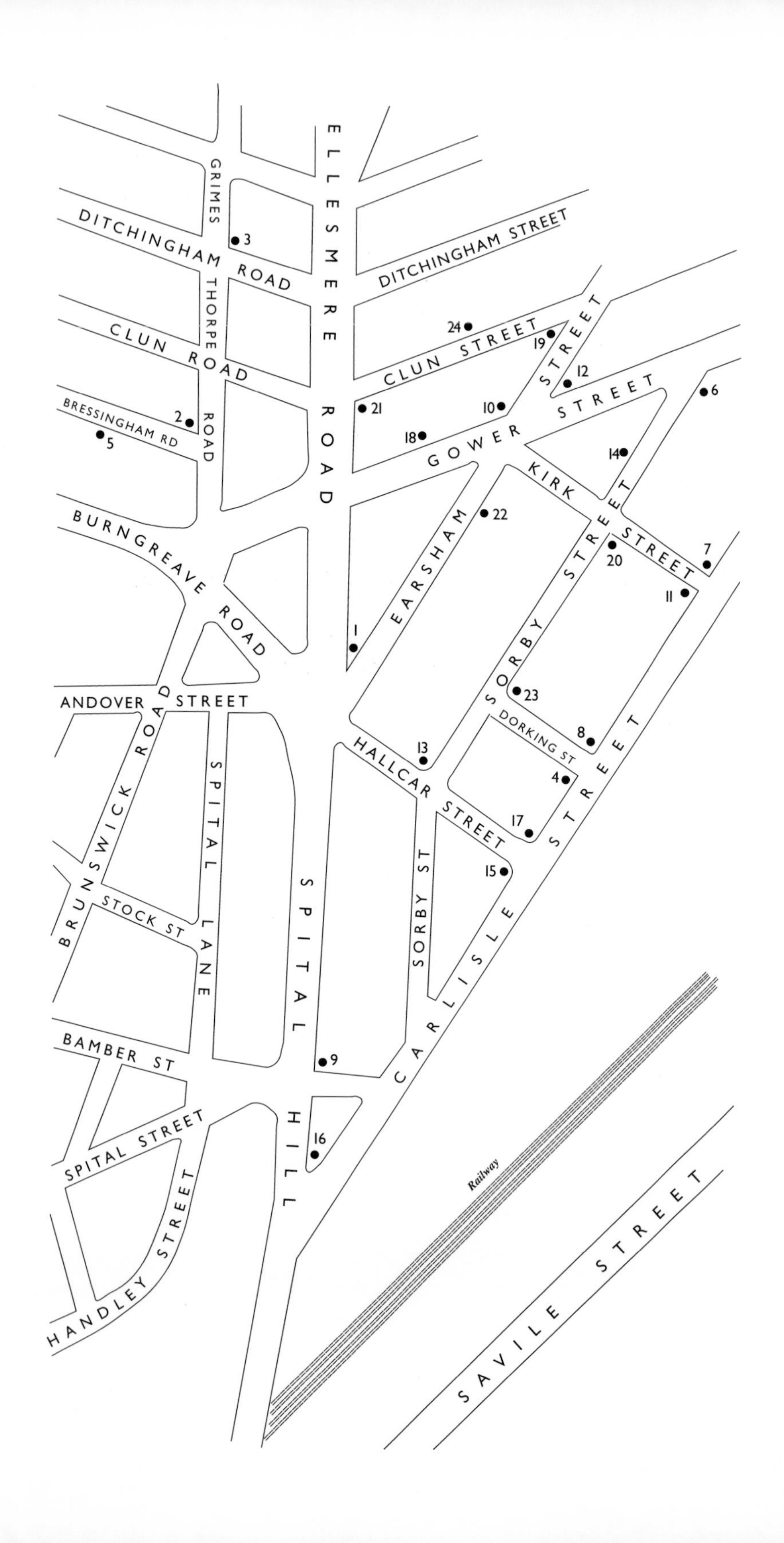
ELLESMERE ROAD
GRIMES
DITCHINGHAM ROAD
DITCHINGHAM STREET
THORPE ROAD
CLUN ROAD
CLUN STREET
BRESSINGHAM RD
BURNGREAVE ROAD
GOWER STREET
KIRK STREET
EARSHAM
SORBY STREET
ANDOVER STREET
BRUNSWICK ROAD
SPITAL LANE
STOCK ST
HALLCAR STREET
DORKING ST
SORBY ST
CARLISLE STREET
SPITAL HILL
BAMBER ST
SPITAL STREET
HANDLEY STREET
Railway
SAVILE STREET
1
2
3
4
5
6
7
8
9
10
11
12
13
14
15
16
17
18
19
20
21
22
23
24

Map 21

1 Albion (became The Golden Perch, now The Old Mill Tavern), 2 Ellesmere Rd (still open)
2 Bressingham Arms, 2 Bressingham Rd (closed 1922)
3 Brunswick, 46 Grimesthorpe Rd (1883–1976)
4 Carlisle Tavern, 67 Carlisle St (1862–1910)
5 Crown Inn, 53 Bressingham Rd
6 Cup, 112 Sorby St (1866–1932)
7 Cyclops, 101 Carlisle St (1864–1922)
8 Dusty Miller, 69 Carlisle St (1862–1932)
9 East House (now Morrissey's East House), 18 Spital Hill (1860—still open)
10 Gower Arms, 47 Gower St (still open)
11 Grapes Inn, 99 Carlisle St (1862–1898)
12 Grapes Inn (or Rovers Rest), 51 Gower St (1868—still open)
13 Guards Rest, 41 Sorby St (1879–1971)
14 Huntsman Inn, 101 Sorby St (1860–1932)
15 Locomotive (became Burngreave Liberal Club), 49 Carlisle St (1862–1932)
16 Midland, 2 Spital Hill (1862–1972)
17 Miller's Arms, 51 Carlisle St (1862–1940)
18 Pheasant, 41 Gower St (open 1879)
19 Puddler's Arms, 73 Earsham St (open1870)
20 Rising Sun, 88 Sorby St (open 1879)
21 Robin Hood, 46 Ellesmere Rd (still open)
22 Royal Oak, 60 Earsham St (1864—still open)
23 Staffordshire Arms, 38 Sorby St (1864—still open)
24 Why Not Inn, 27 Clun St (open 1864)

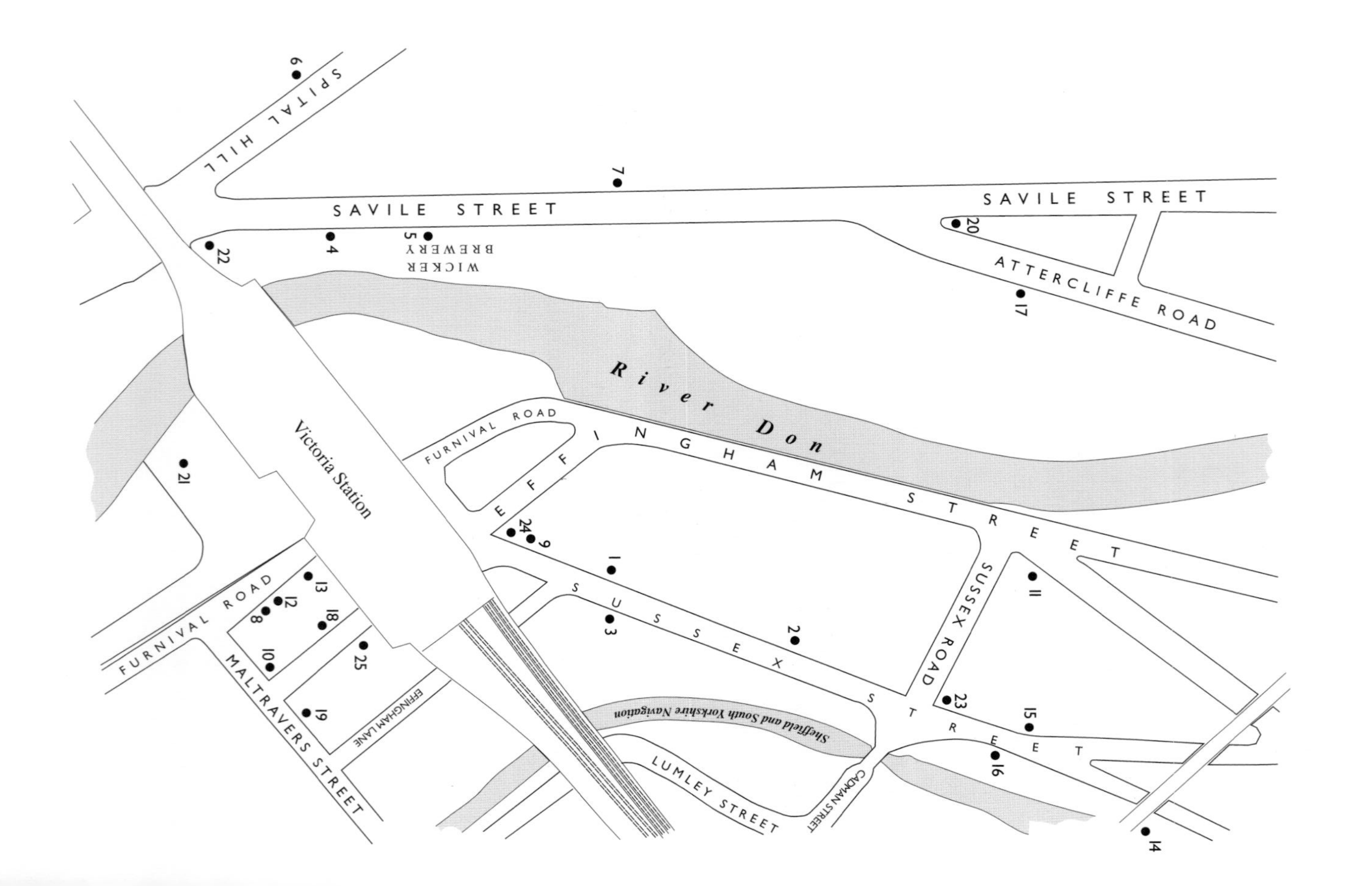
SPITAL HILL
SAVILE STREET
SAVILE STREET
WICKER BREWERY
ATTERCLIFFE ROAD
River Don
Victoria Station
FURNIVAL ROAD
EFFINGHAM STREET
SUSSEX STREET
SUSSEX ROAD
FURNIVAL ROAD
MALTRAVERS STREET
EFFINGHAM LANE
Sheffield and South Yorkshire Navigation
LUMLEY STREET
CADMAN STREET
1
2
3
4
5
6
7
8
9
10
11
12
13
14
15
16
17
18
19
20
21
22
23
24
25

Map 22

1 Effingham Arms, 19 Sussex St
2 Engineer's Arms (Providence Inn), 45 Sussex St
3 Gas Tank Inn, 8 Sussex St (1841–1901)
4 George Inn, 20 Savile St (closed 1920)
5 Hole in the Wall (formerly Wicker Brewery Hotel), 70 Savile St (closed 1992)
6 Lodge Inn, 47 Spital Hill (1852–1969)
7 Midland Railway Inn, 119 Savile St
8 New Bull and Oak, 26 Furnival Rd (open 1833)
9 New Gas Tavern, 5 Sussex St
10 New Inn, 23 Maltravers St
11 New Inn, 2 Effingham Rd
12 New Market Inn (Station Inn), 28 Furnival Rd
13 Norfolk House, 38 Furnival Rd
14 North Pole Inn (now offices), 62 Sussex St
15 Parkside Inn, 73 Sussex St
16 Prince of Wales, 103 Sussex St
17 Queen, 20 Attercliffe Rd (closed 1930)
18 Sheaf Inn, 11 Effingham Rd
19 Sportsman's Inn, 31 Maltravers St
20 Twelve O'Clock Tavern (or Inn), 1 Attercliffe Rd (open 1825)
21 Victoria Station Hotel (Royal Victoria), Victoria Station Rd (still open)
22 Victoria Arches Tavern, 2 Savile St (changed to The Cricket Ball Inn, 1914) (1860–1918)
23 Vulcan Tavern (or Inn), 53 Sussex St
24 Waterman's Rest, 1 Sussex St
25 White Horse, 18 Effingham St

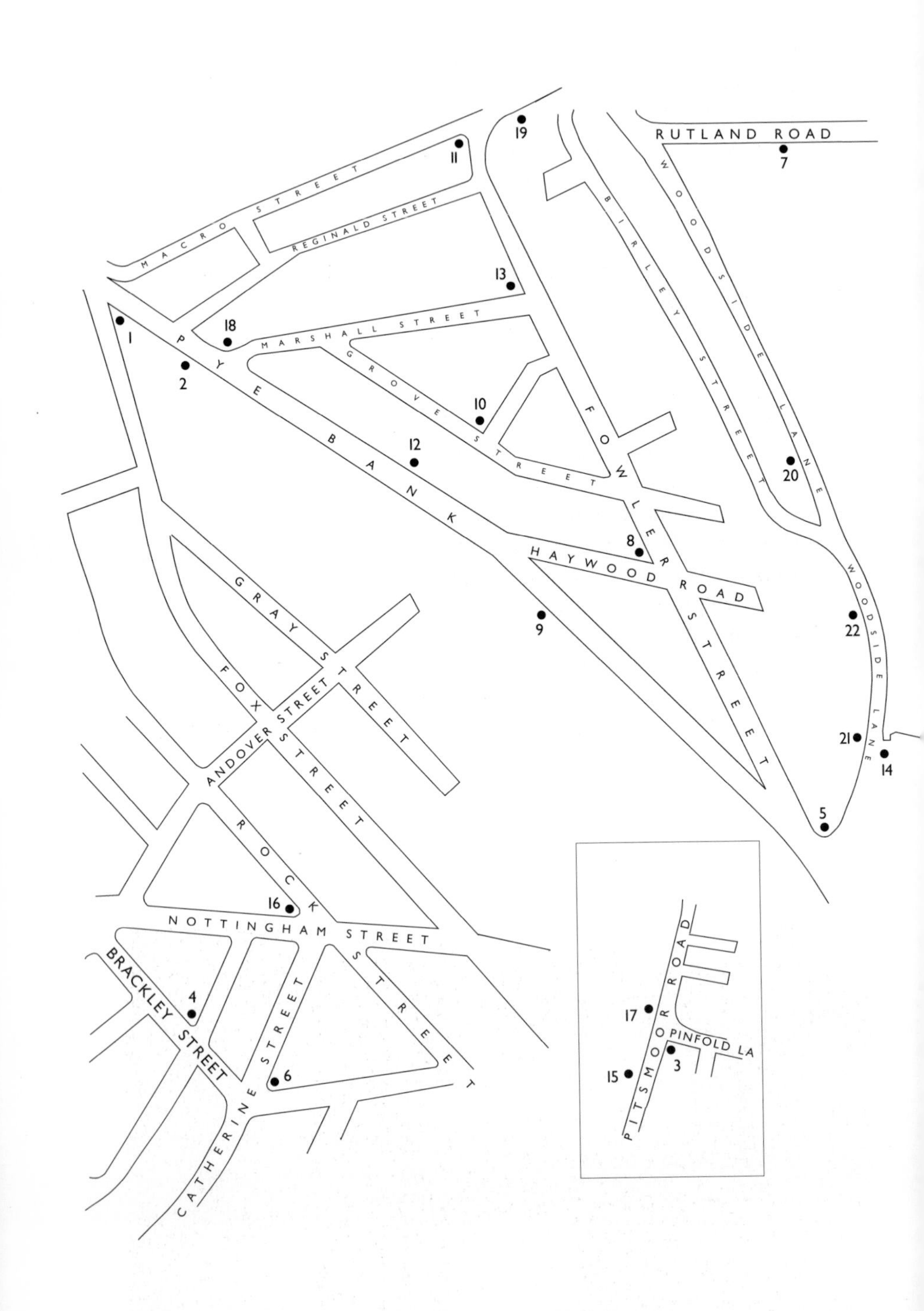

RUTLAND ROAD
MACRO STREET
REGINALD STREET
MARSHALL STREET
GROVE STREET
PYE BANK
BIRLEY STREET
WOODSIDE LANE
FOWLER STREET
HAYWOOD ROAD
GRAY STREET
FOX STREET
ANDOVER STREET
ROCK STREET
NOTTINGHAM STREET
BRACKLEY STREET
CATHERINE STREET
PITSMOOR ROAD
PINFOLD LA
1
2
3
4
5
6
7
8
9
10
11
12
13
14
15
16
17
18
19
20
21
22

Map 23

1 Ball, 50 Pye Bank (1825–1957)
2 Barrel, 86 Pye Bank
3 Bay Horse, 463 Pitsmoor Rd (still open)
4 Brackley Arms, 14 Brackley St
5 Bridgefield, Fowler St (closed 1960)
6 Catherine Arms, Catherine St (still open)
7 Forest Inn, Rutland Rd (last beerhouse in Sheffield)(still open)
8 Fowler Street Hotel, 37 Haywood St
9 Fox and Duck, 174 Pye Bank (still open)
10 Grove, 49 Grove St
11 Locomotive, 2 Fowler St
12 Marshall Tavern, 133 Pye Bank (closed 1960)
13 Old Albion (Guard's Rest), 38 Fowler St
14 Pear Tree, 163 Woodside Lane
15 Pitsmoor, 448 Pitsmoor Rd (still open)
16 Rock House, 170 Rock St (still open)
17 Toll Gate, 408 Pitsmoor Rd (still open)
18 Tunnel, 89 Pye Bank
19 Wellington, 78 Macro St
20 White Lion, 54 Woodside Lane
21 Woodman, 158 Woodside Lane (1833–1962)
22 Woodside Tavern (became working mans club), 126 Woodside Lane (closed 1940)

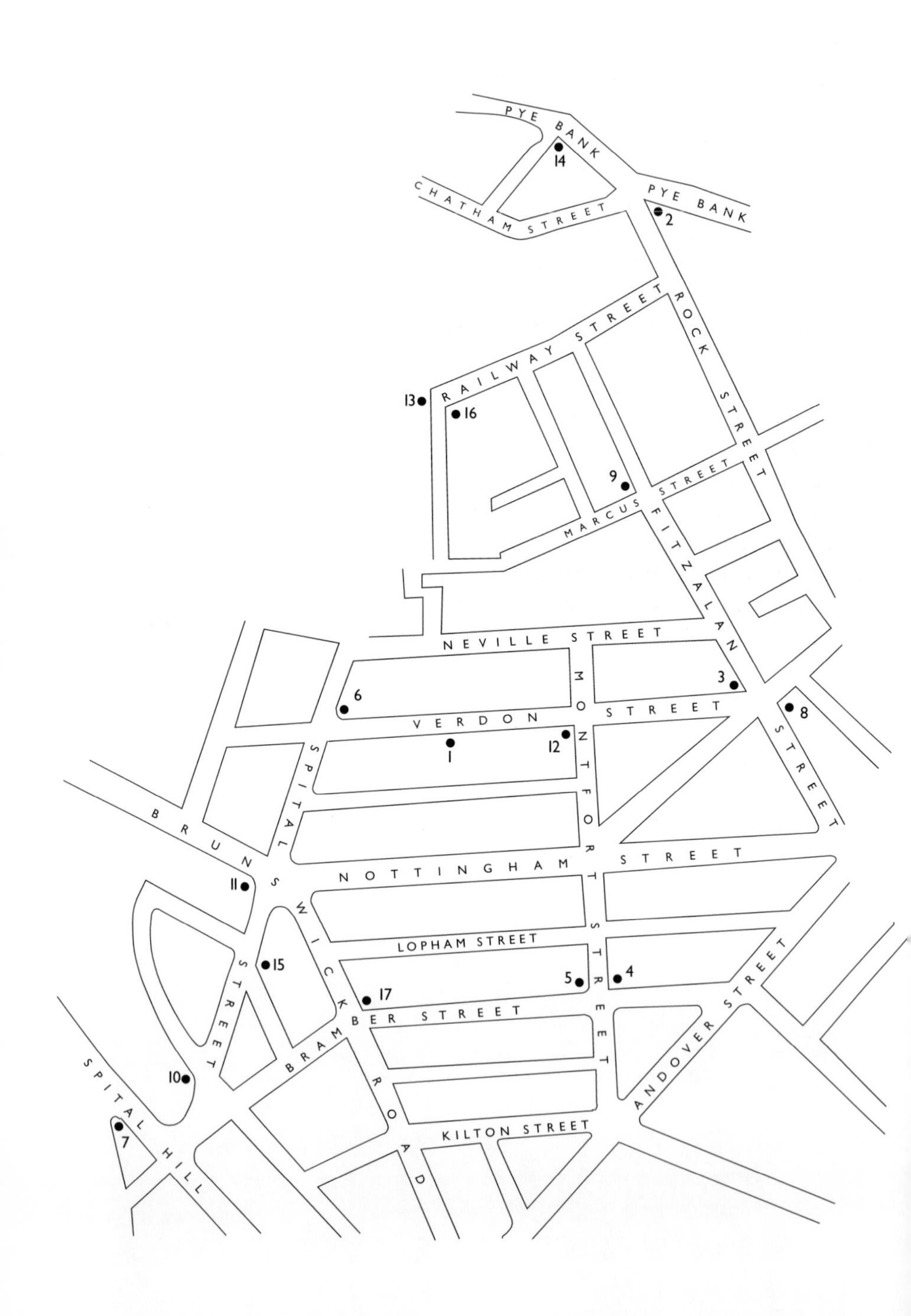
PYE BANK
14
CHATHAM STREET
PYE BANK
2
RAILWAY STREET
ROCK STREET
13
16
9
MARCUS STREET
FITZALAN
NEVILLE STREET
6
3
8
VERDON
MONTFORT STREET
STREET
1
12
SPITAL
STREET
BRUNSWICK ROAD
NOTTINGHAM STREET
11
LOPHAM STREET
15
5
4
17
STREET
BRAMBER STREET
ANDOVER STREET
10
SPITAL HILL
7
KILTON STREET

Map 24

1 Albion, 46 Verdon St (1855–1967)
2 Barrel, 52 Pye Bank
3 Bellevue Hotel, 116 Fitzalan St
4 Bowling Tavern, 53 Montford St (closed 1974)
5 Brunswick House, 50 Montford St
6 Cromwell View, 80 Spital St
7 East House (now Morrissey's East House), 18 Spital Hill (1860—still open)
8 Fitzalan Inn, 123 Fitzalan St (closed 1966)
9 Fitzalan Tavern, 58 Fitzalan St
10 Griffin Inn, 5 Spital St (closed 1966)
11 Merry Heart, 110 Spital St
12 New Inn, 10 Montford St
13 New Ball Inn, 18 Osborne St
14 Rock Inn, 42 Pye Bank (closed 1958)
15 Spital Inn, 24 Spital St
16 Sportsman, 155 Railway St (closed 1960)
17 Vine, 81 Brunswick Rd (closed 1961)

Note : The following pubs were known to be in this area though the actual location is unknown:

Ball, Fitzalan St
Blue Ball, 25 Pye Bank (open 1833)
Iron Man, off Pye Bank

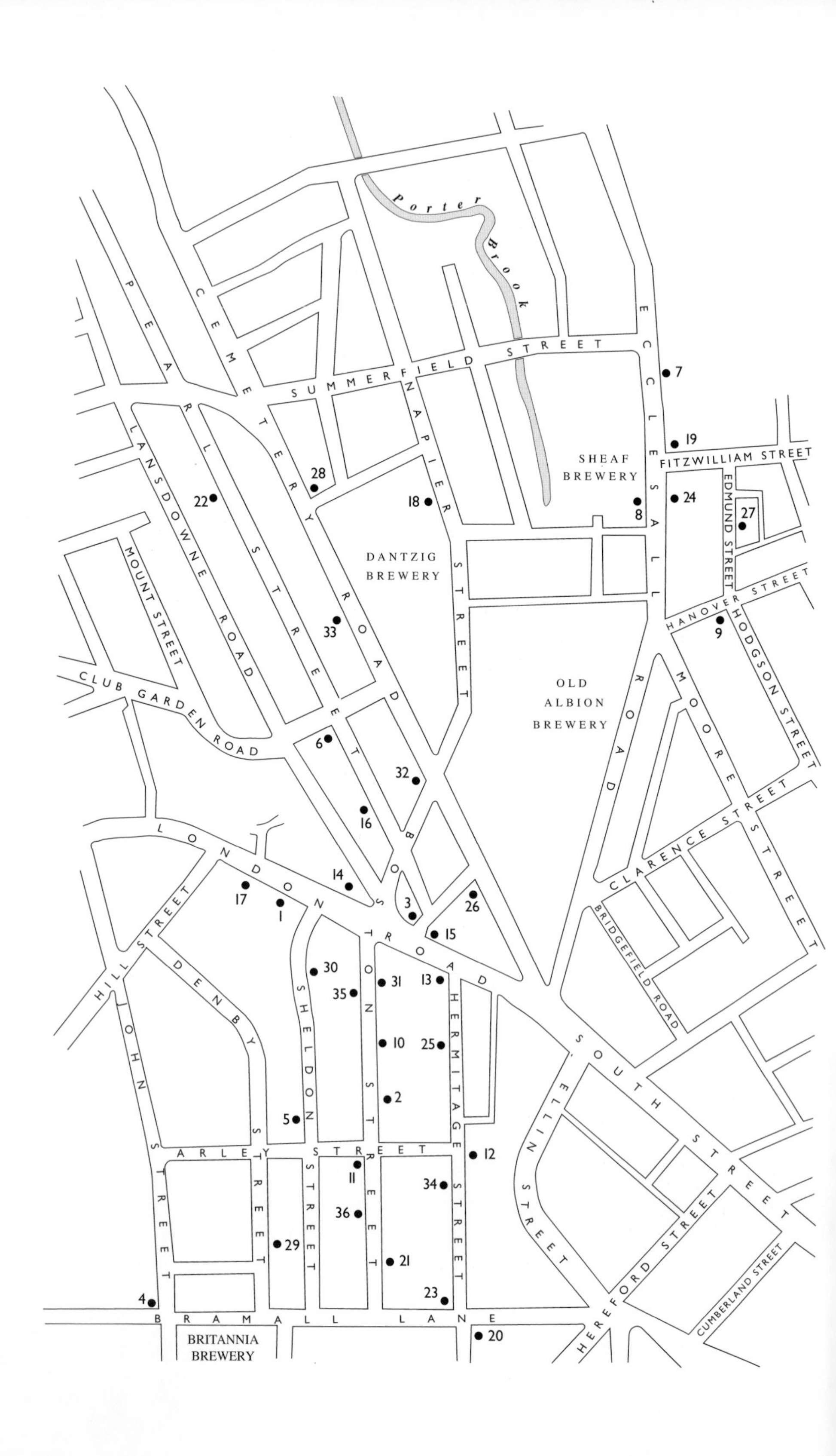
Porter Brook
SUMMERFIELD STREET
ECCLESALL ROAD
FITZWILLIAM STREET
SHEAF BREWERY
EDMUND STREET
PEARL STREET
CEMETERY ROAD
NAPIER STREET
LANSDOWNE ROAD
MOUNT STREET
DANTZIG BREWERY
HANOVER STREET
HODGSON STREET
MOORE STREET
OLD ALBION BREWERY
CLUB GARDEN ROAD
LONDON ROAD
BOSTON STREET
CLARENCE STREET
BRIDGEFIELD ROAD
HILL STREET
DENBY STREET
JOHN STREET
SHELDON STREET
HERMITAGE STREET
SOUTH STREET
ELLIN STREET
ARLEY STREET
HEREFORD STREET
CUMBERLAND STREET
BRAMALL LANE
BRITANNIA BREWERY
1
2
3
4
5
6
7
8
9
10
11
12
13
14
15
16
17
18
19
20
21
22
23
24
25
26
27
28
29
30
31
32
33
34
35
36

Map 25

1 Albion Hotel, 75 London Rd (still open)
2 Angler's Rest, 46 New George St (1841–1901)
3 Boston (Derby), 10 Lansdowne Rd (closed 1963)
4 Cricketer's Arms, 106 Bramall Lane (still open)
5 Cricketer's Inn, 37 Sheldon St (open 1839)
6 Daniel's Rest, 29 Cliffe St
7 Devonshire Arms, 118 Ecclesall Rd (still open)
8 Earl Grey, 97 Ecclesall Rd
9 Ecclesall Tavern, Hanover St
10 George Hotel, New George St
11 George Street Tavern, 1 Arley St
12 Greyhound Tavern, 38 Hermitage St
13 Hermitage Inn, 11 London Rd (Harvey's Tavern, 1832, now Harvey's Bar, still open)
14 Horse and Groom, 80 London Rd (1833–1916)
15 Lansdowne, 2 Lansdowne Rd (closed 1991)
16 Mason's Arms, 47 Pearl St (1858–1960)
17 Milton Arms, 81 London Rd
18 Napier Hotel, 95 Napier St (still open)
19 New Inn, 108 Ecclesall Rd
20 Norfolk Arms, 1 St. Mary's Rd
21 Old Mill Tavern, New George St (1833–1900)
22 Pearl Street Tavern, 93 Pearl Street
23 Queen Adelaide, 32 Bramall Lane (open 1835)
24 Ram Hotel, 100 Ecclesall Rd
25 Rising Sun, 67 Hermitage St
26 Royal Oak, 17 Cemetery Rd (still open)
27 Sheldon Inn, 10 Edmond St
28 Solferino, 130 Cemetery Rd
29 Sportsman Inn, 10 Denby St (still open)
30 Sportsman Inn, 84 Sheldon St
31 Spring Tavern, 74 New George St
32 Star, 39 Cemetery Rd
33 Star of Brunswick, 65 Cemetery Rd
34 Star of Lemont, 29 Hermitage Rd
35 Talbot, 51 New George St
36 Umpire, 9 New George St

Note: New George Street became Boston Street

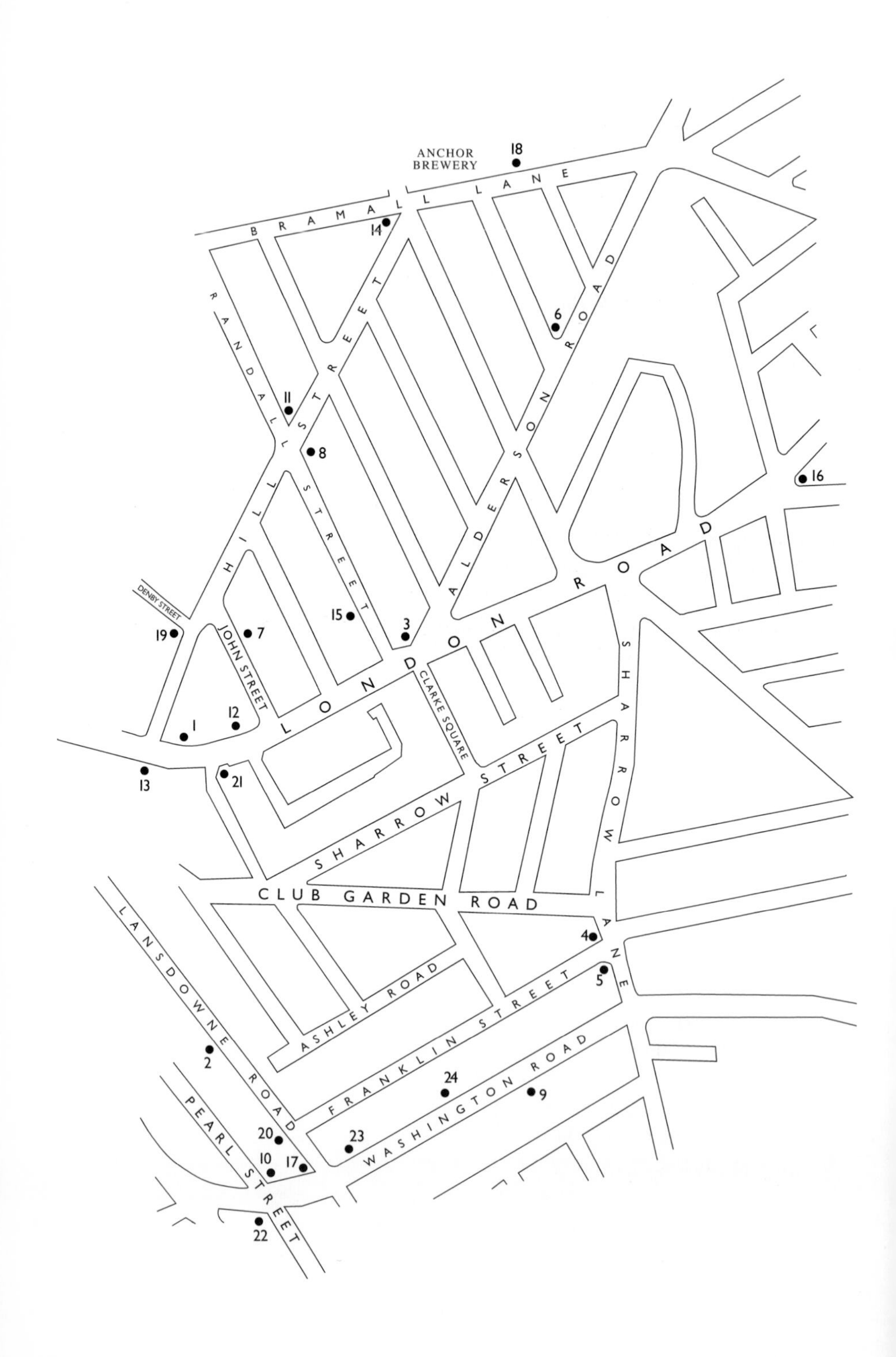
ANCHOR BREWERY
18
BRAMALL LANE
14
RANDALL STREET
HILL STREET
ALDERSON ROAD
6
11
8
DENBY STREET
19
JOHN STREET
7
15
3
16
LONDON ROAD
CLARKE SQUARE
SHARROW LANE
1
12
13
21
SHARROW STREET
CLUB GARDEN ROAD
4
5
LANSDOWNE ROAD
ASHLEY ROAD
FRANKLIN STREET
2
24
9
WASHINGTON ROAD
PEARL STREET
20
23
10
17
22

Map 26

1 Barrel, 123 London Rd (1882—still open)
2 Club Gardens Inn, 60 Lansdowne Rd (1833–1967)
3 Cremone, 155 London Rd (1833—still open)
4 Cross Guns (Great Gun), 115 Frankin St (still open)
5 Franklin Hotel, 118 Sharrow Lane (closed 1970)
6 Golden Lion, 69 Alderson Rd (still open)
7 Great Britain, 28 John St
8 Harwood House, 82 Hill St (open 1841)
9 Industry Inn, 130 Washington Rd
10 Mackenzie Tavern, 189 Cemetery Rd
11 Old Albion, 103 Hill St
12 Old Crown Inn, 137 London Rd (still open)
13 Pheasant, 96 London Rd (still open)
14 Railway Hotel, 184 Bramall Lane (still open)
15 Randall Hotel, 29 Randall St
16 Royal, 1 Abbeydale Rd (still open)
17 Royal Oak, 136 Lansdowne Rd (1860–1967)
18 Sheaf House Hotel, 329 Bramall Lane (1816—still open)
19 Sheldon, 27 Hill St (1841—still open)
20 Sun, 110 Lansdowne Rd
21 Tramway, 112 London Rd (still open)
22 Vine, 162 Cemetery Rd (still open)
23 Washington, 23 Washington Rd
24 Victoria, 115 Washington Rd

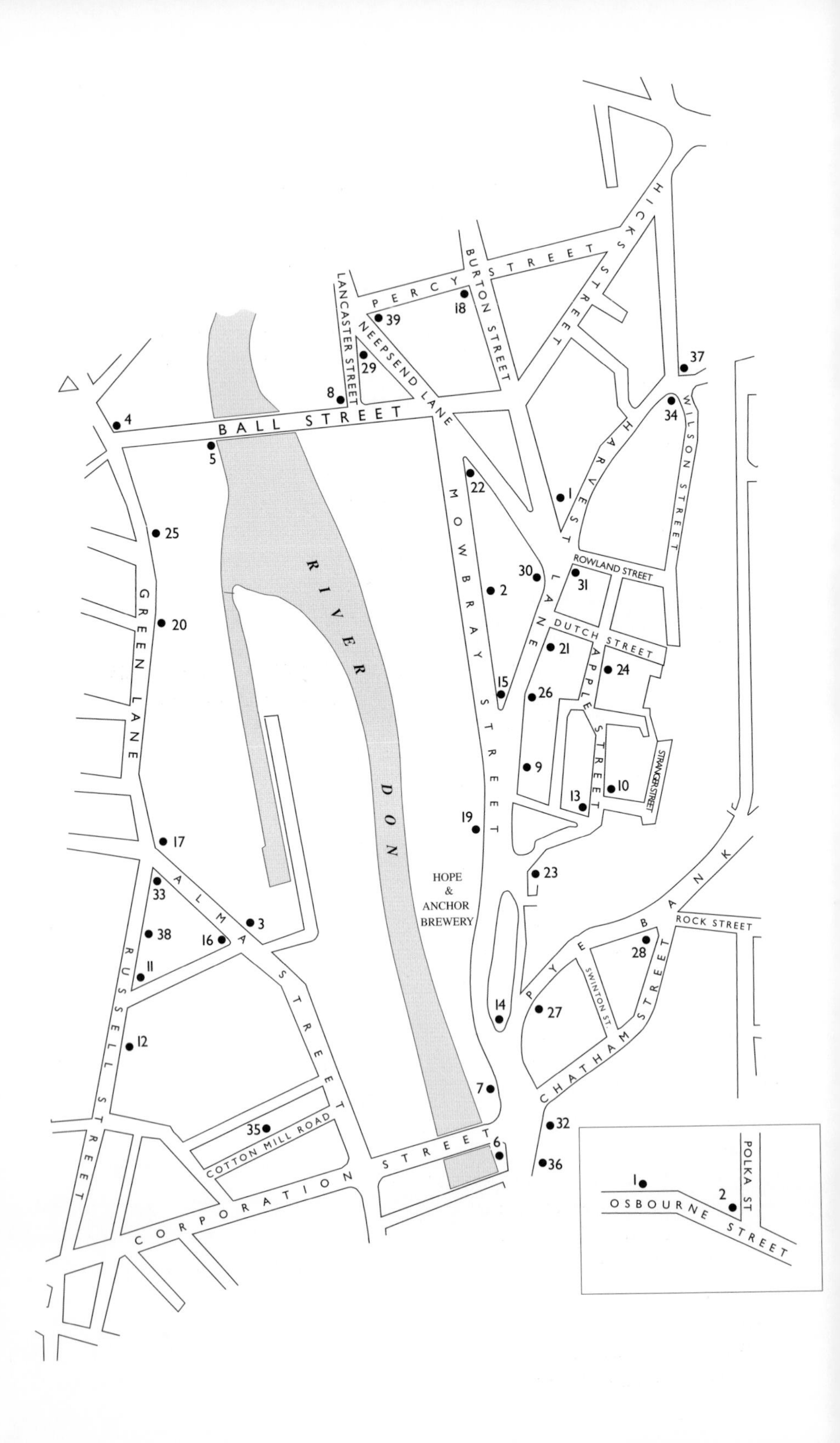

HICKS STREET
PERCY STREET
BURTON STREET
LANCASTER STREET
NEEPSEND LANE
BALL STREET
RIVER DON
HARVEST LANE
WILSON STREET
ROWLAND STREET
MOWBRAY STREET
LANE
DUTCH STREET
APPLE STREET
STRANGER STREET
GREEN LANE
ALMA STREET
RUSSELL STREET
HOPE & ANCHOR BREWERY
PYE BANK
ROCK STREET
SWINTON ST.
CHATHAM STREET
COTTON MILL ROAD
CORPORATION STREET
OSBOURNE STREET
POLKA ST

Map 27

1 Acorn, 20 Burton Rd (closed 1912, became a boys club)
2 Adelaide Tavern, 48 Mowbray St (closed 1924)
3 Alma (now The Fat Cat), 23 Alma St (still open)
4 Ball Inn, 84 Green Lane (open 1833)
5 Boatman, 20 Ball St
6 Bridge Inn (or Bridgehouse Inn), 181 Nursery St (open 1825)
7 Brown Cow (became Morrissey's Riverside Inn, 1995), 11 Mowbray St (still open)
8 Cardigan, 47 Ball St
9 Crown Inn, 52 Harvest Lane (1833–1902)
10 Eagle Tavern, 10 Orchard St (closed 1912)
11 Ebenezer Tavern, 42 Russell St (closed 1905)
12 Engineers, Russell St
13 Greaves Hotel, 23 Orchard St (1796–1925)
14 Hope and Anchor Hotel, Mowbray St (open 1833)
15 Industry Inn, 2 Mowbray St
16 Inkerman Tavern, 12 Alma St
17 King William (possibly once King William 1V), 1 Alma St (open 1825)
18 Malton Hotel, 35 Burton St (closed and demolished in 1980's)
19 Mowbray Inn, Mowbray St
20 Napoleon Tavern, 34 Green Lane (1825–1912)
21 New Inn, 94 Harvest Lane (closed 1959)
22 Norfolk Hotel, 64 Mowbray St
23 Old Harrow, 34 Harvest Lane (closed 1959)
24 Pheasant, Apple St (closed 1919)
25 Pheasant, 50 Green Lane
26 Redford Arms, 88 Harvest Lane
27 Red Lion(or Ball Inn), 34 Pye Bank
28 Rock Inn, 42 Pye Bank (closed 1958)
29 Royal Oak, 12 Lancaster St
30 Sawmaker's Arms, 1 Neepsend Lane (closed 1966)
31 Scissorsmith's Arms, 114 Harvest Lane (closed 1919)
32 Sportsman, 14 Bridgehouses (open 1825)
33 Spotted Cow, 70 Russell St
34 Stag, 2 Wilson St
35 Union Tavern, Cotton Mill Rd (open 1833)
36 Union,12 Bridgehouses (open 1833)
37 Wheatsheaf, 149 Harvest Lane
38 White Hart, 62 Russell St (now The Kelham Island Tavern) (still open)
39 Woolpack, 2 Percy St

Inset

1 Ball, 21 Osbourne Street
2 Crown Inn, Polka Street

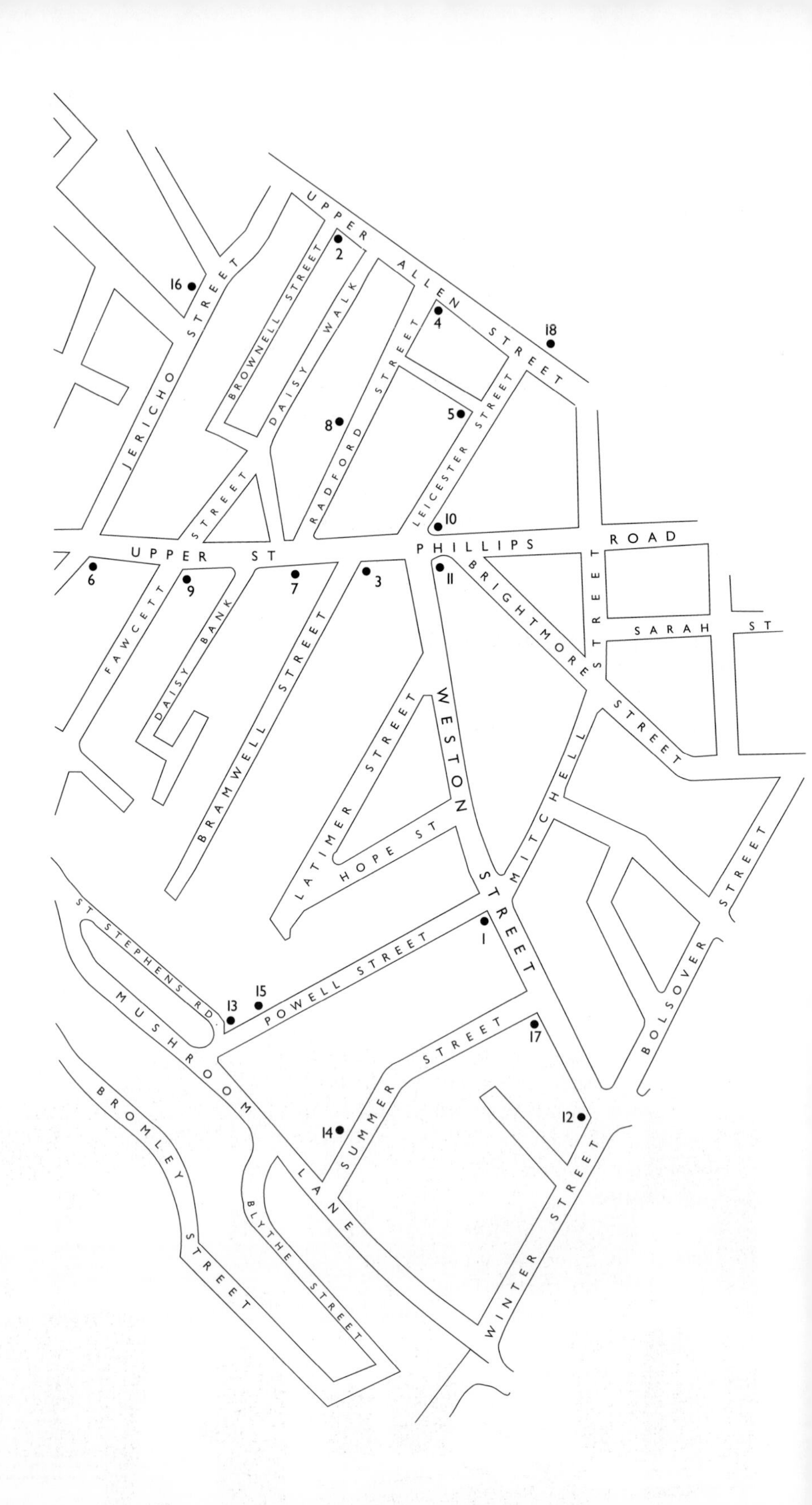
UPPER ALLEN STREET
JERICHO STREET
BROWNELL STREET
DAISY WALK
RADFORD STREET
LEICESTER STREET
UPPER ST
PHILLIPS ROAD
BRIGHTMORE STREET
SARAH ST
STREET
FAWCETT
DAISY BANK
BRAMWELL STREET
LATIMER STREET
WESTON STREET
HOPE ST
MITCHELL STREET
BOLSOVER STREET
ST STEPHENS RD.
POWELL STREET
MUSHROOM LANE
SUMMER STREET
BROMLEY STREET
BLYTHE STREET
WINTER STREET
1
2
3
4
5
6
7
8
9
10
11
12
13
14
15
16
17
18

Map 28

1. Bathfield Hotel, 80 Weston St (still open)
2. Black Horse, 180 Upper Allen St (1833–1960)
3. Bramwell, 99 Upper St Phillips Rd (closed 1958)
4. Brown Cow, 1 Radford St
5. Falcon, 18 Leicester St
6. Hammond, 143 Upper St Phillip's Rd (closed 1958)
7. Harp Tavern, 109 Upper St Phillip's Rd (1833–1920)
8. Old House at Home (became St. Phillip's Club), 34 Radford St (open1796)
9. Prince of Wales, 127 Upper St Phillips Rd
10. Rocket Inn, 106 Upper St. Phillip's Rd (1830–1920)
11. Salutation, 85 Upper St Phillip's Rd (closed 1965)
12. Star and Garter, 82 Winter St (still open)
13. St Stephen's Tavern, St Stephen's Rd
14. Summer Tavern, Summer St
15. Sunny Bank Hotel, 74 Powell St
16. Victoria, 42 Jericho St
17. Weston Park Hotel, 96 Weston St
18. Woolsack, 277 Upper Allen St

Note : The following pub was known to be in this area though the actual location is unknown:

Queen's Head Hotel, 1 Queen St, Portmahon

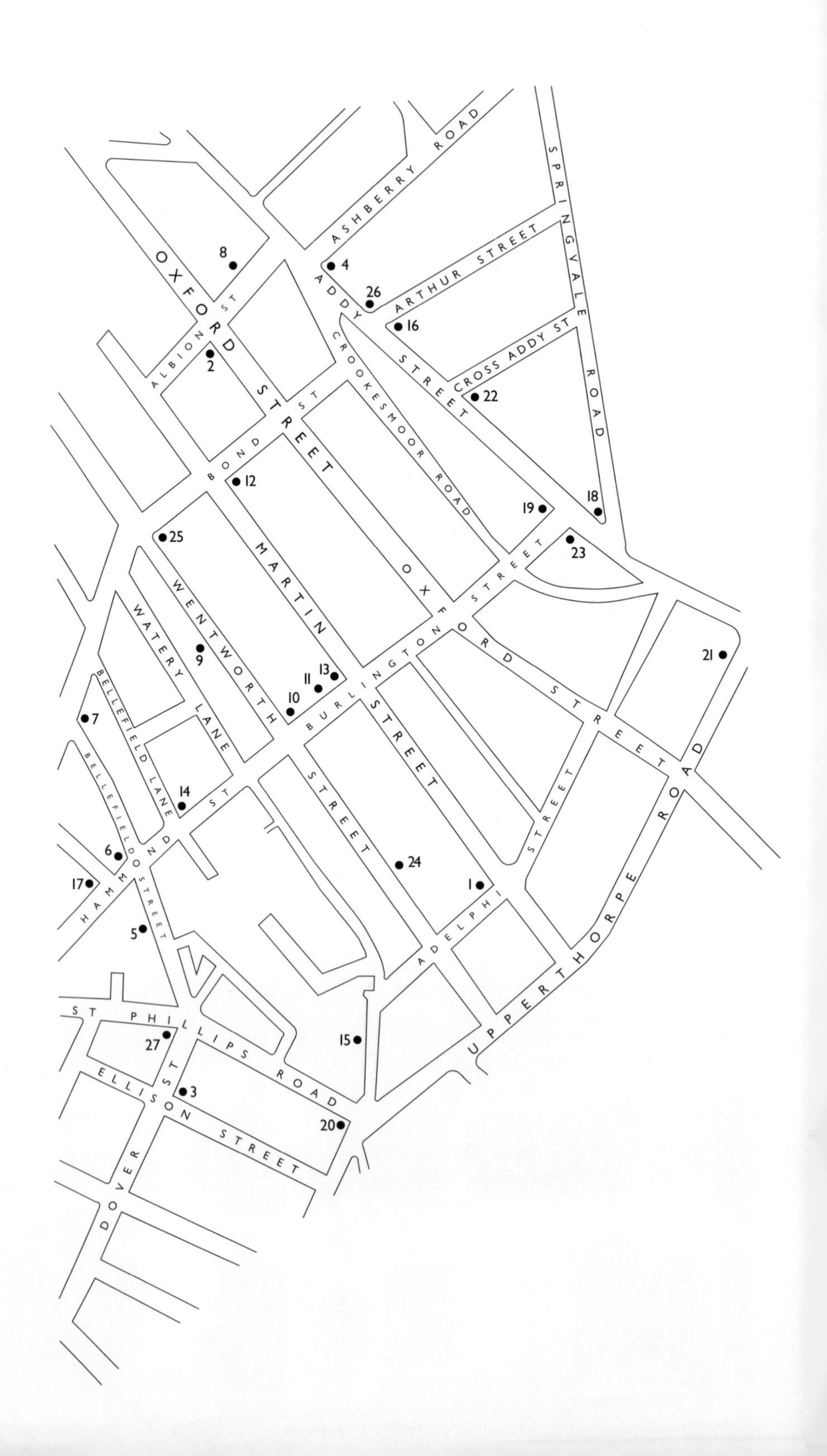

OXFORD STREET
ALBION ST
ASHBERRY ROAD
ADDY STREET
ARTHUR STREET
SPRINGVALE ROAD
CROSS ADDY ST
CROOKESMOOR ROAD
BOND ST
MARTIN STREET
OXFORD STREET
BURLINGTON STREET
WENTWORTH STREET
WATERY LANE
BELLEFIELD LANE
BELLEFIELD STREET
HAMMOND ST
STREET
ADELPHI STREET
UPPERTHORPE ROAD
ST PHILLIPS ROAD
ELLISON STREET
DOVER ST
1
2
3
4
5
6
7
8
9
10
11
12
13
14
15
16
17
18
19
20
21
22
23
24
25
26
27

Map 29

1 Adelphi, 15 Martin St (closed 1917)
2 Albion, 26 Oxford St
3 Alexandra, 23 Dover St (closed 1917)
4 Ashberry, 1 Ashberry St
5 Bellefield Inn, 14 Bellefield St (1830–1962)
6 Bellefield Hotel, 37 Bellefield St (1825–1962)
7 Bellefield House, 70 Fawcett St
8 Bloomsberry, 37 Albion St (open 1838)
9 Bricklayers Arms, 77 Wentworth St
10 Burlington Hotel, 7 Burlington St (closed 1957)
11 Corner Pin, 23 Burlington St (open 1833)
12 Hallamshire, 124 Martin St
13 King's Head Hotel, 105 Martin St
14 New Inn, 2 Bellefield Lane (open 1841)
15 Nottingham House, 23 Watery St
16 Royal, 2 Arthur St
17 Royal Albion, Hammond St/Finlay St
18 Scarborough Arms, 34 Addy St (1841—still open)
19 Spread Eagle, 37 Addy St (closed 1960)
20 St Phillip's Tavern, 228 St Phillip's Rd (open 1825)
21 Upperthorpe Hotel, 137 Upperthorpe Rd (1833—still open)
22 Victoria Hotel, 80 Addey St
23 Vine Hotel, 35 Addey St
24 Wentworth House, 18 Wentworth St
25 Wentworth Inn, 156 Wentworth St
26 Whitby Hotel, 106 Addey St (1846–1960)
27 White Hart, 140 St Phillip's Rd (still open)

Note : The following pub was known to be in this area though the actual location is unknown:

Queen's Head Hotel, Portmahon

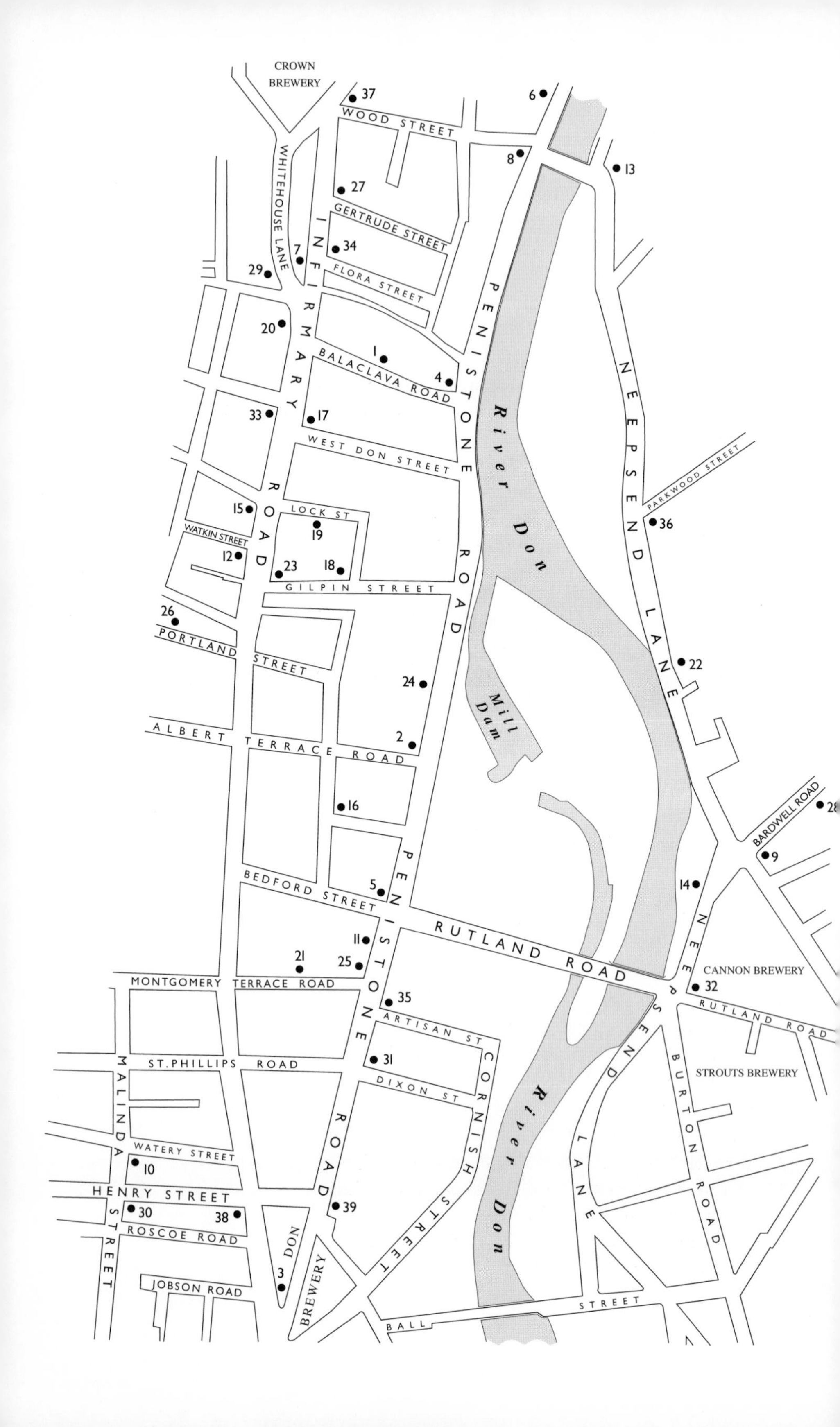

CROWN BREWERY
WOOD STREET
WHITEHOUSE LANE
GERTRUDE STREET
INFIRMARY ROAD
FLORA STREET
PENISTONE ROAD
BALACLAVA ROAD
WEST DON STREET
River Don
NEEPSEND LANE
PARKWOOD STREET
LOCK ST
WATKIN STREET
GILPIN STREET
PORTLAND STREET
Mill Dam
ALBERT TERRACE ROAD
BARDWELL ROAD
BEDFORD STREET
RUTLAND ROAD
CANNON BREWERY
MONTGOMERY TERRACE ROAD
ARTISAN ST
CORNISH STREET
STROUTS BREWERY
ST.PHILLIPS ROAD
DIXON ST
MALINDA STREET
BURTON ROAD
WATERY STREET
HENRY STREET
ROSCOE ROAD
DON BREWERY
JOBSON ROAD
BALL STREET

Map 30

1 Adam and Eve, 17 Balaclava St
2 Albert Hotel, 117 Penistone Rd (1840–1913)
3 Bank Inn, 1 Penistone Rd
4 Barrack Tavern, 217 Penistone Rd (open 1825)
5 Bedford Hotel (became a cafe, 1913), 71 Penistone Rd (closed 1903)
6 Bridge Inn, 317 Penistone Rd (closed 1913)
7 Butcher's Arms, 1 Langsett Rd (closed 1959)
8 Clifton (formerly Army Stores), 281 Penistone Rd (open 1845)
9 Crown, 116 Neepsend Lane (rebuilt adjacent site of Rutland Hotel, closed 1992—offices)
10 Denison Arms, 33 Watery St (1845—still open)
11 Don Inn, 67 Penistone Rd (open 1833)
12 Dragon Inn, 139 Infirmary Rd (closed 1959)
13 Farfield (became The Owl, reverted to The Farfield), 376 Neepsend Lane (still open)
14 Gardener's Rest, 105 Neepsend Lane (still open)
15 Gatefield, 167 Infirmary Rd (1845–1959)
16 General Gordon Inn, 30 Cross Bedford St
17 George IV, 216 Infirmary Rd (1833–1992, re-opened 1994)
18 George Street Tavern, 1 Cross Gilpin St
19 Grapes, 15 Lock St
20 Kelvin Grove, 227 Infirmary Rd (1833–1959)
21 Montgomery Hotel, 1 Montgomery Terrace
22 Neepsend Tavern, 144 Neepsend Lane (1839–1974, became sauna suite)
23 Old Five Alls, 168 Infirmary Rd
24 Old Light Horseman, 155 Penistone Rd (closed 1991)
25 Owl, 51 Penistone Rd
26 Portland Arms, 59 Portland St
27 Princess Royal, 28 Langsett Rd
28 Prince of Wales, 12 Bardwell St
29 Queen, 1 Whitehouse Lane
30 Rosco Tavern, 27 Henry St (open 1841)
31 Royal Lancer, 66 Penistone Rd (closed 1988)
32 Rutland Hotel, 80 Neepsend Lane
33 Sportsman, 133 Infirmary Rd (1830–1913)
34 Target, 12 Infirmary Rd
35 Traveller's Inn, 72 Penistone Rd (open 1697)
36 Victoria Gardens (or Hotel), 248 Neepsend Lane (closed 1992, now offices)
37 Wellington Inn (formerly The Hero & His Horse), 58 Langsett Rd (still open)

38 Wellington Inn (now Cask & Cutler), 1 Henry St (still open)
39 Wheatsheaf, 18 Penistone Rd (1841–1897)

Note : The following pubs were known to be in this area though the actual location is unknown:

Don House, Infirmary Rd
New Inn, Penistone Rd

Closed in 1992, now offices

SPIRITS

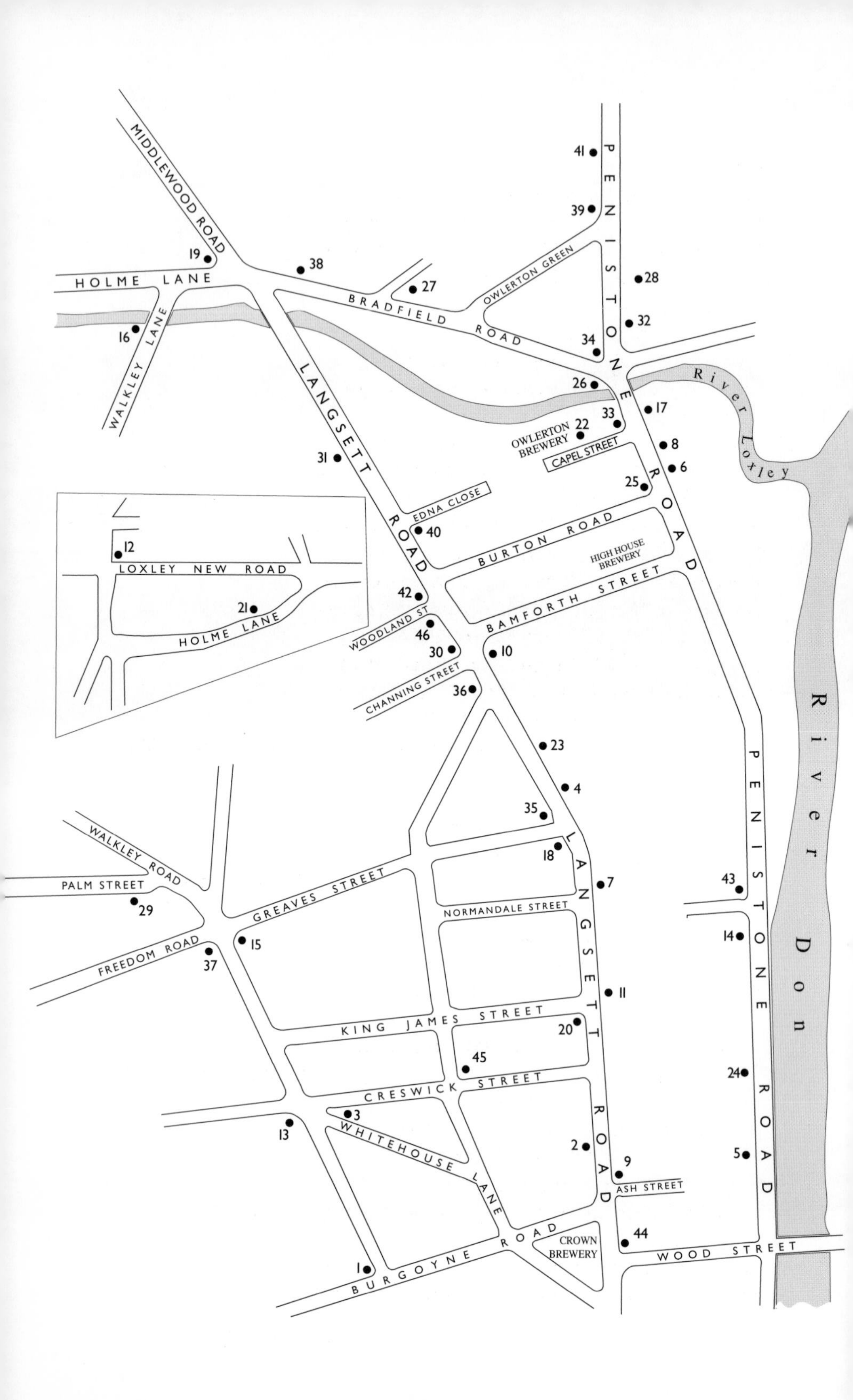

MIDDLEWOOD ROAD
HOLME LANE
WALKLEY LANE
BRADFIELD ROAD
OWLERTON GREEN
PENISTONE ROAD
River Loxley
LANGSETT ROAD
OWLERTON BREWERY
CAPEL STREET
EDNA CLOSE
BURTON ROAD
HIGH HOUSE BREWERY
BAMFORTH STREET
LOXLEY NEW ROAD
HOLME LANE
WOODLAND ST
CHANNING STREET
River Don
WALKLEY ROAD
PALM STREET
GREAVES STREET
NORMANDALE STREET
FREEDOM ROAD
KING JAMES STREET
CRESWICK STREET
WHITEHOUSE LANE
ASH STREET
CROWN BREWERY
WOOD STREET
BURGOYNE ROAD

Map 31

1 Bath Hotel, 148 Burgoyne Rd (still open)
2 Beehive, 115 Langsett Rd (demolished c1968)
3 Bellevue Hotel, 282 Whitehouse Lane (still open)
4 Bold Dragon Inn, 264 Langsett Rd
5 Bridge Inn, 317 Penistone Rd (closed 1913)
6 British Queen, Penistone Rd
7 Burgoyne Arms, 246 Langsett Rd (still open)
8 Cambridge Hotel, 452 Penistone Rd (1836–1992)
9 Crabtree Vaults, 74 Langsett Rd
10 Cuthbert Arms, 296 Langsett Rd (closed 1974)
11 Cuthbert Bank Hotel, 164 Langsett Rd (still open)
12 Elm Tree, Loxley New Rd (still open)
13 Firwood Cottage, 279 Whitehouse Lane (still open)
14 Forester's Arms, 373 Penistone Rd
15 Freedom Hotel, 26 Walkley Bank Rd (still open)
16 Freemason's Arms, 383 Walkley Lane (still open)
17 Garrison Arms, 456 Penistone Rd (1850–1913)
18 Hampton View, 231 Langsett Rd (closed 1972)
19 Hillsborough Inn, 2 Holme Lane (open 1851)
20 Lyceum, 153 Langsett Rd (closed 1972)
21 Malin Bridge, Holme Lane (The Cleakum Inn, 1833, rebuilt after 1864 flood, still open)
22 Mason's Arms, 14 Capel St (still open)
23 Mason's Arms, 270 Langsett Rd (still open)
24 Minerva, 103 Penistone Rd (1833–1959)
25 New Barrack Tavern, 601 Penistone Rd(closed 1992—re-opened 1995 as Hillsborough Barrack Inn)
26 New Inn, Penistone Rd (open 1833)
27 Old Blue Ball, Bradfield Rd (still open)
28 Old Crown, 710 Penistone Rd (still open)
29 Palm Tree Tavern, 35 Palm St (still open)
30 Prince of Wales, 301 Langsett Rd (1833–1921)
31 Queen's Ground (Queen's Hotel), 401 Langsett Rd (1833—still open)
32 Red Lion, 622 Penistone Rd (open 1835)
33 Rose Inn, 627 Penistone Rd (1851—still open)
34 Royal, 2 Bradfield Rd (closed 1990)
35 Royal, 233 Langsett Rd (1833–1921)
36 Royal Exchange (became a club), 283 Langsett Rd (closed 1921)
37 Royal Oak, 23 Walkley Bank Rd
38 Shakespeare, 196 Bradfield Rd (1854—still open)
39 Sportsman Group, 851 Penistone Rd (1833–1989)

40 Traveller's Rest, 406 Langsett Rd (closed 1921)
41 Victoria, 923 Penistone Rd (closed 1982)
42 Victoria, 325 Langsett Rd (closed 1972)
43 Weir Head Tavern (became Hillfoot Club), 377 Penistone Rd (closed 1936)
44 Wellington (formerly Hero & His Horse), 58 Langsett Rd (still open)
45 White Horse, 87 Creswick St
46 Woodland Tavern, 321 Langsett Rd (1845–1921)

Note : The following pubs were known to be in this area though the actual location is unknown:

Grapes Inn, Langsett Rd (open 1869)
Stag, Malin Bridge, destroyed by flood, 1864

The Mason's Arms, Capel Street

The Mason's Arms, Langsett Road

One of the few Penistone Road pubs still in existance

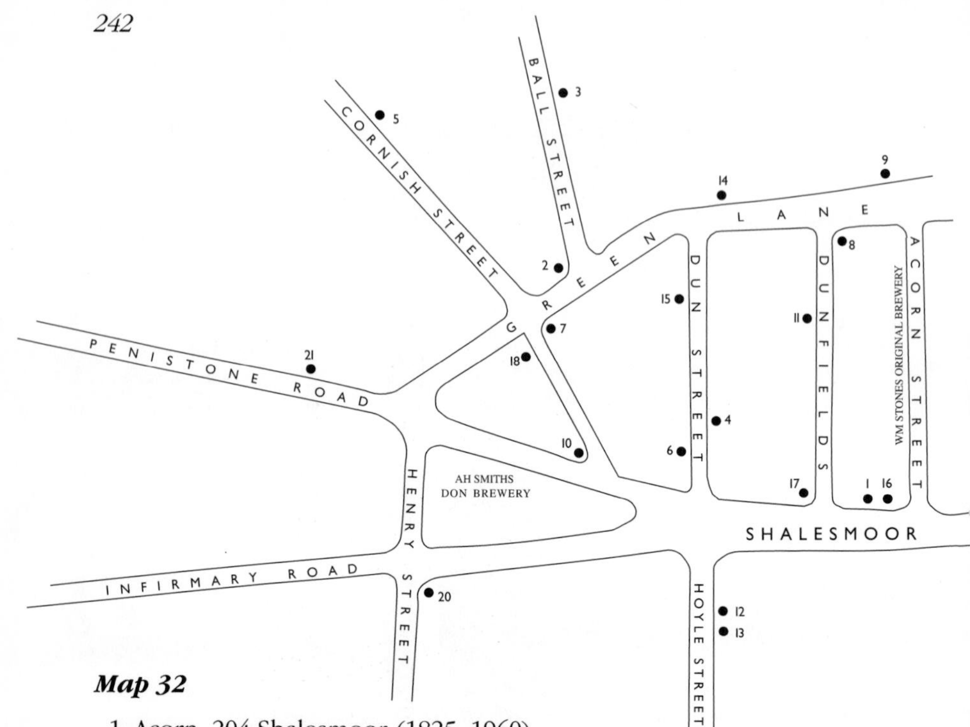

Map 32

1 Acorn, 204 Shalesmoor (1825–1960)
2 Ball Inn, 84 Green Lane (open 1833)
3 Boatman, 26 Ball St
4 Bull's Head, 18 Dun St
5 Cornish Inn, 56 Cornish St (open 1833)
6 Cup (also known as The Gardeners Rest), 17 Dun St
7 Foundry Arms, 101 Green Lane
8 Moulder's Arms, 43 Green Lane (1830–1904)
9 Napoleon Tavern, 34 Green Lane (1825–1912)
10 New Inn, 2 Penistone Rd (open 1833)
11 New Red House, 25 Dunfields
12 Peacock, 11 Hoyle St
13 Pheasant, 9 Hoyle St (open 1833)
14 Pheasant, 50 Green Lane
15 Queen's, 37 Dun St (1825–1970)
16 Red Lion, 202 Shalesmoor (1833–1917)
17 Ship Inn, 284 Shalesmoor (1833—still open)
18 Sportsman, 17 Cornish St (open 1833)
19 Talbot, 40 Hoyle St
20 Wellington (now Cask & Cutler), 1 Henry St (still open)
21 Wheatsheaf, 18 Penistone Rd (1841–1897)

Note : The following pub were known to be in this area though the actual location is unknown:

Cleekham Inn, Cornish Place (open c.1800)

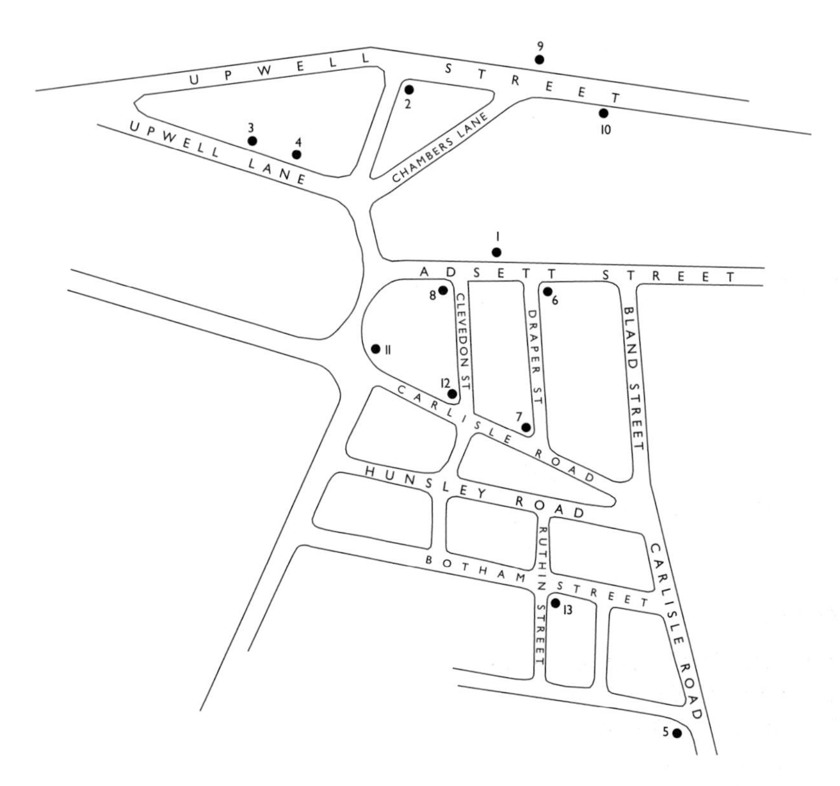

Map 33

1 Albion, 23 Adsett St (1860–1914)
2 Ball, 66 Upwell St (1830—still open)
3 Beehive Hotel, 20 Upwell Lane (closed 1972)
4 Bowling Green Hotel, 2 Upwell Lane (still open)
5 Crown, 41 Carlisle Rd (open 1860)
6 Dolphin, 34 Adsett St (open 1860)
7 Hodson Hotel, 110 Carlisle Rd (1860–1970)
8 Prince of Wales, 20 Adsett St
9 Sheffield Arms, 107 Upwell St (1830—still open)
10 Upwell Inn, 132 Upwell St
11 Victoria Hotel, 146 Carlisle Rd
12 Wellington Inn, 124 Carlisle Rd (open 1868)
13 Who Can Tell, 33 Botham St (closed 1974)

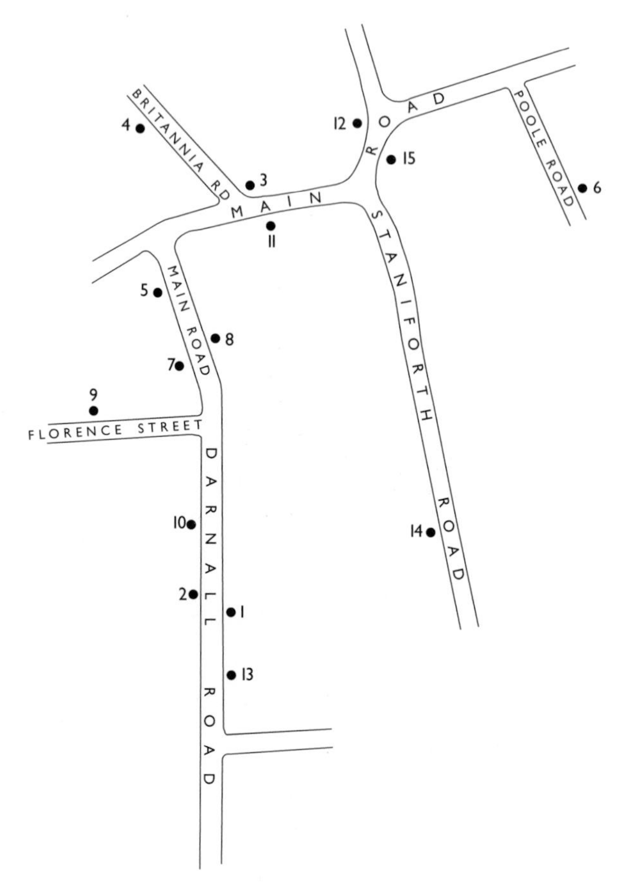

Map 34

1 Albert Inn, 132 Darnall Rd (still open)
2 Ball Inn, 287 Darnall Rd (still open)
3 Duke of York, 135 Main Rd, Darnall (still open)
4 Halfway House, 80 Britannia Rd, Darnall (still open)
5 Industry Inn, 89 Main Rd, Darnall (still open)
6 King's Head, 63 Poole Rd (still open)
7 Meadow Inn, 81 Main Rd, Darnall (still open)
8 New Inn, 56 Main Rd, Darnall
9 Norfolk Arms, 26 Florence St
10 Old Cricket Ground Inn, 289 Darnall Rd
11 Old Bradley Well, 150 Main Rd, Darnall (still open)
12 Rose and Crown, 245 Main Rd, Darnall (still open)
13 Sportsman, 134 Darnall Rd (still open)
14 Staniforth Arms, 261 Staniforth Rd (still open)
15 Wellington Inn, 222 Main Rd, Darnall (still open)

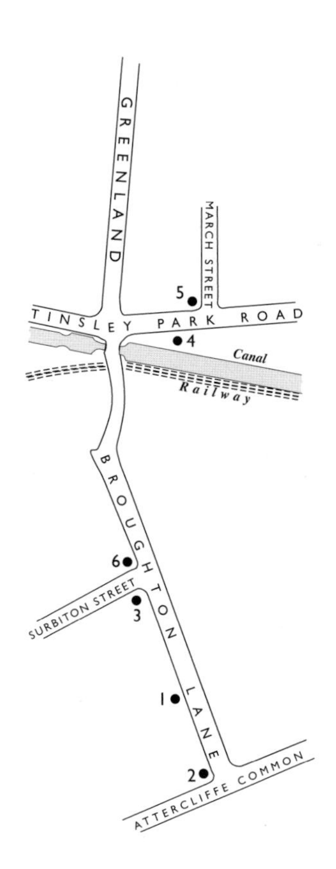

Map 35

1 Bird in Hand, 49 Broughton Lane (open 1861)
2 Broughton Hotel, 1 Broughton Lane
3 Enfield Arms, 95 Broughton Lane (1825—still open)
4 Fisherman's Rest, 93 Tinsley Park Rd (closed 1980's)
5 Friendship Inn, 4 Tinsley Park Rd (still open)
6 Railway Hotel (then The Stadium, now The Noose & Gibbet), 97 Broughton Lane (still open)

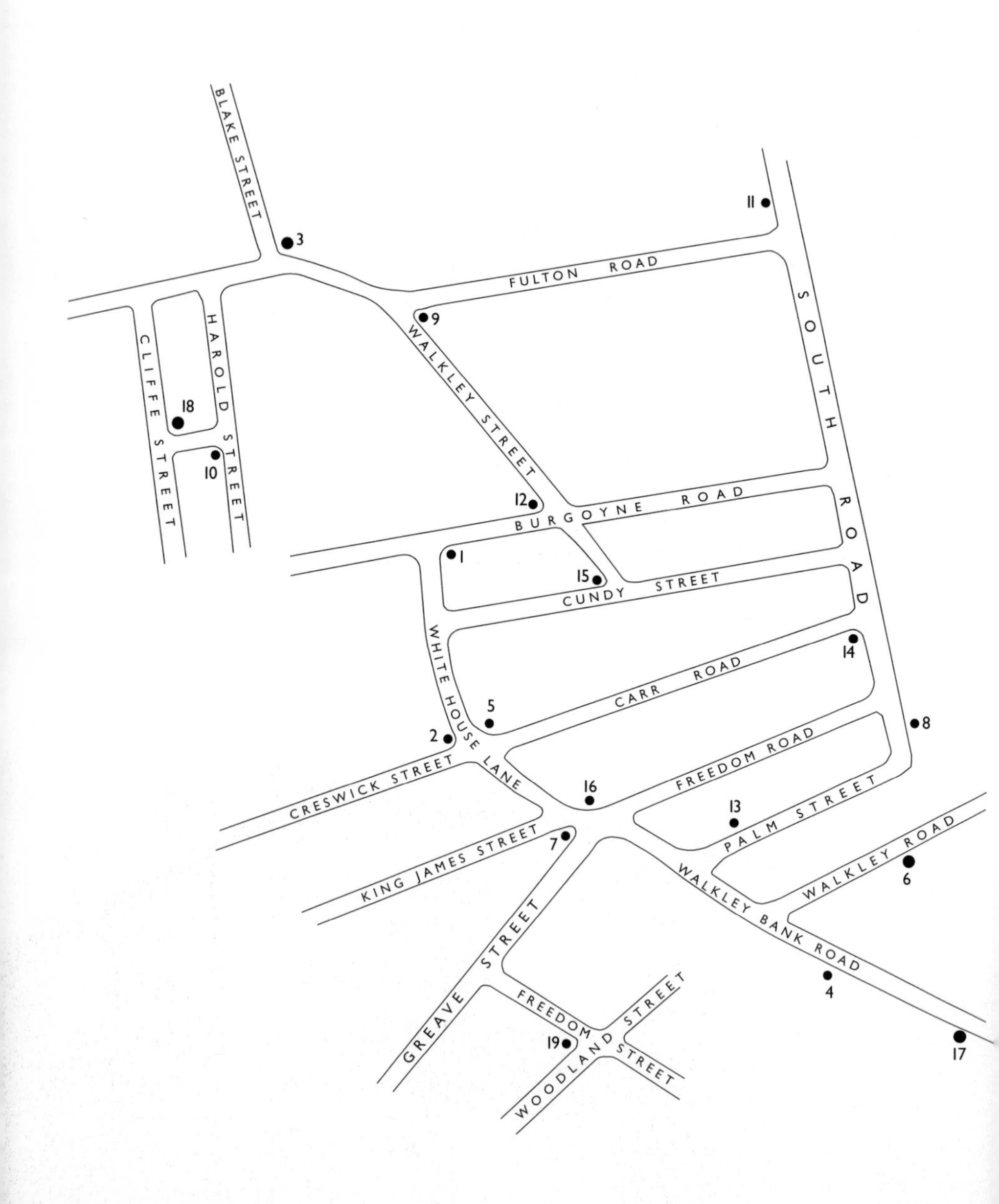
BLAKE STREET
FULTON ROAD
HAROLD STREET
CLIFFE STREET
SOUTH ROAD
WALKLEY STREET
BURGOYNE ROAD
CUNDY STREET
WHITE HOUSE LANE
CARR ROAD
FREEDOM ROAD
CRESWICK STREET
KING JAMES STREET
PALM STREET
WALKLEY ROAD
WALKLEY BANK ROAD
GREAVE STREET
FREEDOM STREET
WOODLAND STREET
1
2
3
4
5
6
7
8
9
10
11
12
13
14
15
16
17
18
19

Map 36

1 Bath Hotel, 148 Burgoyne Rd (still open)
2 Bellevue Hotel, 282 Whitehouse Lane (still open)
3 Blake Hotel, 53 Blake St (still open)
4 Crown Inn, 2 Walkley Bank Rd (still open)
5 Firwood Cottage, 279 Whitehouse Lane (still open)
6 Florist, 185 Walkley Rd (still open)
7 Freedom Hotel, 26 Walkley Bank Rd (still open)
8 Freedom House, 371 South Rd (still open)
9 Fulton Inn (Prospect House), 1 Walkley St (still open)
10 Harold Hotel, 18 Hardy St
11 Howard Hotel, 94 Howard Rd
12 Municipal Inn, 175 Burgoyne Rd
13 Palm Tree Tavern, 35 Palm St (still open)
14 Rose House, 316 South Rd (still open)
15 Royal Hotel, 114 Walkley St (still open)
16 Royal Oak, 23 Walkley Bank Rd
17 Sportsman Inn, 100 Walkley Bank Rd (still open)
18 Sportsman Inn, 1 Hardy St
19 Springwood Inn, 67 Freedom St

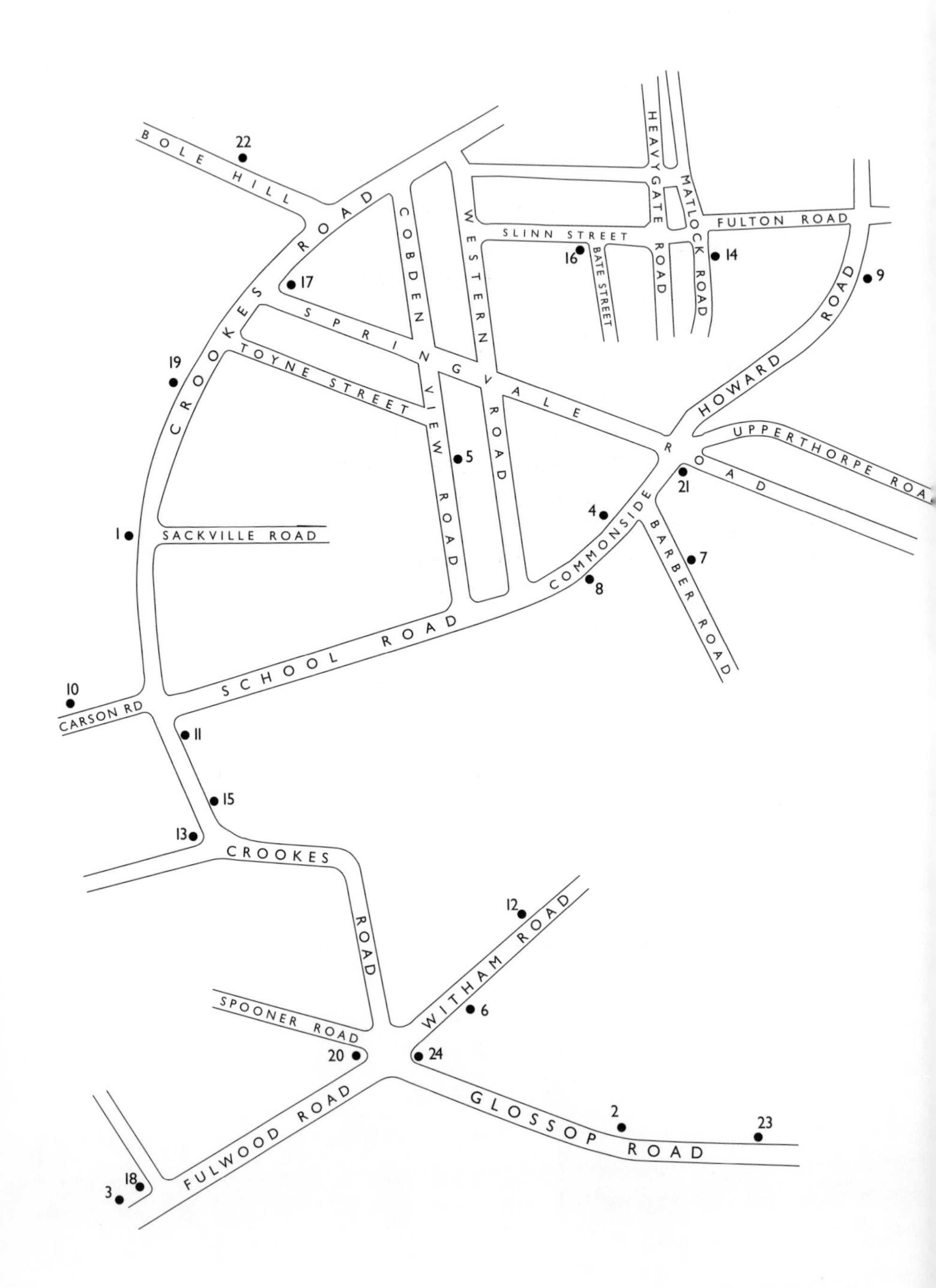

BOLE HILL
22
CROOKES ROAD
17
COBDEN VIEW ROAD
WESTERN ROAD
HEAVYGATE ROAD
MATLOCK ROAD
FULTON ROAD
SLINN STREET
16
BATE STREET
14
9
HOWARD ROAD
SPRINGVALE ROAD
TOYNE STREET
19
5
UPPERTHORPE ROAD
21
4
1
SACKVILLE ROAD
COMMONSIDE
BARBER ROAD
7
8
SCHOOL ROAD
10
CARSON RD
11
15
13
CROOKES ROAD
12
WITHAM ROAD
6
SPOONER ROAD
20
24
FULWOOD ROAD
GLOSSOP ROAD
2
23
18
3

Map 37

1 Ball Inn, 171 Crookes Rd (still open)
2 Broomhill Tavern, 484 Glossop Rd (still open)
3 Bull's Head Inn, 396 Fulwood Rd (still open)
4 Closed Shop, 52/54 Commonside (still open)
5 Cobden View Hotel, 40 Cobden View Rd (still open)
6 Fox and Duck, 227 Whitham Rd (still open)
7 Hadfield Hotel, 28 Barber Rd (still open)
8 Hallamshire House, 49 Commonside (still open)
9 Howard Hotel, 94 Howard Rd
10 Mason's Arms, 2 Carson Rd (still open)
11 Noah's Ark, 94 Crookes Rd (still open)
12 Nottingham House, 164 Whitham Rd (still open)
13 Old Grindstone, 3 Crookes Rd (still open)
14 Old Heavygate Inn, 114 Matlock Rd (1696—still open)
15 Original Grindstone, 22 Crookes Rd
16 Princess Royal Hotel, 43 Slinn St (still open)
17 Punch Bowl, 236 Crookes Rd (still open)
18 Ranmoor Inn, 330 Fulwood Rd (still open)
19 Rock Cottage, Crookes Rd
20 South Sea Hotel, 3 Spooner Rd (still open)
21 Springvale Hotel, 1 Commonside (still open)
22 Walkley Cottage, 46 Bole Hill Rd (still open)
23 West End Hotel, 412 Glossop Rd (still open)
24 York Hotel, 247 Fulwood Rd (still open)

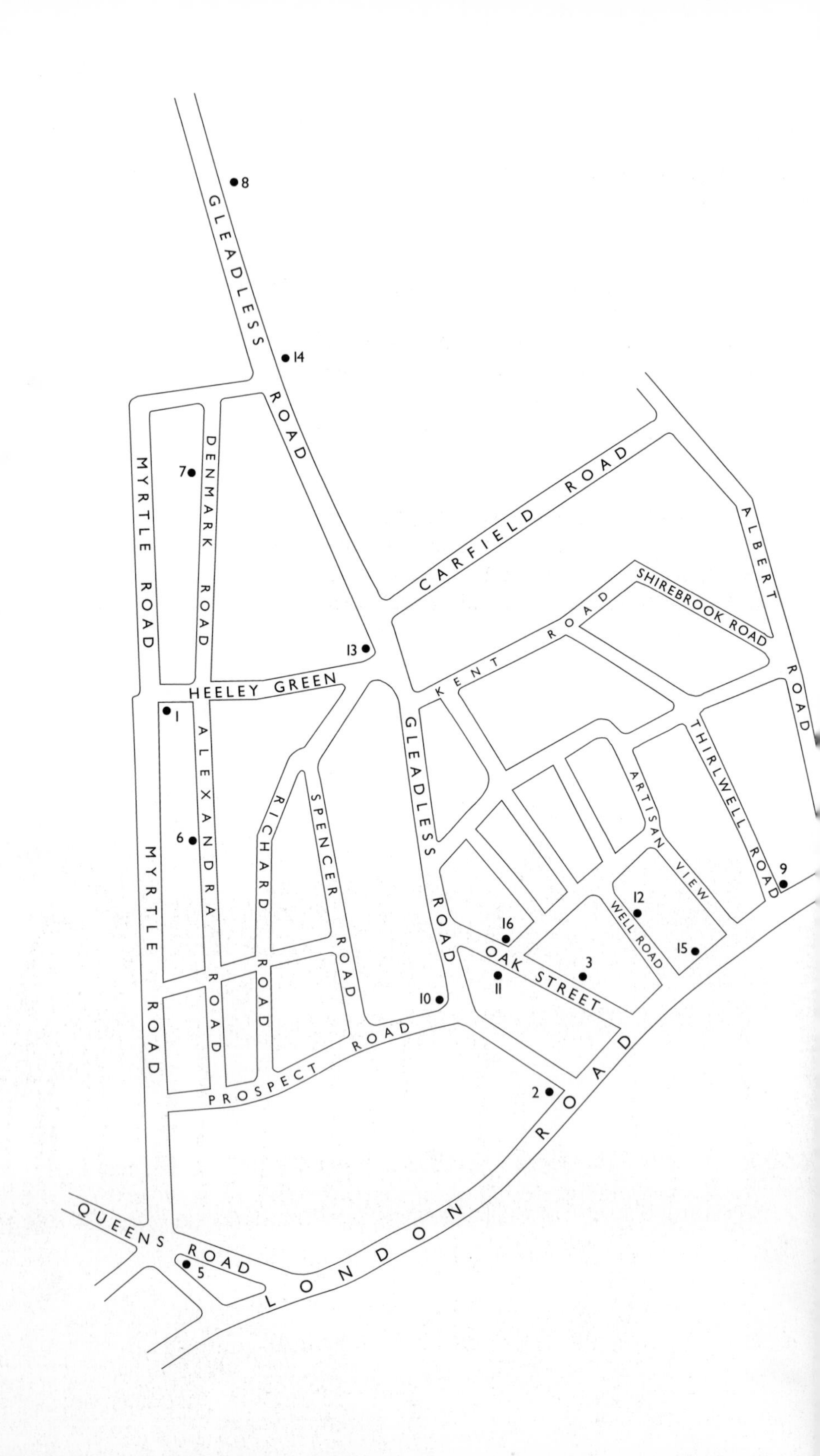

GLEADLESS ROAD
CARFIELD ROAD
ALBERT ROAD
SHIREBROOK ROAD
KENT ROAD
MYRTLE ROAD
DENMARK ROAD
HEELEY GREEN
ALEXANDRA ROAD
RICHARD ROAD
SPENCER ROAD
GLEADLESS ROAD
ARTISAN VIEW
THIRLWELL ROAD
WELL ROAD
OAK STREET
PROSPECT ROAD
LONDON ROAD
QUEENS ROAD
MYRTLE ROAD
1
2
3
5
6
7
8
9
10
11
12
13
14
15
16

Map 38

1 Ball Inn, 230 Myrtle Rd (still open)
2 Bridge Inn, 509 London Rd (still open)
3 British Oak, 30 Oak St
4 Crown Inn, 2 Albert Rd (still open)
5 Earl of Arundel and Surrey, 528 Queen's Rd (still open)
6 Myrtle Inn, 33 Alexandra Rd (closed 1970)
7 Newfield Inn, 123 Denmark Rd (still open)
8 Prospect View, 500 Gleadless Rd (still open)
9 Red Lion, 653 London Rd (still open)
10 Sheaf View Hotel, 25 Gleadless Rd (still open)
11 Sportsman Inn, 63 Oak St
12 Sportsman's Inn, 83 Well Rd
13 Victoria Hotel, 203 Gleadless Rd (still open)
14 Waggon and Horses, 236 Gleadless Rd (still open)
15 White Lion, 615 London Rd (1780—still open)
16 Ye Old Shakespeare Inn, Oak St (still open)

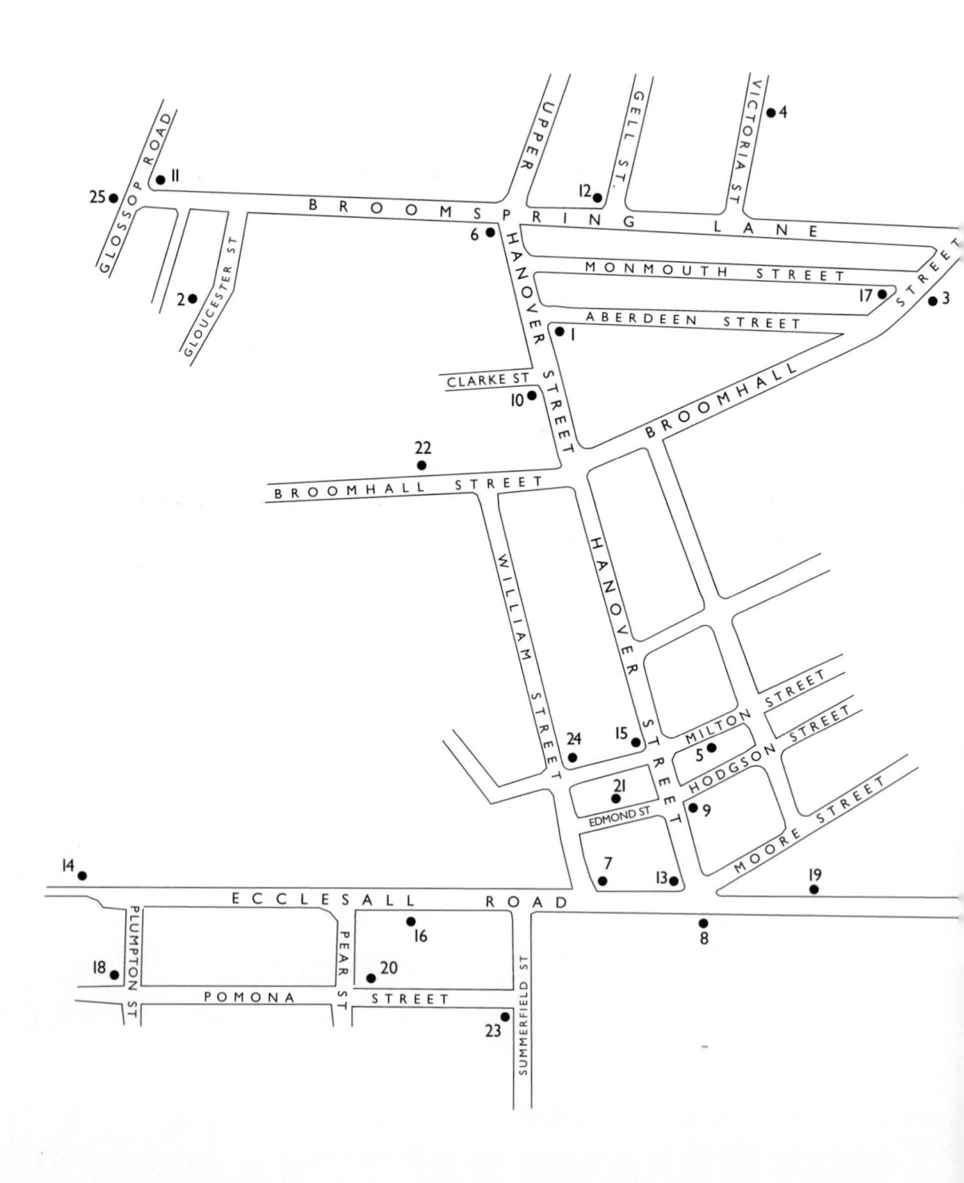
GLOSSOP ROAD
BROOMSPRING LANE
UPPER HANOVER STREET
GELL ST.
VICTORIA ST
GLOUCESTER ST
MONMOUTH STREET
ABERDEEN STREET
CLARKE ST
BROOMHALL STREET
BROOMHALL STREET
WILLIAM STREET
HANOVER STREET
MILTON STREET
HODGSON STREET
EDMOND ST
MOORE STREET
ECCLESALL ROAD
PLUMPTON ST
PEAR ST
POMONA STREET
SUMMERFIELD ST
1
2
3
4
5
6
7
8
9
10
11
12
13
14
15
16
17
18
19
20
21
22
23
24
25

Map 39

1 Aberdeen House, 3 Aberdeen St
2 Albany Hotel, 40 Gloucester St
3 Bath Hotel, 139 Broomhall St (closed 1968)
4 Bath Hotel, 66 Victoria St (still open)
5 Bay Horse, 143 Milton St (1825–1910)
6 Broomspring Tavern, 63 Broomspring Lane
7 Devonshire Arms, 116 Ecclesall Rd (rebuilt 1980s—still open)
8 Earl Grey, 97 Ecclesall Rd
9 Ecclesall Tavern, Hanover St
10 Hanover, 132 Upper Hanover St (still open)
11 Ivy Cottage (now Springfield Tavern), 184 Broomspring Lane (still open)
12 Mason's Arms, 50 Broomspring Lane
13 New Inn, 108 Ecclesall Rd
14 Nursery Tavern, 276 Ecclesall Rd (still open)
15 Old Albion, 244 Hanover St
16 Pomona Garden Hotel, 213 Ecclesall Rd (rebuilt 1980s—still open)
17 Poplar Tree Tavern, 180 Broomhall St
18 Prince Hotel, 100 Pomona St
19 Ram Hotel, 100 Ecclesall Rd
20 Rising Sun, 72 Pomona St
21 Sheldon Inn, 10 Edmond St
22 Stratford Hotel, 234 Broomhall St
23 Summerfield Hotel, 16 Summerfield St
24 Sunnyside Hotel, 26 William St
25 West End, 412 Glossop Rd (still open)

A

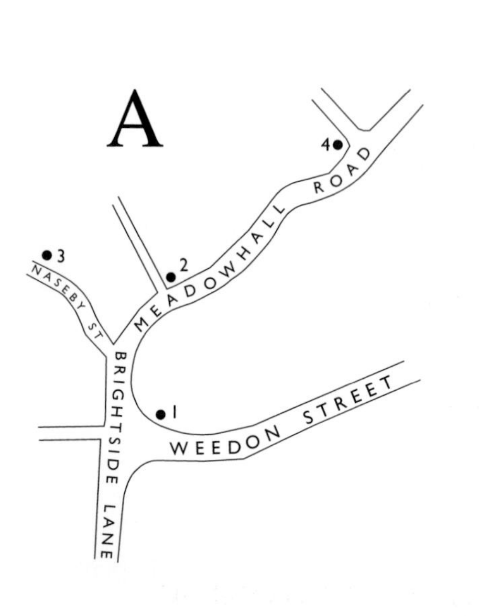

MEADOWHALL ROAD
NASEBY ST
BRIGHTSIDE LANE
WEEDON STREET
1
2
3
4

B

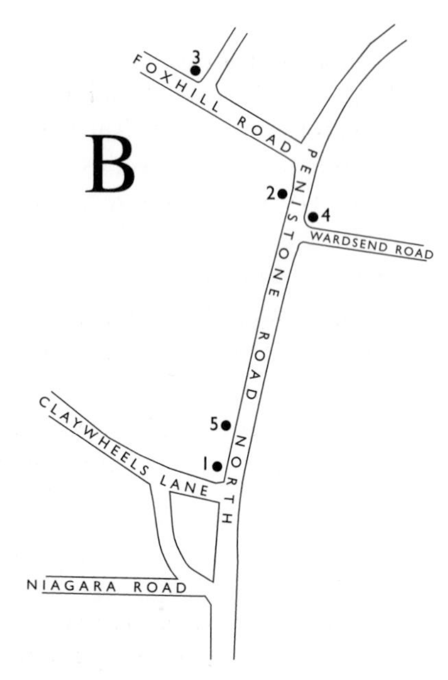

FOXHILL ROAD
PENISTONE ROAD NORTH
WARDSEND ROAD
CLAYWHEELS LANE
NIAGARA ROAD
1
2
3
4
5

C

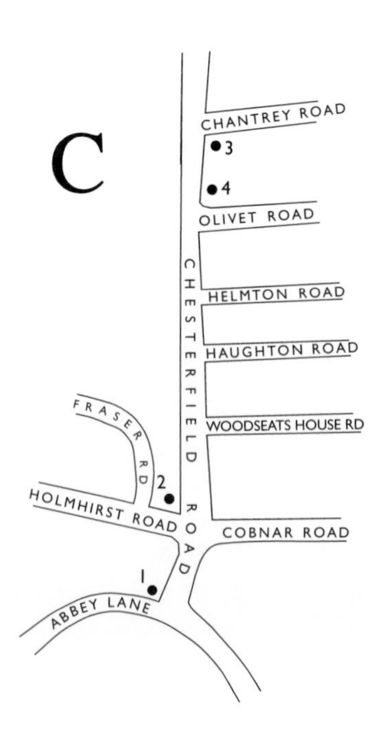

CHANTREY ROAD
OLIVET ROAD
HELMTON ROAD
HAUGHTON ROAD
WOODSEATS HOUSE RD
CHESTERFIELD ROAD
FRASER RD
HOLMHIRST ROAD
COBNAR ROAD
ABBEY LANE
1
2
3
4

D

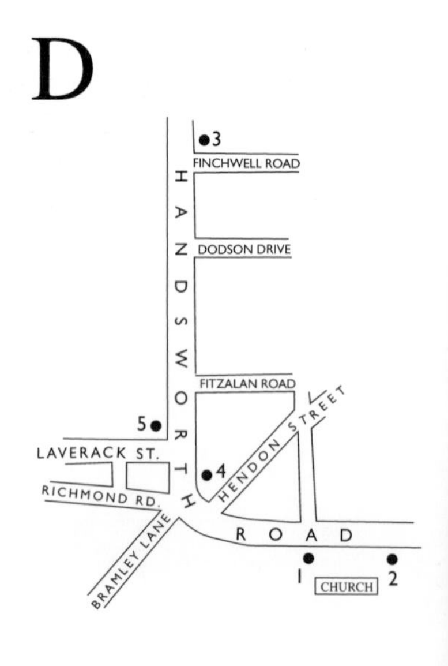

FINCHWELL ROAD
DODSON DRIVE
FITZALAN ROAD
HANDSWORTH ROAD
HENDON STREET
LAVERACK ST.
RICHMOND RD.
BRAMLEY LANE
CHURCH
1
2
3
4
5

Map A

1 Bridge Inn, Weedon St
2 Crown, 21 Meadowhall Rd
3 Station Inn, Naseby St (or Station Lane)
4 White Swan, 105 Meadowhall Rd
All except The Station Inn are still open

Map B

1 Gate, Penistone Road North
2 New Bridge Inn, Penistone Road North
3 Pheasant, Foxhill Rd
4 Railway, Penistone Road North
5 Travellers Inn, Penistone Road North
All are still open

Map C

1 Abbey, 944 Chesterfield Rd
2 Big Tree (formerly The Mason's Arms), 842 Chesterfield Rd
3 Chantrey Arms, 733 Chesterfield Rd
4 Woodseats Hotel, 743 Chesterfield Rd
All are still open

Map D

1 Cross Keys, 400 Handsworth Rd
2 Old Crown, Handsworth Rd
3 Norfolk Arms, 225 Handsworth Rd
4 New Crown, 343 Handsworth Rd
5 Turf Tavern, 336 Handsworth Rd
All are still open